So Far So Good

A 20ᵗʰ Century Autobiography

So Far So Good

A 20th Century Autobiography

Richard C. Dinmore, M.D.

PRINTED BY
TATTERED COVER PRESS

Acknowledgments

I would like to thank the many people who have helped me in the writing of this book. The early drafts were reviewed by Mathew Kailey of Denver, Colorado, Judy Berman of Berman Editorials, Boulder, Colorado, and Kim Lo of Charlottesville, Virginia. All made valuable suggestions and helped with historical accuracy. In the early days of my writing, as I was developing the initial manuscript, my daughter, Katherine Dinmore, was the first to insist that I put the manuscript on a computer disc. Thank you, dear Kathy.

Of invaluable help was my daughter, Ellen Struthers, who, in order to make the final editing process possible, typed the entire manuscript into *MS Word* and then scrupulously reviewed every word, sentence, paragraph, and section for coherency while making innumerable suggestions on how to flesh out my story and improve the syntax, continuity, punctuation, spelling, and readability. My appreciation for the countless hours she has spent improving the book cannot be adequately expressed. I would also like to thank Abby Hoke of AE Book Design Denver, Colorado, who created the designs for the interior of the book and the cover.

Lastly, two books that I often consulted during my labors were *On Writing Well*, by William Zinsser, and *The Elements of Style*, by William Strunk Jr. and E. B. White—two classics the amateur writer ignores at his peril.

Richard C. Dinmore, MD
Col. USAF (Ret)
Douglas County
Colorado
January 2016

Dedication

To Eileen for sixty-two years of patience, love, and understanding.

To Margaret, Clayt, Ellen, John, Kathy, and Liz so that knowledge of the past can help them deal with the future.

And to optimists the world over who, like the man who jumped off the Empire State Building and muttered, as he passed the twenty-fifth floor, "so far so good."

May you live in interesting times.
Chinese curse

The fool doth think he is wise, but the wise man knows himself to be a fool.
William Shakespeare

CONTENTS

Grandparents and parents—Bronxville, New York, 1921—return to San Francisco—Los Angeles, Phoenix, and Windsor Square—Lad—the ranch at Harper Lake—1932 and FDR—Angeline—Beverly Hills—Jackie Cooper—John with Jack at the *Treasure Island* location—interesting friends—Frances Marion—John's literary bent—Lyle Pressey—summer at Sonoma Mission Inn—my father to Honolulu—we join him in 1937—Punahou School—San Francisco in 1941—return to Honolulu—Pearl Harbor

Honolulu after December 7, 1941—Japanese Americans in Hawaii—my father and the Businessmen's Training Corps (BMTC)—to the mainland in 1942—University of California, Berkeley—Zeta Psi fraternity—enlisted as a qualified aviation cadet—the Presidio at Monterey to Maxwell Field for preflight—learning to fly—graduation and commissioning—transition training in "gooney birds"—joining the 349th Troop Carrier Group—meeting Eileen Frances Quinn—overseas—home from Europe—VE Day in San Francisco—demobilization—home to Honolulu terests of the children—gall bladder surgery—the last of Nixon—changes in the specialty of Obstetrics and Gynecology—vacation in Hawaii with the Lewises— new offices with Jim Myers—Margaret's marriage—recertification by American Board of Obstetrics and Gynecology—trip to Europe with the Wrights—return to the Air Force

PREFACE

At the beginning of the third millennium in the United States, there is a popular appreciation of the so-called Greatest Generation, a term first used by Tom Brokaw as the title of his excellent book, *The Greatest Generation*. It inspires me, as a member of that generation—those born during the Roaring Twenties, who matured during the worst depression in the country's history, and who ultimately helped to win the most horrific war in world history, in which an estimated fifty million people perished—to chronicle my part in and possible contribution to it. Though it is a generation to be proud of, I have some reservation about the label, "the greatest."

In the last quarter of the eighteenth century, the imperishable legacy of our Founding Fathers was that freedom, liberty, and the general welfare of the people could best be preserved by electing ordinary citizens from their midst to govern. The instruction manual for this notion was the most remarkable document ever conceived by the mind of man—the United States Constitution. The concept of governance by three separate branches of government—the executive, the legislative, and an independent judiciary, co-equal but with appropriate checks and balances, one upon the other—was a work of genius. Furthermore, the Founding Fathers, our national heroes, and their ragtag army knew that if England won the Revolutionary War, they probably would have been convicted as traitors to their mother country and, very likely, hanged.

In the first quarter of the nineteenth century, our fledgling country again triumphed over the greatest military and naval power in the world in a war that should never have been fought. In the second quarter of that century, the remarkable saga of the western transmigration and the establishment of the borders of the continental United States were epic events. In the third quarter, the preservation of the Union at a cost of six hundred thousand lives (approximately 1.5% of the population at the time), the abolition of slavery, the building of the transcontinental railroads, and the establishment of the supremacy of the national government over the individual states, gave meaning to the words United States. Finally, in the last quarter of the nineteenth century, the genius of Thomas Edison and the utilization of electricity, Andrew Carnegie and the production of steel, John D. Rockefeller's development of oil and oil derivatives, Cornelius Vanderbilt's vast railroad networks, and J.P. Morgan's financial wizardry all marked the beginning of the industrial revolution that was to make the United States the preeminent industrial power on earth.

In the first quarter of the twentieth century, the devastation of World War I notwithstanding, the United States emerged as the most powerful nation in history. The astounding advances of science, technology, and medicine began, and continue to this day. The development of the automobile, more than any other invention, was ultimately responsible for a standard of living higher than the world had ever seen. Even the tragedy of the First World War spawned advances in science and technology that earlier generations could not have dreamed. The second quarter of the century, however, saw that the excesses of capitalism, without restraint, led to a financial collapse and the worst depression in the nation's history. There was a fatal flaw in Adam Smith's belief that in capitalism an "unseen hand" self-regulated a marketplace economy. That kindly, old eighteenth century philosopher's idea did not take into account the human frailties of greed, selfishness, and indifference. Only the sacrifices of the people and demands for armament of World War II ended the Depression. During the third quarter of the twentieth century, the evils of racial inequality were, at long last, addressed. Equal civil rights began to be achieved due to the efforts of a relatively few very brave and very committed African Americans. In the final quarter of the century, for good or ill, the country, even after the tragedy of the Vietnam War, continued to try to introduce principles of freedom to areas of the world that neither understood nor wanted our good intentions. The unintended consequences of this naïve notion predictably incited dislike and even hatred among one-sixth of the world's population, a sentiment that reached its zenith in the tragedy of the destruction of the Twin Towers in New York on September 11, 2001.

Each generation in our nation's history, therefore, has had its triumphs and tragedies. So to agree that my generation, the second generation of the twentieth century, was "the greatest," is a label that may be premature if not presumptuous. History will decide. Of greater relevance in the new millennium is how we will use the gifts previous generations have given us by their courage and foresight. The key to that question lies with an educated, moral people mindful of the past, grateful for the present, and optimistic about the future.

Author's Notes

In the months spent writing this biography, I have often recalled Winston Churchill's observation that writing any literary work is first a diversion, then a chore, and finally, a tyrant. Nonetheless, I think that the story of one's life during the last seventy-five years of the twentieth century and first decade of the twenty-first should be passed along to one's children and grandchildren. The epic events of those years—the Great Depression and the most destructive war in the history of the world, World War II—affected not only the "Greatest Generation" but also will have a ripple effect on generations yet to come.

My life began with a privileged childhood, but I didn't realize just how privileged it was until I left home at about the age of nineteen to make my way in the world. My parents were not wealthy, but we never had to worry about the necessities of life and there was always enough money to enjoy most of the luxuries. My childhood was, in a word, wonderful. I was never abused physically, emotionally, or mentally. My parents were firm and clearly imparted what was expected of me, but they were never unreasonable. There were carefully defined rules of behavior and decorum. If the rules were broken, punishments followed, and they were usually in the form of writing themes. Sometimes we were sent to bed without supper, and I remember only one or two half-hearted spankings for serious breaches. The 1930s were, for my brother and me, essentially carefree, due entirely to a benevolent providence and a wealthy grandfather.

In 1929, the euphoria and prosperity that had followed the allied victory in World War I came to an abrupt end with the collapse of the world's financial markets. In the United States, undisciplined spending, borrowing, and greed demonstrated the fallacies of Adam Smith's theory of a self-regulating marketplace. Almost overnight the country was plunged into the worst depression in its history, and the administration of President Herbert Hoover lacked the imagination to take corrective action—massive unemployment and near panic followed.

In Germany, far worse happened. Economic chaos after World War I resulted in a cultured, sophisticated people becoming mesmerized by a charismatic megalomaniac named Adolf Hitler. Hitler, blaming the Communists and the Jews for all of Germany's problems, began preaching a bizarre doctrine of "Aryan Supremacy" and that National Socialism could be Germany's salvation. Thus the world watched as the horrors of Nazism led inexorably to the most destructive war in world history.

Politically in the United States, the misery of the Great Depression caused the American notion of rugged individualism associated with unconstrained capitalism to give way to a kind of benign socialism under the leadership of the century's greatest president, Franklin Delano Roosevelt. But even in our country, and in spite of the Constitution, a crypto-fascist organization, The German-American Bund, sprang up. It appeared for the same reason it had appeared in Germany—fear. The Bund disappeared as fast as it had appeared when the country was drawn into World War II.

As for me, I was involved in many of the landmark events of the twentieth century. I grew up in Hollywood during the most flamboyant years of the motion picture industry. I lived in Honolulu during the attack on Pearl Harbor. I was a troop carrier pilot in the 9th Air Force in Europe during World War II. After the war, I attended college and then medical school; then I spent thirty-five years in the practice of medicine specializing in obstetrics and gynecology.

At the time of my birth in 1923, the fastest speed attainable by any man-made object was about two hundred miles per hour. There were no electronic calculators or computers or televisions. Antibiotics had not been discovered and any infection, even a trivial one, could be life threatening. (President Calvin Coolidge's son, for example, had died from an infected blister on his foot.) Major surgery, blood replacement, and general anesthesia were extremely hazardous. Motion pictures were silent and radio, as a mass media, was in its infancy. The horse cavalry was still an important part of the United States Army. Wyatt Earp, the last of the legendary western lawmen, was still alive. It took five-and-a-half days to cross the continent by train and thirty hours, at best, by air. It was four years before Lindbergh's epic solo flight to Paris from New York. Jim Crowism, lynching, and the Ku Klux Klan were still evils to be dealt with—and not only in the South. There were no great bridges in San Francisco. World War I, the "war to end all wars" had concluded five years earlier, and the Great Depression was still six years in the future. The sale of liquor was illegal and boot-legging, the father of organized crime, was a growing industry. It was a time of boisterous optimism, of "flappers," "It" girls, the Charleston, and unbelievable prosperity. The population of the country was about 120 million and the future seemed untroubled and assured.

I
1923-1942

FAMILY HISTORY

Walter Robert Dinmore (1870-1923), my paternal grandfather, died the year I was born. He was from Philadelphia and came west to California to seek his fortune in the 1890s. I know nothing of his family. He was, by all accounts, a thorough scoundrel and a neglectful parent with few redeeming qualities. He and my grandmother, our beloved Nana, were divorced years before I was born. He was apparently successful in his early years and was at one time the sole representative for Mumm's Champagne in California. The problem was that he drank about as much of it as he sold. One article about him in the *San Francisco Chronicle* referred to him as a *bon vivant*, a euphemism for a drunk with a little money. He took a selfish pride in exhibiting my father to his cronies. My father remembered waking up on pool tables after being shown off to Walter's friends and then promptly forgotten at the beginning of an evening debauch. Save for that recollection, I have no memory of my father ever speaking of Walter Dinmore. There was certainly no love between my father and Walter, but the relationship between Walter and his daughter, my Aunt Mary Margaret, Marne, as we called her, was poisonous—he could not stand the sight of her and the feeling was mutual. His gift to her on her sixteenth birthday was a lemon wrapped in toilet paper. There was a story that was probably true of Walter greeting my maternal grandfather, Nathan Jacob, on the street one day in San Francisco by saying, "Hello Nathan, what do you hear from the children?" (referring to my parents). He was cut dead by Nathan who said, "I don't know you, sir, nor do I wish to." Walter died at the age of fifty-two with chronic myocarditis and atherosclerosis.

Nanny Mae Lewis (1870-1947), my paternal grandmother, was much loved by all the family. Her parents, the William Lewises, had come across the plains in the 1840s from St. Louis and were among the first settlers in Petaluma, California. In her last few years, Nana lived at the Crocker Home in San Francisco. She was confined to her chair with various disabilities, but by using a hot plate within arm's reach she could make the most delicious penuche I ever tasted. Nana was a marvelous cook, and on more than one occasion during the time she kept house for my father in New York in 1917, entertained Babe Ruth with spaghetti dinners. Spaghetti was a particular passion of The Babe's.

During my junior year of high school, I would stop by the Crocker Home after school to visit Nana and to learn the rudiments of bridge. Nana was a master at the game. She was the first to tell me of a simple counting method—assign four points to an ace, three to a king, two to a queen, and one to a jack; if the total was thirteen or higher, one had at least an opening bid. Response bidding was more complicated, but I never forgot the "rule of thirteen." Nana was great fun; she loved people, loved to laugh, and loved parties. She smoked incessantly and was habitually shrouded in a cloud of blue-gray haze. Years after she died from congestive heart failure, my cousin, Penn Arnett, told me she was also the bookie at the Crocker Home and thus supplemented her meager income.

Nathan Jacob (1860-1928), my maternal grandfather, was a successful and wealthy businessman in San Francisco. His parents were German Jews who came to San Francisco via Cape Horn from Baden, Germany, in the 1840s. He was an autocrat, consistent with the mores of the late Victorian era but, nevertheless, a sort of clown. His distinguished appearance belied a great sense of fun. My mother often said that he would have been very happy on the stage. He could imitate anyone, and on one occasion, by reversing his collar and adopting a thick Irish brogue, heard a drunk's confession and solemnly absolved him. Nathan passionately loved his city and enjoyed nothing more than walking around while admiring it. He disliked

Southern California and, for reasons known only to himself, always called Los Angeles "Cafeteria." His devil-may-care brother, Uncle Aaron, was a good enough boxer to spar with Jim Corbett at the Olympic Club and was once caught *flagrante delicto* with Virgil Earp's mistress. Common sense prevailed, and before Earp could draw his gun, Uncle Aaron bailed out the nearest window. Another relative, an uncle of my grandfather I believe, was one of the fabled vigilantes. My mother worshiped her father, and one of the few hiatuses in her diary entries was the eight days after his death, of a cerebral hemorrhage, in 1928.

Of my maternal grandmother, Lulu Finn (1873-1905), I know very little. Her parents were born in Ireland and came to San Francisco in the 1850s. She was convent reared and said to be quite beautiful. She died suddenly when my mother was about nine years old. As commonly happened, her birth certificate and death certificate were destroyed in the San Francisco fire and earthquake of 1906. My grandfather loved Lulu deeply and never remarried.

For a few days after the great 1906 disaster in San Francisco, my mother, with her father and her baby sister, Midey, camped out in Golden Gate Park; then the girls were sent to relatives in San Jose for several weeks. When order was restored in the city, my grandfather and the children returned to their home on Washington Street, where they continued to live until 1913, at about which time, when my mother had a "fit of hysterics" after being told she could not take her own maid with her on her first trip to New York (which was too much even for an indulgent father to tolerate), and since my grandfather had no idea how to raise two willful, spoiled, and motherless daughters, and knew nothing about housekeeping, he discharged all the servants, except Tibbets, the chauffeur, and moved into a suite of rooms at the Fairmont Hotel, where he lived until his death in 1928.

My father, Henry Clayton Dinmore (1893-1957), who was always called "Clayt," was not tall but, as my daughter once said, "had movie star good looks." I never thought too much about that, but I respected and loved him, and we had countless good times during my childhood and youth. In later years, when I was struggling through medical school, he made the financial sacrifices that made it all possible.

I knew my father well, though he was not given to introspection and we did not share profound philosophical discussions. My father probably had less to do with forming my character, and that of my brother, than did my mother. Nonetheless, he was affectionate, fun-loving, even-tempered, impeccable in his dress and person, attractive to both men and women, generous to a fault, hard-working, and successful—though never quite to the level of his aspirations. His career was compromised by an education in a second-rate parochial school, by not continuing his education past the twelfth grade, and by the difficult days of the Great Depression. He was not an intellectual, but he loved books and read extensively. He was an excellent athlete, a strong swimmer, carried a ten handicap at golf, and was an enthusiastic, vigorous tennis player. I was never able to beat him consistently at golf, including our last game together, a few weeks before he suffered a fatal heart attack. His health was always robust as was his appetite, which, unfortunately, ran to foods rich in cholesterol. If there was gravy, ice cream, butter, eggs, or organ meats within a hundred yards, he would find them. He was intelligent, but sometimes his enthusiasm clouded his judgment, which led to his being victimized by slippery or inept associates. I missed his support and camaraderie for many years after his unexpected and premature death. My only consolation was that he died the way a San Franciscan should: his last view must have been of the Golden Gate Bridge from the twelfth floor of the Moffitt Hospital.

My mother, Estelle Louise Jacob (1895-1969), who was from infancy always called Tyke, was quite different from my father, yet they complimented one another. They had known each other casually during their high school years in San Francisco, but there was no romance until they met in New York after World War I. My mother's formal schooling at

Miss Hamlin's (now The Hamlin School) ended before her graduation, but she remained an avid reader throughout her life. She was very bright, philosophical, witty, and artistic, but she lacked the discipline of a trained mind. She studied the piano all her life with excellent teachers and played beautifully. She was affectionate, fun-loving, and extravagant—which was encouraged by an indulgent father—as well as a compulsive shopper. She loved poetry and wrote it with considerable skill, wit, and humor and always attracted intelligent, often unconventional, friends. She was intuitive but, like my father, occasionally victimized by scoundrels if they were amusing, attractive, and well-mannered. For her, the ultimate virtues were loyalty and kindness, and the ultimate sins were cruelty and self-importance. The last ten years of her life were not particularly happy. A lifetime of extravagance and a contempt for practicalities resulted in constant financial worries. Unlike my father, her health was not robust and was characterized by chronic recurring upper respiratory infections or, as she called it, "Irish lungs." In her later years, as old friends faded away, her only joys were times with her grandchildren, the piano, letters, books, and infrequent visits with old and dear friends. In a candid self-assessment in her diary she wrote:

> I think that people do not change very much. We may overcome a few faults and we pass through many phases but the essential us remains the same. I know I have always been extravagant, inconsistent, apt to run to extremes, fond of a certain amount of solitude, afraid of girls, more comfortable with men, very reserved to the point of being secretive about certain things while running off at the mouth about superficial things, lazy, nasty tempered at times and subject to fits of complete physical and mental depression usually followed by spurts of great energy and a sense of well being. These things I have always been and probably always will

be. Experience teaches us, saddens us or toughens us but, as for me, I love life and I think people are all interesting though I don't like very many of them. Those that are nice are very nice but those that are horrid are poisonous. But all are interesting.

Although my mother was a dedicated liberal democrat all her life, she was not an activist. But I do remember a time when she took prompt action when I reported to her that our Boy Scout troop leader at Hawthorn School, a retired army cavalryman, had suggested to us that we did not want to vote into our troop a Jewish boy named Paul Ginsberg. Paul happened to be the biggest, strongest, best athlete of our seventh grade class and well-liked by all. When hearing this, my mother, in a fury, immediately went to the office of our school principal, Miss Pogson, and demanded that the Scout Master be fired at once. He was and was never seen again at our troop meetings.

Until stricken at the age of seventy-three with a rapidly progressive and fatal illness known as Creutzfeldt-Jakob disease, she continued an active correspondence, played the piano, and indulged in her sole form of exercise—a life-long passion for walking.

In sum, my parents' thirty-seven year marriage was a happy one, marred only by a one-year separation in 1939. After they reconciled, my father gave up drinking entirely and, in 1950, he put a stop to his lifetime habit of heavy smoking. A few years before my father died, both my parents resumed a long-dormant interest in the teachings of the Catholic Church. Many talks with priests whom they respected brought them a great deal of spiritual comfort.

My Early Years

My father had moved to New York before the Unites States entered World War I and was variously employed as an automobile mechanic during the day and as an understudy to a popular musical comedy dancer, Maurice, at night. He had developed an inguinal hernia trying to lift an engine block, so he was disqualified from naval flight training during the war. By the time he and my mother married in 1920, at St. Bartholomew's Episcopal Church in Manhattan, he had become a successful broker in the coal business. A few months after they were married, they moved to Bronxville, a suburb north of New York City, and in 1921, my brother was born, and I followed two years later. In 1926, after having lived in New York for six years, my parents returned to San Francisco.

My parents often spoke of their six years in New York as the happiest and most carefree of their thirty-seven years together with "the children small and the parents young." They had a large circle of interesting friends: young businessmen, writers, actors, musicians, and artists who came and went so often that my mother once said she felt as though they were running a roadhouse. Well-known actor Alfred Lunt and the popular young composer George Gershwin were acquaintances, and my father played a few rounds of golf with the professional golfer Gene Sarazen at the Westchester Country Club. Their life was bohemian and compatible with the Roaring Twenties—including the making of bathtub gin. My father once described a typical workday in this way: from Bronxville by train to his office in the Grand Central Terminal building, lunch at the Oyster Bar, then home to Bronxville without ever seeing the light of day. But, from what I have come to understand, it was a wonderfully exciting time to live in New York with the best in art, theater, music, and literature, and yet with a kind of intimacy and friendliness perhaps lacking today.

I was born at the Woman's Hospital the afternoon of November 21, 1923, although my arrival nearly came almost a month earlier when my mother went into false labor on opening day of the 1923 World Series

at the new Yankee Stadium. (It is interesting to note that in those days it
was common practice for women who lived out of town to check into the
hospital, as though it were a hotel, a week before the delivery date and wait
for the onset of normal labor.)

I'm not sure why my parents decided to move back to San Francisco
in 1926. Although my father was doing well in the coal business, I think
perhaps there was a measure of homesickness, or they missed childhood
friends and family members, or my mother had a desire to be nearer her
beloved father, whose health was beginning to fail.

At any rate, one thing I know is true, San Franciscans are notoriously
hard to transplant permanently. For my family, no matter where we lived,
San Francisco was always "home." My parents and all but one grandparent
were born either in the city or in Petaluma. Summer and Christmas vacations at the Fairmont were the high point of the year. The sounds of the
city, the smell of cable car grease, the great restaurants, entering the warm
and cozy apartments on chilly and foggy evenings, crossing the bay on
ferry boats, walking along Fisherman's Wharf, the "pea soup" fogs, Golden
Gate Park and the Japanese Tea Garden, dinners with old friends and family, are all vivid memories that will stay with me the rest of my life.

I believe there was never a more exciting city than San Francisco was
in the late 1930s. The great bridges opened in 1936 and 1937, and the
World's Fair on Treasure Island opened two years later. The view from the
Top of the Mark (the Mark Hopkins Hotel) at sunset, with the lights of
the Bay Bridge and the lights of the fairgrounds in the bay shining across
the water, is a vision as clear to me now as it was seventy-five years ago.

1926-1933

Although I was quite young, a few things stand out in my memory
of the first five years after we returned to California. One of my earliest
memories, at about age three or four, is of my grandfather holding a flash-

light beneath his chin, in a dark closet, making scary faces as my brother and I screamed with laughter. I remember my grandfather being very funny and jolly. I remember the large rooms at the Fairmont Hotel and its beautiful lobby with enormous marble pillars and red plush furniture. I remember a trip to Petaluma and the family home on B Street with its dark living room where my paternal great grandmother, Mary Louise Hall Lewis, lived. I remember the farm a few miles out of town that she and my great grandfather had built in the 1840s. I remember being ushered into my great grandmother's presence and feeling a little scared. She was in her mid-nineties and I think I was intimidated, as are most children by adults of great age.

In 1927, we moved to Southern California. My mother once told me that my father was not comfortable working for his father-in-law and wanted to be on his own. His older sister, my Aunt Mary Margaret (Marne) was married to Len Owens, who was successful in real estate in Los Angeles. Uncle Len was also the brother of the famous screen writer, Frances Marion. Uncle Len encouraged my father to join him Los Angeles. It seemed that everyone in LA was making a lot of money in the mid-1920s, especially in real estate.

In 1928, Uncle Len and my father decided that an especially good opportunity presented itself in Phoenix, Arizona, in an upscale subdivision called Windsor Square. They devoted all their energies to the development of the project and it opened with a good deal of publicity two months before the stock market collapsed in October, 1929. This project was, in a word, a disaster—my father and Uncle Len lost a great deal of money. Though timing was the main problem, Uncle Len's patronizing attitude did not endear him to the locals. It was a pity that the combination of disastrous economic times and a bad attitude doomed the project because years later, and under different management, Windsor Square became a success. We spent the better part of a year in Phoenix, but my only clear recollections now of the place are of the heat and someone actually frying an egg on the sidewalk. My mother, who was never able to tolerate heat, and who, at heart, was a big-city person, was unhappy in such a small (population sixty-five thousand) desert town.

We returned to Los Angeles in 1930 and got our Collie pup, Lad. Laddie, as we called him, was a special friend—beautiful, intelligent, and vain. He was given to occasional "benders" and would disappear for a few days only to reappear exhausted, dirty, and full of remorse and guilt. He was with us for fifteen years.

My father's next venture that I remember well was an interest in a one-thousand acre alfalfa ranch in the Mojave Desert near Harper's dry lake. The nearest town was an uninteresting little place called Hinkley. The development of this property with the non-availability of enough water, the Depression, and the inexperience of my father and his three associates at farming more or less doomed this project as well. It was not the debacle that Windsor Square had been but neither was it the success that everyone dreamed it would be. However, for my brother and me, going to the ranch, riding horses, swimming in the large reservoir, shooting jack rabbits, and watching one of the ranch hands hypnotize a sidewinder snake and then catch it by hand were all part of a great adventure.

My clearest memories begin when we moved back to Los Angeles to the first address I was taught to memorize: 843 3rd Avenue. I recall the election of President Franklin Roosevelt in 1932 and that both my parents voted for Herbert Hoover. At that time of near economic panic, they were reluctant to support a politician unknown in the West. It was not too long, however, before they became and remained dedicated supporters of FDR.

My parents soon acquired a large circle of friends, just as they had in New York and San Francisco, and it seemed there were parties, or at least visitors, every night. At that time, there was no television, not much of interest on the radio for adults, and constant worry about money, or the lack of it, so visiting and playing games were about all there was to do. Movies and the motion picture industry were always a source of interest and probably a more important diversion to Southern Californians than to those who lived elsewhere. My parents knew a lot of motion-picture people in addition to Uncle Len's sister, Frances. Some were already famous, others were to become so. Walter Pidgeon was an occasional guest as was Lloyd Nolan, the brother of an old chum in San Francisco. Contract bridge was very much in vogue and games of pinochle, penny-ante poker, backgammon, and Russian Bank were widely enjoyed. Everyone smoked incessantly and probably drank too much; yet, even to this day, though I quit smoking decades ago, the smell of secondhand tobacco smoke still evokes wonderful memories of parties, cocktails, music, laughter, and animated conversation.

By the early 1930s, my brother and I had finally outgrown governesses. Our last one, Antoinette, left when we returned to California from Phoenix. In 1931, Angeline came into our lives. She was our maid and cook for many years. Angeline's husband, Bob, who was neither a high achiever nor given to strenuous work, was occasionally our chauffeur as my mother had never learned to drive. Angeline, who resembled the great Hattie McDaniel (the winner of an Oscar for her portrayal of Mammy in *Gone With The Wind*), was our loyal and affectionate friend during my pre-teen years. She wiped away my tears, bandaged my scraped knees, and listened to all my childhood woes. She was a superb cook and I remember trying, but never succeeding, to learn how to roll a pat of butter into a ball between two serrated wooden paddles—a pre-dinner ritual every night. Angeline was rotund, and I recall hugging her as a measure of my growing up. By the time I could get both arms around her, I was about as big as I was going to get.

1933-1937

In the summer of 1933, we moved into our bungalow in Beverly Hills at 626 North Foothill Road, and my memories of people and events from that time are clear. The house was not large—it had two bedrooms with a connecting bath, a library with guest water closet, a living room, a dining room, and a maid's quarters—but it was very comfortable. The back yard was large and very much to Laddie's taste. The house was owned by the silent screen star Buddy Rogers and rented for ninety dollars a month. Years later, in the 1970s, a friend who knew a little about the real estate market in Beverly Hills told us that the land alone, about nine thousand square feet, was valued at something in the range of a quarter of a million dollars.

The house was three blocks from our grade school, Hawthorn, a place that also holds nothing but good memories. My parent's social life continued as it had always been with parties, visitors, and guests, many of whom I have never forgotten. I had many friends my age, but somehow adults—writers, musicians, artists, and intellectuals—were always much more interesting. To this day, I can almost hear the fascinating conversations, the music, the laughter, and the uninhibited political discussions.

One day, in the fall of 1933, I was riding my bike about a block from Hawthorn and saw a familiar person learning to ride his bike in his driveway. It was Jackie Cooper. At that time Jack was one of the big stars at MGM. One of us said hello to the other and that was the beginning of a friendship that lasted several years. Jack was a year older than me and a year younger than my brother. He was a generous and loyal pal and not in the least impressed with his celebrity. We had wonderful times together. He had a mock-up of a World War I fighter plane in his back yard that had all the controls of a real airplane plus two fake Lewis guns mounted forward of the cockpit. We logged a lot of hours playing in that plane. He also had a large collection of model airplanes, some given to him by fans and some made by experts at the movie studio. He had a collection of real cowboy handguns, rendered harmless by the removal of the firing pins, and we wore them, holstered, constantly. In the summer of 1934, I was invited to spend a week with Jack and his mother, Mrs. Bigelow, and Jack's ever-present bodyguard, a huge, amiable, ex-Los Angeles policeman, at a rustic cabin in Palm Springs. The horses were saddled at the front gate each morning and off we went, with side arms of course, to play cowboys and Indians. Sixty-seven years later, on a return trip to Palm Springs, I was a little surprised to see more than the one street paved than I remembered. In 1934, the town was a popular, quiet retreat for Hollywood celebrities where they would escape the hurly-burly of the fans and the press.

A year later, Jack invited my brother John, who was about the same height and weight as he, to be his stand-in while filming *Treasure Island* at Catalina Island, the location site for Robert Louis Stevenson's classic. The picture starred Jack, Wallace Beery, Nigel Bruce, Otto Kruger, and Lewis Stone and was directed by John's special hero, Victor Fleming. Fleming obliged John by shooting a beret (which he hated and my mother liked) full of holes with his .22 caliber pistol so that it could never be worn again.

It was around this time that Jack was at our house for dinner one night and told us, with his usual enthusiasm, about a new teenage sensation he knew slightly who was about to debut on the Eddie Cantor radio show that night. He assured us that we would hardly believe the talent of the thirteen-year-old girl. He was right; her name was Judy Garland.

Many fascinating friends of my parents are still in my memory. Max Rabinowitz was a concert pianist and a musical director at Paramount. He had escaped the Russian revolution through China with his close friend, Jascha Heifetz, the most celebrated violin virtuoso of the day. Max and his wife, Galina, were frequent guests. They were a mercurial, demonstrative, funny couple given to violent arguments, but their marriage survived until Galina was wooed and won by the celebrated author James Hilton. I remember her saying one night that most Americans would never know how close the country came to a revolution during the depths of the Depression. In the early 1930s there was simply no work for one-fourth of the country's workforce—thirteen million desperate, proud, but frightened men. Many were literally starving. Had it not been for Roosevelt, or if some charismatic megalomaniac had appeared on the scene, anything might have happened. Galina had seen this sort of thing in her native country of Russia, so her opinion was worth noting.

Of course the Roosevelt haters of the day dismissed such talk as hyperbole. Nonetheless, I remember men in our alley scavenging garbage cans and one sickly, jaundiced man coming to our door to ask if he could cut our lawn, not for wages but for a sandwich. I was too young to fully understand the significance of these events, but, whether or not Roosevelt's programs or World War II pulled the country out of the depression, there is no doubt that Roosevelt's buoyant spirit replaced despair with hope. Though many of our friends were liberals and Democrats, most were not. Conservatives at that time considered Roosevelt to be anything from mentally deranged to simply wrong-headed. Discussions with our Republican friends were, to say the least, lively.

Mary and Igor Gorin and my parents were friends for many years. Igor Gorin had the most magnificent and powerful base-baritone I've ever heard. He had not only starred at the Metropolitan and other famous operas but also performed on concert stages throughout the world. He was heard regularly on the Bell Telephone hour weekly radio broadcasts. When he was in full voice, I remember ashtrays and other bric-a-brac rattling on the tables. One evening, the new sensation, the tenor Mario Lanza, was being discussed and I recall Mr. Gorin saying that without training, discipline, and expert management, there would soon be no voice. He was exactly correct. Lanza, who also reportedly had a problem with alcohol, began to slip in the late 1940s and died a decade later, silencing, prematurely, one of the great voices of the age.

We entertained two young British adventurers, Gerald Gordon and Geoffrey Mardin, in 1937. Gerald Gordon was dynamic, ruggedly handsome (much like a blond Lawrence Olivier), and very funny. At twenty-five, he had already published a travel book and was gathering material for a second. He was escorting an exquisite young starlet of Chinese-English heritage, Lotus Liu. Lotus was animated, beautifully educated, funny, and a little ribald at times. She was absolutely gorgeous and in her presence I was simply dumbstruck. She eventually had a few small parts in forgettable movies but never achieved stardom. Geoffrey Mardin was reserved and aristocratic, but in a typically British understated way, just as amusing as Gerald. They were on their way around the world and I think both knew that war with Germany was just a question of time. Geoffrey might have been the son of a peer; he certainly looked the part at any rate. I can remember laughing until we ached at his description of an evening at one of London's oldest and most prestigious clubs—the Carlton Club. As a junior member, Geoffrey had noted that members, often retired military types, withdrew to the map room after dinner to point out old campaigns in India. Geoffrey, having nothing better to do, did the same and, touching a map, it suddenly rolled up with a tremendous clatter. For weeks, older members derided that "dammed young fool." Nothing like that had happened in two hundred years at the Carlton Club. I have often wondered how or even if those two attractive young men survived the war.

Hugh Stillwell was a thoughtful, pipe-smoking, intellectual whose life story had elements of tragedy and comedy. A childhood illness (probably scarlet fever) left him severely hearing impaired. His family had been wealthy, so Hugh was well-educated in spite of his precarious health. After inheriting his family's considerable estate in the late 1920s, he was diagnosed with tuberculosis and was advised by his physician that, having but few years to live, he might as well spend the money and live life to the fullest, which he did. By the time the Great Depression was at its worst, all the money was gone and, mysteriously, so was the tuberculosis. Suddenly he was well, although deaf, completely untrained to do any useful work, and penniless. In spite of his desperate situation, he was composed, philosophical, and wonderful company. All of his friends saw to it that he ate properly. He was at our house for dinner at least once a week and I remember him talking with my mother for hours about current events, politics, people, books, theater—everything. Though he lived in a makeshift garage, his wardrobe was still impressive and he had a rare sense of style, the perfect picture of a successful middle-aged academic. He was a fascinating conversationalist, well informed, and a uniquely comfortable person to be with. During the very difficult days of the early 1930s, he eked out a living as a "reader" at one of the motion picture studios. ("Readers" in Hollywood at that time were people employed to read every novel that was published, synopsize it, and have their synopses evaluated to see if the story had motion picture potential.) Unfortunately, after we moved to Honolulu, we lost touch so I have no idea how his last days were spent.

Fred Salleté was an immaculately dressed, perfectly manicured and barbered individual who was an occasional visitor. He was the only man in my life I ever saw who wore spats. I have no idea what he actually did, but he was wealthy, had a small talent at the piano, and was fond of our family. I remember him as being the virtual embodiment of the character Elliot Templeton in Somerset Maugham's *The Razors Edge*. He was so perfect in manners and comportment that a ghastly *faux pas* like belching or farting in his presence would have been too awful to contemplate. I recall my mother briefing a business associate of my father, who was about to meet Fred for the first time, that he was going to meet a big, burly, uncouth fellow but, withal, a salt of the earth. I wasn't present at the meeting when Fred minced in, but I wish I had been.

"Buzz" Brown was a cutter at MGM who, in his off time, had written a play and often came over to talk to my mother about character development and plot lines. I never read the play but heard enough discussions to know that it was about the ruination of a young man due to a domineering, perfectionist mother—a classic case of "smotherhood." It was called *Roses Have Thorns*, and whether or not it was ever produced I don't know. Buzz's Christmas gift to John and me was always the same, a carton containing ten packs of chewing gum: Spearmint for me and Black Jack for John. All that gum all at once seemed a very exciting gift.

Bill Younger, or Uncle Bill as my brother and I were invited to call him, was a dynamic, handsome, very dashing screen writer who had been my mother's principal beau in San Francisco in the years before World War I. I think they had been quite in love as teenagers until he broke the code of behavior as it existed in San Francisco at that time. He appeared slightly drunk before escorting her to a party. No proper young debutante could tolerate such an affront, so she refused to go and that ended the romance. I don't think she saw him again until we returned to Los Angeles in 1930. He had achieved success as a writer for the movies and they saw a great deal of each other working on the script for a soggy epic about prohibition called *The Wet Parade*. I have no idea whether Uncle Bill and my mother just resumed an old friendship or had something more serious between them. Whether or not it was career disappointments, unrequited love, an unhappy marriage, alcohol, or some combination of all, Uncle Bill committed suicide by "accidentally shooting himself while cleaning a pistol," or so said the press reports. I remember my mother weeping inconsolably for days after it happened.

By far, the most exciting, the most unforgettable person in my young life in the 1930s was Frances Marion, Aunt Frances to us, although "Aunt" was not quite accurate since she was the sister of Uncle Len, who was my uncle by marriage. Nonetheless, she preferred the title "Aunt." Her third husband, the great love of her life, was Fred Thomson. "Uncle Fred," whom I vaguely remember, had been America's foremost decathlon champion before the 1912 Olympic Games. After the Olympics, he studied at the Princeton Theological Seminary and became a Presbyterian minister. During World War I he was an army chaplain, and it was in Europe, in 1918, that he renewed an acquaintance with Aunt Frances, who was the first American war correspondent (man or woman) in Germany after the war. Their chance meeting soon became a romance and they were wed in New York eight months later. Uncle Fred, with his physique and good looks, soon found himself in the movies and rapidly became (along with Tom Mix) one of the great cowboy stars. He and his great white stallion, Silver King, had worldwide fan appeal. Tragically, he died of pneumonia, complicated by tetanus, on Christmas Day, 1928, at age thirty-eight, leaving Aunt Frances to raise their two sons, Fred and Dick, alone. Aunt Frances and Uncle Fred had built their fabled "House on the Hill," which, along with Mary Pickford's and Doug Fairbanks' "Pickfair" and the Harold Lloyd estate "Green Acres," were the million dollar show places of the 1920s.

As head of the story department at Metro Goldwyn Mayer, Aunt Frances wielded great influence in the movie industry. She was, without doubt, the most creative and accomplished person I have ever known. She not only wrote all of Mary Pickford's films but also wrote or adapted hundreds of screen plays, and probably wrote the first actual scenario in Hollywood history. She was also a novelist and short story writer and even wrote a textbook on how to write and sell screenplays. Along the way, she collected two Oscars. Aunt Frances excelled at every other aspect of film making: acting, directing, and producing. And there was much more. She also excelled in many other art forms—she sculpted, painted, played the piano beautifully, spoke three languages, had a lovely contralto, and was a magnificent cook. The only art form at which she didn't excel was dancing. One leg was a trifle shorter (possibly from a mild case of poliomyelitis in childhood) than the other and she had a slight but noticeable limp. But above all, from my point of view, she was fun and funny! Her impersonations of well-known celebrities and studio heads were devastating and hilarious. Of course, Hollywood being the place it was—a hotbed of intrigue, rumors, and easily bruised egos—she had to be circumspect in her pantomimes and she performed them only for people she knew well and trusted completely. She enjoyed children and knew the things that interested them, from old-fashioned taffy pulls in the kitchen to the thrill rides at the Venice amusement park to carefree vacations at her father's summer resort at Aetna Springs.

My brother and I were close enough in age to Aunt Frances's two sons to be compatible with them. Aunt Frances and my mother shared a close friendship, and during the 1930s she, with her beau John Merideth, was at our house, or my parents at hers, one or two nights a week for pinochle, bridge, or Russian Blank. There were plans to take a round-the-world trip on the Grace Line that had to be shelved when President Roosevelt declared a bank holiday in 1932. Long after we moved to Hawaii and until my mother's death, Aunt Frances and my mother kept an active correspondence.

The parties at Aunt Frances's beautiful estate on Selma Drive were legendary. She knew every celebrity in Hollywood and, in fact, had given many of those celebrities their start in the industry. The word "glamorous" has, through over-use, become almost meaningless. The adjective is, I think, essentially feminine; I don't know what a glamorous man would be. The word implies many things: sensuality, beauty, intellect, style, allure, and an element of mystery. It defies precise definition, but one knows when one is in the presence of glamour. In my lifetime, I have known only one person who personified the word, and that was Frances Marion.

As usual, my father continued working hard after the failure of the ranch at Harper Lake. Having learned the hard way of the importance of water in farming, he found it was a valuable background for his next job—selling large Venn-Severen Diesel engines to the farmers in the Imperial Valley. Sometimes I played hooky to make rounds with him to towns like Barstow, Victorville, and Lancaster.

During the most difficult days of the depression, our family survived almost unaffected due to the guaranteed income from my grandfather's estate plus, of course, what my father was able to earn. We knew a little of hard times but very little; by the standards of the day, we were relatively affluent. We were incredibly fortunate but we knew it and were everlastingly grateful.

It was during the 1930s that I got to know my brother best. We were not as close as some brothers, but John would have taken my part and I his in any confrontation with an outsider. And because he was my older brother, he was always able to out-poke, out-pinch, and out-wrestle me in our childish tussles, which left me in tears to be consoled by Laddie.

John's best friend from the time we moved to Beverly Hills was Arthur Marx, the son of the legendary Groucho Marx. I remember that John idolized Mr. Marx, who became a hero figure to my brother. Groucho was an odd sort of hero for a youngster like John, who had never known a day of want in his life and was raised in relative luxury. Nevertheless, John identified with the tough, cynical Jewish man who had grown up in the Upper East Side of New York City and who, with his famous brothers, achieved super stardom on the New York stage and in the movies. Groucho was brilliant, very funny, and a compulsive punster. "Don't conscience strickens before they're hatched," and "Senator Johnson is incongruous," were two of his puns that I've never forgotten. Groucho played the guitar skillfully but ping-pong poorly and was not happy when I beat him with my "schmuck serve," as he called it. Groucho had few illusions about the goodness of man but was generous to his children and to their friends. Groucho was as funny and inventive off screen as he was in his films. John recounted an evening when he, Art, and Mr. Marx went to a movie (a horror film of the Dracula/Frankenstein genre), which Groucho had a special liking for. At the scariest moment of the film, with the audience on the edge of their seats as the heroine was about to have her throat cut by "the Fiend," Groucho let loose with an earth-shaking sneeze (although his "ahh-choo" sounded a bit more like "aw-shit") that momentarily terrified everyone in the house. It was the sort of antic only the masterful Groucho Marx could muster and the sort of thing that endeared him to my brother.

John loved books and read insatiably and beyond his years. He was an excellent athlete with talent in swimming, boxing, and tennis. At Dartmouth he won the welterweight boxing title. I enjoyed reading, too, but, unlike my brother, I re-read favorite books over and over. I'm sure I read every Albert Payson Terhune dog story at least three times.

John was very bright, very perceptive, and was a skilled writer. He had a rare critical sense and there were adults who wouldn't go see a movie he had panned in his reviews in the high school paper. With time, training, and experience he might have become a second George Jean Nathan, the famous drama critic and editor. John had a sense of humor reminiscent of H. Allen Smith, the well-known journalist and humorist. John probably should not have married so young, but after his years in the navy during World War II, he and Nini Agee fell in love and, at age twenty-five, he married and started a family. Instead of sharpening his talents without worrying about feeding the family, he did the honorable thing and got jobs: selling insurance, selling household goods at Sears Roebuck, selling automobiles, and working as a telecommunications consultant. The jobs paid the bills but frustrated any possibility of a career in literature.

During the war, John was a quartermaster on an escort carrier, the USS *Attu* (CVE 102). Two months before the end of the war, the *Attu*, part of Task Group 30.8, under the command of Admiral "Bull" Halsey, was driven through a severe storm. It was reported that one ship (though there were possibly three) foundered and many lives were lost. It was also suggested that had not Admiral Halsey been a national hero, he might have been admonished for his decision to go through the storm. This mistake on the part of Halsey was hardly mentioned in the press, as was true of most of our failures, defeats, and mistakes during the war. Presumably, too much bad press would have adversely affected civilian morale.

John wrote a report in longhand within forty-eight hours of his experiences in that storm. I found it a year or so ago among some old letters. Since he actually had the wheel of the ship during some of the most harrowing moments, the report is, I think, of unique interest and has some value. Reports such as this did not surface during the war. I believe the immediacy of the piece gives it an impact that an official report, cautiously written, would probably lack. It not only demonstrates his undoubted writing skills but also gives one an appreciation of the steadfast courage

of Navy personnel. Not all harrowing moments in war involve an armed
enemy. Although this incident was reported in the press, the official ac-
counting did not fully describe the seriousness of Halsey's mistake and the
effect it had on the fleet.

> While en route to our rendezvous off Okinawa in the morn-
> ing (mid-watch) of June 5, 1945, we received word of an
> impending typhoon. At 0100, the wind had risen to fifty
> knots, bearing off our port beam, and steering was becoming
> difficult. At 0230, acting on orders from the task force com-
> mander (?Halsey), the Captain c/c to 300 degrees T. and
> PGC. This course headed us directly into the center of the
> storm and steering became very difficult. The apparent wind
> was now bearing between 210 and 180 degrees or abaft our
> port quarter. The barometer dropped during the period to
> 28.80 and continued to drop. The wind velocity (apparent)
> now was hitting as high as 60K. sometimes directly astern,
> and the ship was rolling heavily.
>
> At 0330, with the barometer still dropping, we entered the
> outer edge of the typhoon on a heading of 270 degrees—ap-
> proximately. With the Captain at the conn, I put the wheel
> hard right to attempt to keep the ship on course. This had
> little or no effect. The storm hit us on the port beam and
> we healed sharply to starboard with an estimated 25 to 30
> degree list. The wind now settled dead astern and reached an
> apparent velocity of 75 knots or, as we later discovered, over
> 95 knots true. The full right rudder had no effect and we
> turned slowly to port finally settling on 220 to 230 degrees
> true. This broke the entire formation and all TBS contact
> was lost. The ship was listing heavily now and we narrowly

missed collision with an oiler lying dead in the water. The Captain ordered full astern rung up on the Engine Order Telegraph and collision was avoided by an estimated 25 feet.

The storm had now reached its peak and begun to subside somewhat as we entered the "eye" of the typhoon. The barometer at this point had dropped to 28.30 and the wind subsided to 50 knots and shifted to the starboard quarter.

During the peak of the storm, aircraft had torn loose on the flight deck. The Captain put the ship in the trough and the heavy listing sent several (9) TBMs over the side, clearing the deck from further danger. Gasoline from several of the overturned planes began to flow around the deck and down the scuppers. One plane, tilting over the forward stack, poured gasoline down the stack causing much apprehension among those who saw it.

During this period of comparative calm (0445-0600) the damage control parties repaired what could be reached and steering control was regained to a certain extent. The crew lay below for coffee and buns.

At 0600 the ship moved out of the "eye" and through the outer edge of the storm without further damage. The wind died down, the barometer began to rise and things in general returned to normal. T/G 30.8 reformed and proceeded on course.

By noon the ship was rolling easily and the work of jettisoning damaged planes was underway. By nightfall the wind

had died to normal and we proceeded without further incident. (John Dinmore, 1945)

At one point after the war, unhappy, frustrated, and in a kind of emotional cul-de-sac, John began seeing a psychiatrist in order to cope with
his alleged passive-aggressive neurosis. Predictably, John was led to believe
that the source of his trouble was an overprotective mother. This simplistic
appraisal didn't do much to solve his problems but did add a great deal to
our mother's depression in her last years. But John's virtues exceeded his
faults. He was loyal to his friends, gallant toward women, respected and
loved by his children, and he had courage and integrity. He also had an
immediate, invariably correct antipathy to the self-important, the phonies,
and the fools. Always a heavy smoker, he died prematurely at the age of
fifty-eight of lung cancer after a life of unfulfilled promise.

Early in 1936, my father renewed an acquaintance with an old school
friend from Petaluma, Lyle Pressey. Pressey, a nephew of the then Governor General of the Territory of Hawaii, Joseph Poindexter, was touting
the great business opportunities in the Islands and encouraged my father
to come with him. Pressey's enthusiasm and the fact that the diesel engine
business in California was in the doldrums were enough to convince my
father to travel to the Islands to evaluate business possibilities.

While my father concluded his affairs in southern California, my
mother, brother, and I spent our last summer vacation in California at
the Sonoma Mission Inn north of San Francisco. It was a fine vacation
with lots of swimming, hiking, and trips down to the city for evenings
with family and friends. My cousin, Virginia Lewis, was married to an
Air Corps pilot, Mike Harding, who was stationed at Hamilton Field, not
far from Sonoma. Mike, a West Point graduate, was the first person to
ignite my interest in the Academy. At that time, the Air Corps was like a
big club. It was still small enough to permit everyone to know everyone

else. Dinners at the Officers' Club were formal and very colorful. General Tinker was the wing commander and when he entered the room, one was immediately aware of his presence. He was about six foot four, swarthy, with prominent black sideburns, and his Cheyenne Indian heritage was very much in evidence.

Mike knew of my interest in airplanes and took pleasure in taking me to the flight line to see the "ultimate" bomber, the B-18. The B-18 was a twin-engine aircraft that entered the weapons inventory before the fabled B-17. I remember Mike showing me his plane and saying he doubted that it would ever be improved upon for "it even has a heater." It was a time when the Air Corps had great popular appeal and was considered very dashing and exciting. General "Hap" Arnold, then a lieutenant colonel, had recently completed his noteworthy mission of a flight of a dozen bombers to Alaska and back, and it was a feat that was still a topic of conversation.

That summer at the Inn, I also met a couple, Mr. and Mrs. Fisher. They were in their eighties, but Mr. Fisher had more *joie de vivre* than most men in their thirties and was a lot more interesting. He remembered seeing Abraham Lincoln and, when a little younger than I, remembered meeting a nonagenarian who had fought in the Revolutionary War. It impressed me then and still impresses me now that I could have met someone who had met a veteran who had fought for our nation at its inception.

In October 1936, my father sailed to Hawaii. His initial impression of the place, absent his family and missing California, was unfavorable. When he came to realize that all the talk of opportunities in Hawaii, with or without Governor Poindexter's help, was smoke and mirrors, he was ready to come home on the first available ship. As fate would have it, a maritime strike totally isolated the Islands for weeks. Returning by air was not an option, so my father was essentially marooned in paradise. He also had had a falling out with the exuberant Lyle Pressey. However, by the time the strike was settled, my father was doing pretty well selling automobiles. He was adapting to the Islands and suggested that we join him the summer of 1937. As 1936 was closing, my mother was warming to the idea and we began to plan the next chapter in our lives.

1937–1942

I doubt that one could adequately describe life in pre-war Honolulu to anyone who never experienced it. Compared to today, it was idyllic. There were four hotels in Waikiki: the Niamalu, the Halekulani, the Moana, and the Royal Hawaiian. Today, in that space, there are over sixty. All of the land between Kalakaua Boulevard and the Ala Wai Canal was filled with inexpensive bungalows. Fort DeRussy was an active coast artillery post. Automobile traffic was busy but not the nightmare it is today. "Tourism" consisted of the Matson Steamship Line's *Lurline* or *Malolo* (later re-christened the *Matsonia*) disgorging seven hundred people on alternate Wednesdays, and their other two ships, *Monterey* and *Mariposa*, on their return trips from Australia, docked every five or six weeks. Other steamship lines, the Grace Line and the American President Line, as well as Japanese passenger lines contributed their share to a lesser extent. In contrast, during the latter decades of the twentieth century, at the height of the tourist boom, three or four hundred people arrived by airplane every half hour. Memories fade, but I still remember the pretty young girls wearing hibiscus in their hair, the flowers everywhere, and the pervasive, subtle, sweet smell of carnations, ginger, gardenias, and plumeria. Pink carnation leis were fifty cents, white carnation leis a dollar, and, for very special occasions, a nine-strand pikake was three dollars. On the days that passenger ships arrived, the downtown area was especially colorful as the lei-making ladies busied themselves making hundreds of leis for the arriving tourists.

My mother, brother, and I arrived in mid-October, 1937. To this day, I remember the fragrance of the carnation and ginger leis that were piled around our necks up to our ears and the beautiful Hawaiian melodies

played by the Aloha Band as we pulled into the dock. There were few places in the world where arrivals and departures were more emotional.

Our home for the next two years was the Pleasanton Hotel, across the
street from the campus of Punahou School, where my brother and I were
to attend high school. The Pleasanton was old, dark, shabby, and as different form our beloved Fairmont Hotel as one could imagine. My mother
was, in a word, miserable. Not only were our accommodations depressing
but also she was unable to tolerate the sub-tropical climate. To make matters worse, we had arrived in the middle of one of the worst spells of *kona*
weather in anyone's memory. Even the locals hate *kona*, or "sick weather,"
when the wind blows from the south instead of from the northwest and
both the temperature and the humidity hover in the mid-nineties.

John and I started the fall school semester late, and catching up was a
struggle for half a year. The transition for me, from Hawthorn, which was
a typical suburban elementary school occupying about a half a city block
in one big building with a large gravel-covered playground, to Punahou's
eighty acres of beautiful grounds, many pavilions for classes, large football
fields, tennis courts, and an Olympic-sized swimming pool, was not an
easy one. My transition to this first-rate school was made even more difficult by academic standards higher than I had ever known.

Punahou was and remains a remarkable and unique school. It was
founded by the missionaries in 1841. Up until that time, the missionaries
sent their children to school in New England, a custom that became intolerable because they often did not see their children for years, sometimes
never, and, of course, the trip sailing 'round the Horn was very dangerous.
Punahou's reputation has always been at the very top of all private schools
in the country. From its inception, Punahou has educated children from
kindergarten through high school, and it has always been coeducational.
Its distinguished alumni roster includes the father of one country, Sun Yat-
sen, often called the George Washington of China, and the president of
another, Barak Obama, the 44th President of the United States.

Non-graduates of Punahou—the wives, husbands, and children of alumni—are often bemused, even amazed, at the lifelong loyalty of its graduates. The school has an enormous "pull" for anyone who attended, which is often greater than most colleges. Graduates come from all parts of the country, even the world, to attend the alumni luau each spring. The nature of this loyalty is hard to pinpoint. Whether it is the physical beauty of the campus, its traditions, or its academic standards that prepare graduates for the most prestigious universities, I am not sure. It's probably all three plus something more—it's difficult to define, yet that intangible "it" exists and flourishes. It was a privilege to attend Punahou and one that I did not fully appreciate at the time.

Getting squared away at Punahou the first year was difficult, I had never been required to work that hard, and starting late made it that much harder. Once, I went to my algebra teacher, Mr. Schmutzler, a crusty, no-nonsense old German, whining about how I needed extra help; he listened, briefly, and said something to the effect that I probably wasn't worth the effort. No teacher had ever talked to me that way and I was stung. It also made me mad. Whatever Mr. Schmutzler had in mind by saying what he did must have worked because I passed algebra and made it into my sophomore year. The year was also made better because I turned out for the swimming team and managed to earn a letter diving.

The second year was better—the realization that Punahou was an unusually fine school was a consolation but, in retrospect, I wasted a lot of time being homesick for San Francisco. Plus, it would have been better for all of us if we had had our own home instead of living at the depressing old Pleasanton, and I know my mother would have been much happier with her own furniture, her piano, and her books.

Difficult academic transitions aside, we teenagers made our own fun by surfing, hiking, and ti-leaf sliding, along with the usual high school activities of sports and parties. I don't recall any of my contemporaries smoking or drinking anything more than an occasional beer. Marijuana or any other drugs were unheard of; staying in excellent physical shape was a consuming interest. A classmate of mine who had been born and raised in the Islands, when asked how she liked the mainland after her first year of college replied, "It's nice but there's nothing to *do* up there." It would be hard to imagine a healthier place to grow up than pre-war Hawaii.

In June after my second year, we returned to San Francisco, leaving my father in Honolulu, so that John could enter the University of California at Berkeley. We took an apartment on California Street a few blocks from the Fairmont, and I enrolled at the Bates School for my junior year. No high school could have been more different compared to Punahou. Bates was in a single, four-story building with commercial apartments sandwiched on either side, and it had no recreation fields. It was a private school and had a good reputation, but it catered to students who had been expelled, for a variety of reasons, from public schools. I signed up for six subjects, and the fact that I wound up with six A's was testimony to the academic standards. (However, it made my transcript look awfully good.) Many years later I learned that my parents had decided on a "trial separation" during this period, but I've never known the exact reason for their decision.

After a few months in San Francisco, and the joy of being in the city again, we were surprised to realize that we began missing Honolulu. By the end of my junior year at Bates, we were looking forward to our return to Honolulu. My mother still had misgivings about the climate but more and more missed my father and the casual lifestyle of Hawaii, as well as its unparalleled beauty. We returned in June 1940, and were quite excited to be "home."

Within a week or so of our arrival, my parents bought a home on Anuenue Street off lower Manoa Road and were to remain in the Islands for the next fifteen years. I re-registered at Punahou and met a former classmate who told me about an opportunity to attend a senior ROTC camp at Schofield Barracks. It sounded like a good idea, so I applied for the six-week encampment.

It was my first exposure to the United States Army, the pre-war peace-time army. Our NCO supervisor was a tough old regular Army buck ser-geant. He was probably in his thirties, but he seemed old to us. He may not have been the brightest soldier in the Army, and he viewed us with ill-con-cealed amusement, but, good soldier that he was, he did his best and was thoroughly competent at his job. We learned the intricacies of close-order drill, basic field hygiene, chemical warfare, firing range discipline, and how to use the Springfield Model '03 bolt action rifle—and a lot about how to clean it properly. Our sergeant would call us out at reveille every morning and invariably say, "All right you guys, fall in alphabetical order, A's first." I don't think he ever knew why we thought this was funny.

If the morning mission was the firing line, we would spend a good part of the afternoon cleaning our weapons using two big GI cans. One was filled with hot soapy water and the other with even hotter clear water. The first time I cleaned my rifle, using brass wire brushes followed by small oiled patches, I thought after one hour of labor I had the cleanest rifle at Schofield. With pride, I presented it to our sergeant for inspection. He flipped it up, squinted down the barrel, and tossed it back saying that it was "coming along."

If the morning mission was a hike up Kolekole Pass with rifles and light field packs, even that was fun. On one occasion, I remember coming down the pass just as the Twenty-Seventh Infantry Regiment was going up in Jeeps and 4x4 trucks. We had been properly schooled in customs and courtesies and knew that if a vehicle with a little white cardboard sign bearing a black "O" was spotted, an officer was on board and rated a salute. There are a great many vehicles in a regiment and a great many officers, so I spent a good part of the afternoon practicing the hand salute.

If the morning mission was chemical warfare, we learned in gruesome detail the effects of phosgene, Lewisite, and mustard gas and how to iden-tify them—the smell of new-mown hay, of garlic, etc., and how to get on a gas mask fast. It amused me to discover forty years later when I rejoined the Air Force and was required to attend lectures on the old agents, as well as some of the newer nerve gases, that the lectures were essentially the same. Morning, afternoon, and at all other times we learned the old admonition to garrisoned infantry soldiers: "If it's on the ground, pick it up; if it moves, salute it, if it doesn't move, paint it white."

I loved every minute of that encampment, from reveille to taps, and even though it only lasted six weeks, it did bolster my self-esteem. It also inspired in me an admiration for the military and a desire to be part of it. My brother, sensing this, took delight in quoting Bernard Shaw's observation that "never a bright child, he early on decided upon a career in the military."

If there is a better year in the life of a teenager than the senior year of high school, I can't imagine when it would be—especially if one's senior year is the last one before a world war and the school is Punahou. No sooner had school started than two pleasant things happened. I was appointed a lieutenant in the ROTC battalion and Franny Stevens and I were elected co-editors of our school yearbook, the *Oahuan*. I think my six weeks at Schofield had something to do with the former and the fact that John had edited the yearbook two years before had a lot to do with the latter. By my senior year I had developed study habits good enough to maintain a weak "B" average without undue effort so that the coveted "senior privileges" were automatic.

Punahou's centennial year was especially exciting in my second semester as a senior. A two-and-a-half hour pageant, which told the story of the school from its inception, was presented two weeks after graduation. After two years of planning, over twelve hundred people were involved in the production. It was quite a show. The stage was three hundred feet long with a revolving center and it filled the football field at Alexander Field. There was an impressive display of lights, music, dancing, and participation of Army units. There were two performances playing to audiences of over five thousand. The actors on stage lip-synched the dialogue read by "actors" in the control booth high above the stage. The designer was a talented young graduate of the Chicago Art Institute, Norman Grant, and the director was Elroy Fulmer, who continued for many years as the director of the Honolulu Community Theater. The pageant was a fitting climax to an unforgettable year.

After the pageant, we began to get ready for a summer vacation in California. John, who had taken a year off from college to work in a local bookstore, was accepted at Dartmouth for the fall semester. My father's automobile business was prospering, so we had few worries. The war in Europe, however, was on everyone's mind. England was taking a terrible beating, and France had already fallen to the Nazis. In Honolulu there were practice blackouts and even talk of martial law. There were as many people who feared a war with Japan as there were who laughed at the idea.

Nevertheless, we sailed in mid-August for the mainland. San Francisco was magical, as usual, and our two short trips to Southern California were as much fun as ever. John saw a lot of Arthur and Mr. Marx, and we enjoyed the usual good times with Aunt Frances, as well as a lovely garden party at the Harold Lloyds' and two evenings with Mr. and Mrs. Nigel Bruce. Mr. Bruce was a jolly, big man who, in person, was not unlike the bumbling characters he played in films. Evenings at his home were informal and great fun. His two daughters, Jennifer and Pauline, were about the same age as John and me, and we had known them when we lived in Beverly Hills. Jennifer, the younger, was bubbly and talented while Pauline, the elder, was more reserved and a raving beauty in the Merle Oberon/Hedy Lamarr mold. The Bruces were chaperoning their houseguest, a beautiful newcomer, Anne Baxter, who was being groomed for motion pictures and ultimate stardom. She was at that time about seventeen, unaffected, and had a good time entering into our silly party games.

Somewhat reluctantly, we sailed back to Honolulu on November 1, 1941. The night we sailed from Los Angeles, I noticed a farewell party in progress with a group of very attractive young people. The party was for

Roberta Paul-Reed, who I came to know the next few days at sea. "Bobby" was on her way to Honolulu to see her fiancé, Yale Lewis, a lieutenant in the Army Air Force stationed at Hickam Field. It was the beginning of a friendship that lasted over sixty years.

Back home there was much discussion about the international situation. One night at dinner with Jan Jabulka, the managing editor of the *Honolulu Advertiser*, and his wife, Vickie, the possibility of war with Japan came up. I remember him saying, "I don't know if we'll have a war or not, but if we do, there won't be a declaration. We'll just wake up some morning and there'll be planes over Diamond Head." There was a military alert the last week of November, and I recall seeing the old water-cooled Lewis machine guns set up behind sandbags at Kau Kau Corner at the intersection of Kalakaua and the Ali Wai Canal. The alert was called off and the guns gone by the first of December.

I had no plans for college, so I passed the last few weeks of November working for my father and working with Norm Grant at the Honolulu Community Theater learning a little about stage craft, lighting, and scenery design. We were soon rehearsing a light comedy, *Mr. and Mrs. North*, which opened December 1, 1941. The play was well attended and closed Saturday evening the 6th of December. There was a cast party following the last performance, and I stayed a little while until, being a nondrinker, I began to feel out of place. I left for home about midnight and collapsed in bed, pleasantly exhausted.

The next thing I remember hearing, about nine o'clock Sunday morning, was the voice of a family friend downstairs saying, "No, I don't think it's a drill. I was driving over here along Wilhemina Rise and I saw ships under attack off Waikiki. I think we may be at war."

Reflections

From about age five through the teen years is that time of life when one's habits, beliefs, and a sense of the fitness of things are molded and learned. Young people of a certain environment assume that they and their contemporaries are pretty much the same; the sons of farmers assume that others their age are interested in agriculture; sons of the politically conservative think that most people are conservative; ministers' children think that most people are religious. When one learns that these assumptions may be wrong, one is beginning to think like an adult. It was certainly true for me. It wasn't until I was more or less on my own during the war and later that I realized my background was both privileged and untypical. We always had one servant and a governess until I was seven or eight and most people did not. We had a multitude of unconventional friends and most people did not. We talked about everything—politics, religion, current events, and people—and most people did not. We thought the old adage, "If you can't say something nice about someone, don't say anything" was saccharine and mindless. People were analyzed, ripped apart, ridiculed, praised, and even canonized simply because they were endlessly fascinating. Manners were drummed into our behavior and the definition that "good manners consist of a series of self-sacrifices" was well learned. One stood up for seniors, kept silent unless invited to contribute, wrote thank you notes, opened doors for women, dressed appropriately, and on and on. One respected the opinions of those qualified to utter them and avoided self-important fools. Competence in any field of endeavor, whether the arts, academia, the military, the learned professions, and even business was respected. The proper use of the English language, written or spoken, was admired and often revered. We simply did not know, for very long, people who lacked the virtues of loyalty, kindness, and decency. Conflicting opinions were vigorously defended but disagreements were rarely disagreeable. In dress and comportment, "fashion was for the many, style for the very few."

These were the standards of my life, and I was to learn (sometimes the hard way) they were not common to all. Making money, if it was the by-product of useful work or talent, was pleasant enough, but acquisitiveness alone was not considered a virtue. The accumulation of material things, if it was one's goal in life, was not the mark of a civilized man. I could not change these sets of values even if I wanted to, for they are the foundation of a lifelong appreciation of excellence in any field of endeavor and a basis for rejecting anything tawdry, tasteless, ignorant, lacking in talent, or without redeeming social value.

Nanny Mae Lewis "Nana" at age 17

Nanny Mae Lewis
Great Grandmother Hall, Great Grandmother Lewis, Mary Margaret Dinmore

Nathan Jacob at 35

Nathan Jacob

Lulu Finn Jacob

Walter Robert Dinmore

Estelle Jacob "Tykey" at age 3

Lulu Finn Jacob with Tyke and Midey

Estelle Jacob at age 18

Me, John, and Mother in 1925

John and me in 1926

Our Family in Bronxville, NY in 1925

Dad and Laddie

My boyhood hero and cousin, Lt. Ned White

Me, cousin Penn, John, and cousin Virginia

Francis Marion

Fred Thomson

Aunt Frances with her children Fred and Dick
in Black-Foxe Military Institute uniforms

Jackie Cooper

Jack and me capturing the "evil-doers"

II
1942-1945

At no time in our country's history had the coming of age of one generation arrive with greater abruptness than it did at 7:55 a.m., December 7, 1941. The fact that we were finally in the war did not surprise many people, but the manner in which we were forced into it did. As seniors in high school, my friends and I knew that, sooner or later, we would become involved in the European war. The Lend Lease Act, which provided U.S. military aid to allies during World War II, was very nearly an act of war. We also knew that war with Japan was a strong possibility. We knew that the United States could not tolerate England and all of Western Europe falling under the oppression of Nazi Germany. As for Japan, few people thought the country had the audacity or capability to strike such a devastating blow against the United States. The average person believed that the Pacific Fleet was virtually invulnerable and tended to believe the Hollywood legend of invincibility. A few American military scholars who had read General Billy Mitchell's remarkably prescient warnings (written in the 1920s) that the Japanese could, and probably would, initiate hostilities exactly as they did, were the only ones not surprised by the attack on Pearl Harbor.

Having no experience with war or knowledge of Japanese culture, I remember thinking, in effect, *the poor fools; do they really think that they can win a war against the United States?* I was arrogant and ignorant to be sure, but that was the way most of my generation reacted. We hadn't the slightest notion that the surrender of Japan would come only after nearly four years of bloody warfare. And few, with the exception of Albert Einstein and a handful of theoretical physicists, had any conception of the weapon that would prove decisive.

Our home in Manoa Valley was about ten miles from Pearl Harbor on a direct line, but any view of the harbor was blocked by the shoulder of Round Top, which was part of Mount Tantalus. On the morning of December 7, 1941, we could neither see smoke nor hear gunfire or bombs. By the time I had dressed and gone down to the front lawn, most of our neighbors were milling around, confused and uncertain, until an ear-splitting sound and a small explosion on Round Top got everyone's attention. What we heard and saw was not a Japanese bomb but an artillery shell that had been fired by the defenders at Pearl. The ear-shattering sound of incoming artillery is unlike any other sound—one never forgets it. With that explosion, everyone went indoors to listen more attentively to their radios.

I recall the staff announcer at KGMB, Webb Edwards, excitedly reporting that the Rising Sun emblem had been confirmed on the wings of the attacking airplanes. Soon thereafter, martial music began to be played, followed by the national anthem. At about 9:30 a.m., Edwards announced that martial law had been declared, that people were to remain home and off the streets, that a total blackout was to be in effect at once, and that KGMB would soon be going off the air.

With the local radio signed off, we turned on our short-wave bands. For the next several hours, the local radio would come on briefly for official announcements: to stay off the streets, to black out our homes, to observe the strict curfew, and the like. But, for the next few days and nights, we learned what was happening in Hawaii from radio stations in Los Angeles and San Francisco via our short-wave radios. There was no panic. There were a few hysterical rumors about Japanese paratroopers landing, but these were discounted as fast as they surfaced. There was never any concern about the necessities of life—food, water, and power. For those of us who were young and had no responsibilities, it was all very exciting. For adults it was quite different. We did not know if the city of Honolulu had been bombed or not. My father didn't know for several days if he still had a business. My mother, who ever since the San Francisco fire and earthquake of 1906 was not stoic about natural or man-made disasters, spent the hours clutching a hot water bottle wrapped in an afghan to her stomach, trying not to be ill, and sleeping in snatches. By mid-week the immediate threat of an invasion was over and people began to move about; the blackout and curfew, however, were in effect until October 1944. On December 8, 1941, we heard President Roosevelt's declaration of war; the thunderous applause in the Congress was oddly reassuring.

I have been asked by people who have no knowledge of the Islands if there was concern about the fact that seventy-five percent of the population were Americans of Japanese descent. It simply never occurred to anyone that they constituted a nest of potential saboteurs. To my knowledge, there was not a single episode of sabotage by Japanese Americans during the entire war. And the bravery of the 442nd Regimental Combat Team, composed almost entirely of American youngsters of Japanese descent, most from Hawaii, is legendary. There undoubtedly was espionage by foreign nationals and Japanese embassy personnel (there were rumors to this effect), but such activities were predictable, and the FBI had most of them in custody rapidly. When the shameful and unconstitutional relocation of Japanese American citizens in California occurred, I remember thinking it was a hysterical over-reaction to a non-existent threat and that it was totally unjustified.

On about December 10, 1941, a call went out for volunteers who were not otherwise employed and who knew their way around Oahu to report to the U.S. Corps of Engineers. The Corps had taken over the entire campus at Punahou as their headquarters. They needed drivers for the coordinators who were in the process of evaluating the damage at Pearl Harbor and other military installations; I volunteered for about two weeks, at which time I was no longer needed. Although my parents did not see Pearl Harbor for many weeks following the attack, my first trip to Pearl was a day later, and I remember looking at the damage from Aiea Heights. The destruction was appalling. Ships were still smoking and the carnage was shocking. Some capital ships were sunk on a level plane so that their decks and main batteries were awash; one was lying on its beam end; other smaller vessels were sunk so that only their bridges or foretops were visible. Litter, oil slicks, and debris were everywhere. On the USS *Arizona*, twenty men were trapped in a water-tight compartment and could not be reached—their tapping was heard for almost three weeks as they slowly, agonizingly, died of starvation and dehydration.

At this point, the future was uncertain and confused. We didn't know whether the evacuation of civilians was to be ordered or offered. There was no imminent danger and, save for martial law and the blackouts, life began to assume a more normal pattern. I was uncertain about my own future, and my desire to get into the Army Air Force was frustrated by my parents' natural desire to keep me out of it and get me into college. Having just turned eighteen I could have enlisted, but I was not interested in joining the ground forces. At that time, pilot training still required two years of college, so I felt my best option was to begin making plans to get to the mainland and at least begin college at the University of California at Berkeley.

I remember the spring of 1942 as a time of frustration and impatience. I filled my time working for my father, taking classes in mechanical drawing at the University of Hawaii, and spending a lot of time sharpening my skills at two-man beach volleyball at the Outrigger Canoe Club. In general, however, I was feeling pretty useless. Finally, I was accepted for the fall term at Berkeley and started the necessary procedures to get to the mainland. It was not an easy time to travel, and there were many delays and a lot of red-tape.

My father joined a volunteer group call the Businessmen's Training Corps (BMTC). The mission of the BMTC, or "overage destroyers," was to act as a civilian defense force in the event of an invasion, which was by no means out of the question in early 1942. The BMTC was issued steel helmets (circa 1918) and .45 Colt automatic pistols, and they practiced close-order drill once a week. Because my father knew little about side arms and I did, we practiced together at the kitchen table stripping, cleaning, and reassembling the weapon. We got so good at it that we could literally do it blindfolded.

Finally, I received tickets to sail on June 5, 1942. The exact time of departure was kept secret until eight hours prior to departure. We left in convoy on the old S.S. *President Johnson*, which had been converted to a troop carrier. We assembled off Diamond Head and were joined the next day by our escort, a World War I vintage *Marblehead*-class four-stack cruiser. We zigzagged most of the way, but the trip was mostly uneventful. But I do recall the S.S. *President Johnson* had some sort of irregularity in one of the propeller drive shafts which produced a moderately severe, constant vibration. After the first night, it was so consistent that it went unnoticed. About the third night at sea, the vibration suddenly stopped and that did awaken everyone. It was later suggested that a submarine had been detected by one of the escort ships but nothing came of it and the convoy continued as before. There were no other alerts and we finally sailed under the Golden Gate Bridge eight days after departing Honolulu.

The S.S. *President Johnson* was a far cry from the luxury of the *Lurline*, and the food was typical Navy chow. But there were half a dozen friends from Punahou and some colorful defense workers aboard, so the time passed quickly. There were obviously none of the amenities of pre-war luxury travel—no movies, no music, no dancing. So we improvised. One memorable evening, a game of "show me what you can do" was conceived. There were one-armed push-ups, sit-ups, and chin-up competitions. But the most memorable was that of a man who claimed he could light his own farts. There was a general murmur of disbelief and incredulity as he withdrew to prepare himself. He soon reappeared and, with a look of steely determination, first kneeled then quickly and simultaneously rolled on his back in a semi-tuck position, then produced a packet of matches, farted, and lit the product, producing a pale blue flame easily seen in the dimly lit area where we all bunked. This amazing trick produced a roar of applause and cheers of approval from the assembly. Our fellow passenger had achieved celebrity status for the rest of the trip.

We didn't know it the day we sailed, but the great victory at Midway was announced that afternoon. From that time until the end of the war, there was no longer a threat of invasion in Hawaii. However, had our Pacific Fleet been defeated at that momentous battle, it is doubtful that a determined Japanese invasion force could have been repelled.

In San Francisco I met John, who had left Dartmouth and was trying to get home to enlist in the Navy. It was not easy for a civilian to get passage to Hawaii and he had to tolerate many delays. But he finally made it home and, while waiting to be called up, got a temporary job on a defense project at Aiea Heights where the Navy was building enormous underground fuel storage tanks. Unfortunately, John suffered a severe on-the-job injury. In order to remove the earth that had been loosened by high-pressure hoses, large, belt-driven muck-rakes were used. With his machine turned off, John, using a hand device similar to a railroad spike, was chipping away dried mud. Without warning, the operator started the machine and John's hand and arm were caught up in the belt. The spike was driven through the palm of his right hand, his right arm fractured, and, while dangling in mid-air, most of the skin of his right shoulder was ground off by the belt. John had to be extricated from the machine. Thankfully, the skill of his surgeon, Dr. Bob Faus (the father of a Punahou classmate), saved the function of his hand. The fractures healed normally, but the denuded skin of his shoulder healed only after multiple skin grafts. It took a full year of recovery before he was fit for service in the Navy.

The war notwithstanding, it was quite a carefree time in San Francisco the summer of 1942. Many Punahou friends were in town on their way to colleges in the Bay Area. There were parties, dinner dancing at the St. Francis Hotel, and even occasional swimming at China Beach, although the water was always freezing.

I registered at the University of California, Berkeley, and classes started in late August. I went through rush week, and pledged my brother's fraternity, Zeta Psi. Truthfully, I made only a half-hearted attempt at my studies. It was a time when concentrating on class work required a mental discipline I totally lacked. One by one, the brothers at Zeta Psi were leaving for the military while the rest of us were simply marking time. We did learn a few important things, however, like how to hold a milkshake in two paper bags, what not to do at gin rummy, one's individual tolerance for alcohol, which, for me, then and always, has been close to nil, and how to smoke. It was the responsibility of the pledges to keep a wooden bowl on the living room table filled with Bull Durham tobacco, papers, and matches. Buying the makings inevitably led to rolling one's own and, when that got tedious, buying tailor-mades. But the nausea and dizziness that the novice smoker contends with makes studying trigonometry unnecessarily difficult.

The fraternity system at a large public university at that time was a study in snobbery, but, of course, we didn't think of ourselves as snobs at all. We all thought of ourselves as democratic jolly good fellows (but *never* as Democrats). No one questioned the time-honored practice of socializing only with other "Greeks" and rarely with "non-orgs." Sorority women were treated with respect, more or less, but "bags" (an unfortunate term used by some young men in frats to reference any non-sorority woman) were fair game for all sorts of indignities.

Stanford University was considered sort of a joke to us—a playground for the wealthy—and, it was rumored, cows occasionally wandered in and out of the classrooms. UCLA, the Los Angeles branch of the University of California, was called "the twig" and, except on football weekends, was regarded tolerantly. The Big Game each year, California versus Stanford, was the most important athletic event on the West Coast and any time the boys from The Farm (Stanford) won, it was a disaster. For the jolly Zetes, a Stanford Beta (Theta Pi) from the East was the ultimate stuffed shirt. It was said that the Betas even played classical music during dinner.

Academically, Zeta Psi, it was said, was invariably at the bottom of all the social organizations on campus—a source of pride for the brethren. Many times we were guilty of violating certain rules that would normally have resulted in our being "campused" (i.e., thrown off campus). But the authorities couldn't do that because we owned our own house.

I failed to maintain a C+ grade average the fall semester, so was not allowed to be initiated as a brother in the fraternity. Coincidentally, at about the time of my nineteenth birthday in November, I learned that the Air Force had lowered its requirement for pilot training. Two years of college were no longer required and one could, by volunteering, enter the Army (the Air Force was part of the Army until 1947) as a "qualified aviation cadet applicant." This solved two problems: by enlisting, I was allowed to leave the University without prejudice, and I would avoid being drafted into the ground services. When I announced my intention to the dean's secretary, she smiled, obviously relieved that there would be less paperwork involved than there would be if I had to be thrown out.

My parents were not pleased with my plans but resigned themselves to the inevitable. For me, after another period of waiting that seemed endless but, in reality, was not more than a few weeks, I got orders to present myself for induction the second week of January, 1943. When the time arrived, we were sworn in and promptly bussed to the Induction Center at Fort Ord, California, for in-processing.

Reflections

Just how much my four-month exposure to fraternity life during the fall of 1942 at the Berkeley campus of the University of California influenced my life is, to this day, unclear. "Rush Week" at the beginning of the school year, when the fraternities and sororities entertained and considered prospective members, was a well-established tradition. My brother and two cousins had been members of Zeta Psi, so I was a "legacy." I would have to have had leprosy, been a member of the young communist party, or been a hopeless nerd *not* to have been invited to join. So I happily accepted the little circular white pledge pin (or "eagle shit") when it was offered and soon moved into the house.

In the months that followed, I learned that the fraternity system at a large public institution was a study in snobbery. Zeta Psi was the first Greek letter fraternity at the University of California and was prestigious for that fact, if for no other. The fraternity was a kind of "old boys club" in the San Francisco area which could lead, in later life, to all sorts of opportunities and entrées—like eventual membership at the Olympic Club and even the Bohemian Club. The tone of the house was jolly, informal, and democratic. We considered other well-known houses, like the Alpha Delts and Betas, stuffy. Academic achievement was not a high priority. We accepted the fact with equanimity that the only group academically lower that the Zetes on campus was the Filipino Boys Club. Weekend parties were routine and, if they were not stag parties, usually included sorority women. Kappa Kappa Gamma (KKG) and Kappa Alpha Theta (KAT) were favorites. The KKGs were tall, elegant, flat-chested, smart, rich, and made lovely wives. The women at the KAT house were not quite so tall, a bit more earthy, not flat-chested, smart, rich, and made lovely wives. I remember one *faux pas* I made at a sorority party which resulted in my being "belted" a week later. We had a nondescript dog at the house whose name was Hair Pie. Being naïve in such matters, I had no idea of the implications of that name. When I called out "C'mere Hair Pie," across the living room at a party, an upper classman collared me and threw me into a corner. "Shut the fuck up," he explained. I had no idea just what code I had broken until someone drew a picture for me a week later.

Charlie Chew, our ageless Chinese cook, guarded his domain with particular vigor and was known to chase any trespasser out of it with a meat cleaver in one hand and a butcher knife in the other. Periodically, the Phi (the house president) ordered a freshman into the kitchen, just behind the head of a large moose on the wall of the dining room, to "wipe the moose's ass." The trick was to avoid Charlie and return with a napkin filled with mustard, ketchup, A-1 Sauce, or any other condiment, smeared into the most nauseating mixture one could conceive.

Alcohol abuse was a constant. The favorite drink was a "McGurk" composed of dollar-and-a-half *per gallon* gin, Coca Cola, and a wedge of lime. My tolerance for liquor was and still is close to zero. I pass from being talkative, to assertive, to argumentative, to sullen, to sleepy, to nauseated, to unconscious rapidly after any more than three drinks.

So, for four months of my life, I learned very little except how to smoke, what not to discard at gin rummy, and that I shouldn't drink—and not much else. Those four months, though occasionally fun, were essentially a cipher and an academic disaster. My grade average of something less than a D- was so poor that I was ineligible for formal initiation into the brotherhood of Zeta Psi, and I remained a pledge until mustered into the Air Force in January, 1943.

1943 and Flight Training

The Presidio at Monterey can be one of the most beautiful places on earth in good weather and one of the most dismal in bad. We got the latter: cold, wet, foggy, and occasional winds of gale-force intensity. The two or three weeks at Fort Ord were the most depressing I can remember. We were issued ill-fitting uniforms, painful boots, and awful food. Our first meal was the classic SOS, which stands for "shit on a shingle," a menu item made first thing every morning in every mess hall at every United States military installation in the world. It consists of either sausage or chipped beef or some other unidentifiable meat in a thick grayish goo ladled over biscuits. With enough pepper, salt, or Tabasco sauce, it could sometimes be made palatable, and there was always plenty of it. A serving of SOS and a "short arm" inspection (to see if the new arrival had active gonorrhea) were the two predictable rituals on arrival at every new installation to which my colleagues and I were assigned during the entire war.

The barracks were cold and smelled of mildew and unwashed bodies. I don't think I ever spent a more miserable two weeks in my life, before or since. I was homesick, depressed, scared, uncomfortable, and I soon developed a severe head cold. It was the only time in my military career that I had serious doubts about the future. We were in a war and it occurred to me that people can get killed in wars. There was absolutely nothing to suggest that we were in the Air Force—no music, no aircraft, no "wild blue yonder," just day after day of rain, wind, and misery. If there was a Base Exchange or canteen, I never found it. There were no letters from home because I hadn't an address. We were read the Articles of War, as required, and it didn't help my frame of mind to learn how many ways one could suffer "death or other punishment as a court martial may direct."

The purgatory at Fort Ord finally ended and we were sent to Camp Hahn, California, just across the highway from March Field in Riverside, where we spent about a month doing soldierly chores like unloading freight trains and moving pile "A" to pile "B" and back again. At least the weather was pleasant and we could occasionally see an airplane take off or land across the highway. About the time we all began to wonder whether we "qualified aviation cadets" had been forgotten by the War Department, we were assembled and advised that we were soon to be sent to the Classification Center—not the one in Santa Anna forty miles away but to Nashville, Tennessee, two thousand miles away. Finally, at long last, we were about to take the first step toward those coveted silver wings.

The trip to Nashville, sitting in coach seats for five days, was tolerable because morale was definitely improving. In St. Louis, we pulled into the station alongside another troop train heading west. They too were qualified aviation cadets, all from the East Coast and all, predictably, heading for the Classification Center at Santa Anna.

Nashville was cold and dreary in midwinter and smelled of coal smoke. Our barrack was heated by two coal-fired space heaters and the "space" was limited to a radius of about ten feet, so picking a cot became a high priority. But compared to Fort Ord, my spirits were high because we were "on our way."

For the next month we were tested in all manner of ways and with all manner of devices to determine who was to be qualified for pilot training, navigator training, or bombardier training. The physical examination was the most thorough I had ever taken. Passing the 1-A Flight Physical was essential because failure ruled out pilot training. Standing in line for the first doctor, a urologist, I heard one of my comrades exiting his cubicle say, "There's the strangest guy in there. He says 'good morning' then grabs your balls." The eye exams were critical and very thorough. One's visual acuity had to be 20/20 uncorrected. Evidence of color blindness or failure of the depth perception test was disqualifying. I was unaware until several years later, when I re-entered college, that I had a considerable astigmatism, but young eyes can compensate almost immediately for that developmental error.

There were manual dexterity tests, balance tests, reaction time tests, and many others, but the one most dreaded was the ARMA. The very initials still create a sense of unease. The ARMA stood for one's "Attitude with Regard to Military Aviation" and was administered by a clinical psychologist or a psychiatrist. It was dreaded because there was not only no way to prepare for it but also it had nothing to do with one's physical condition or one's motivation, and the results were final. A few "bad" answers and the qualified cadet applicant was on his way to Biloxi, Mississippi, and the infantry. Three days after the last exam, the results were posted. I had made the list for pilot training.

Our next station was to be Maxwell Field, Alabama, headquarters of the South East Training Command. After an all night trip from Nashville, we arrived at about sunup. The first thing I saw on waking was the gleaming hilt of a saber and a pair of white gloves accompanied by an upperclassman screaming at us to get our "ugly butts" off the train and into some kind of formation. We were dirty, disheveled, and unprepared for the beginning two months of strenuous military training. The objective, as with all boot-camp training, was to grind a man down to almost nothing the first month and then, hopefully, build him up into something that would one day become a commissioned officer. For a month, I saw little of Maxwell Field or anything else except the neck of the man in front of me. There were alternate days of close-order drill and calisthenics, with Sundays "at ease" to polish shoes and brass and do laundry in preparation for the week ahead. If there were academics, I don't remember them, nor could they have been too challenging.

By the time we arrived at Maxwell, after weeks of relative inactivity, we were not in the best physical condition. That was to change quickly. The first day of calisthenics, we were required to run around the perimeter of Maxwell Field, a distance of about six miles, up and down a gully known as the Burma Road. Our physical training instructor was a muscular, cheerful individual and former Olympic steeplechase champion who ran the entire course up and down the line, much of it backwards, exhorting us on to more speed. In the physical condition we were in, a number of people vomited or simply passed out from total exhaustion. But because we were motivated, young, and strong, we were running the course without difficulty a week or so later.

After the initial shock on arrival and the hazing the first month, the Maxwell experience was a wonderful time for all of us. Our every-other-day wing parades were usually to honor a visiting VIP. I recall Lord Halifax appearing on one occasion and General "Hap" Arnold on another, and on yet another we had a mass calisthenics demonstration for President Roosevelt. Everyone knew that he suffered from poliomyelitis but most did not know how incapacitated he was. He arrived by train and we were instructed to face away from him until he was properly seated to watch us perform. I was not more than a hundred feet away from him and he seemed to enjoy the demonstration. It was the second time I had seen the president. Once before, when I was in the seventh grade in Beverly Hills, the entire school marched two blocks up to Sunset Boulevard to wave and applaud as his motorcade sped by, but not too fast for us all not to see him wave and smile at the children.

Shortly before our graduation review at Maxwell, our next assignments were posted. I was ordered to Carlstrom Field in Arcadia, Florida, for primary flight training.

As far back as my memory reaches, I can remember wanting to do but one of two things as an adult: fly for the Air Force or become a doctor. I was lucky enough to fulfill both my childhood dreams.

As a pre-teen, my hero was my cousin Edward "Ned" White, a graduate of the University of California, a Zete, and an Air Corps fighter pilot, or "pursuit pilot," as they were called in the 1930s. I vividly remember Ned at the National Air Races held in Los Angeles in 1932, flying his P-26 Peashooter. The featured celebrity at that show was the famous World War I German ace, Ernst Udet. Tragically, Ned was one of the twelve pilots killed when the Air Corps was called upon to fly the Air Mail in 1932. The civilian authorities, in a monumental blunder, tasked the military with a mission in aircraft that were ill-equipped and unsuited for the job. Ned's death did nothing to dissuade me from my dreams of flying. I remember fantasizing that I was the pilot of every model plane I built.

Primary flight training in Florida was literally the most carefree time in my life. It was also the only time in my life that I habitually woke up a minute or two before an alarm clock or a bugle or else an ill-tempered NCO rousted me out. To face another day flying was all that mattered. My instructor was a free-spirited civilian, Jim Sutton, who enjoyed flying as much as anyone I ever knew. Aerobatics, night flying, basic instrument flying—all of it was the most natural thing in the world to me. From the first moment of dual training to my last flight two and a half years later, I was always comfortable in the air. Neither did I ever have problems with spatial orientation—perhaps my years practicing springboard diving was a helpful preparation. I understood the phenomenon of vertigo, so trusting the instruments was automatic. I could never understand not trusting them.

Unfortunately, there were personality clashes between the cadets and some of their instructors. Some of the latter were military pilots who would rather have been anywhere but in the training command and took out their frustration on their students. Swearing at their students' shortcomings and screaming at anything less than perfection were common occurrences. More than one student "washed out" solely for this reason. But then there were others, like Jim Sutton, who were fun, tolerant up to a point, and made life much easier. In fact, I never had an instructor at the three flight schools (primary, basic, and advanced) with whom I did not get along.

After soloing, which most of us did after six hours of dual instruction, to be able to check out a plane and join friends at "five thousand feet ten miles south of the field" for a forbidden but universally practiced "rat race" was simply pure joy. The beloved Stearman PT-17 was forgiving, indestructible, and, when properly rigged, one of the best aerobatic planes ever built. Precision in flight was not difficult—to make a standard three-degree turn, one had only to drop the tip of the upper wing on the horizon. There were wires and struts for every turn—thirty, forty-five, and sixty degrees. Crossroads on the ground guaranteed precision in loops and cloverleaf turns, Immelmanns, and figure-of-eights. There was only one small problem: the Continental 220 hp engines had float-type carburetors, so that extended inverted flight was impossible without constantly pushing the primer. We all felt that we were Baron von Richthofen, Max Immelmann, or Eddie Rickenbacker incarnate. The most popular combat aircraft of the day was the P-38 Lightning, and all of us were sure that we would become fighter pilots and preferably in that aircraft. I can't remember ever talking to my friends about the merits of flying bombers or, worse yet, transports. The academic work in ground school—meteorology, theory of flight, engineering, navigation, and other subjects—was considered a necessary interruption but, happily, was not too difficult.

Following primary training, we moved to Bainbridge, Georgia, for the next two months of basic training in the infamous Vultee BT-13 "Vibrator," with its interesting stall characteristics. After basic, we were sent to Albany, Georgia, for the final two months of advanced flight training. We were given the option of stating a preference for either single-engine or twin-engine training and, because the P-38 had two engines, I thought the latter was logical. At Turner Field in Albany, we flew the stable, boring AT-10s and the Curtis AT-9s, which were neither stable nor boring.

Graduation day for the Class of 43-K was December 5, 1943. On the day that we had been training for for the better part of a year, we were simultaneously rated pilots and commissioned second lieutenants. Eddie Rickenbacker was our graduation speaker, and I remember an emotional and motivating address. We were given two weeks leave, so I headed for Los Angeles with the hope of getting a ride to Honolulu. Unfortunately, there was no way that was possible. Nonetheless, I had a pleasant leave with Aunt Mary Margaret visiting friends and family.

Several of my newly commissioned friends and I were ordered to the Troop Carrier Command and transitional training at Bergstrom Field in Austin, Texas. Not knowing exactly what the Troop Carrier Command was, we assumed that we would be taught to fly fighter cover for the paratroopers. It was not exactly one-on-one "knights of the air," but it was good enough. It came as a shock on arrival to see a field full of C-47s without a P-38 in sight. My closest friend and I bravely walked into the adjutant's office to request an immediate transfer and were told by a cranky captain to get out of his sight. He had been dealing with hot pilot "butter bars" like us all day and was not amused.

1944-1945

None of my immediate group had ever flunked a check ride or a ground school class or been warned of any deficiency. However, trying to rationalize why we had been assigned to transport aircraft, instead of combat aircraft, was an exercise in futility. But, after the first week, as we learned to fly the C-47, our disappointment gave way to interest and, finally, respect for the sturdy old "gooney bird." It was one of the most durable and versatile airplanes ever built and probably had as much to do with ultimate victory as did the fighters and bombers. Obviously, strategic plans for the invasion of Europe were advanced by the beginning of 1944 and the roles of paratroops and glider-born airborne infantry were to be critical.

After completion of transition training, I was assigned to the 314th Squadron of the 349th Troop Carrier Group forming at Alliance, Nebraska. Our squadron commander was Captain (later Brigadier General) Walter Hurd, who had recently returned from three years in the China-Burma-India theater of operations. Having survived countless missions flying the infamous "Hump," Walt was an unusually skilled and experienced pilot. He was also the most able commander I ever served under, and we remained friends for fifty years after the war. Walt taught me professionalism and the necessary skills beyond just taking off, driving, and landing an airplane. He also probably saved my life on one mission at Pope Field in the summer of 1944 when we were flying a night "flack corridor" indoctrination mission and flew into unexpected violent weather. I was flying on Walt's wing, but because I did not have all my gauges ready for instrument flying, I tucked my wing in as close as I dared to Walt and stayed there. I knew instinctively that a pilot of his experience would not allow himself to be caught unprepared. In a little while all was well, but we lost an entire three-ship element as the planes plunged into the sea and were never found.

Alliance, Nebraska, was an ill-chosen site for the training of paratroopers. At a field elevation of about four thousand feet and a combat drop altitude of about eight hundred feet, there was never a training mission that didn't result in broken ankles, legs, and even backs. The air was too thin to slow a deployed parachute. Naturally, the airborne troops blamed the Air Force for these unhappy accidents. This irrational dislike manifested itself in intense hostility, and it became dangerous for anyone wearing a pair of wings to be caught off base. Air Force people were outnumbered twenty to one.

In late spring of 1944, we were ordered to Pope Field at Fort Bragg, North Carolina. The men I lived, worked, and flew with for the next two years were, for the most part, serious, conscientious, and dedicated to our mission. The first cadre of pilots, Captain Harvey Kennedy and 1st Lieutenants McCarron, Benedict, Crumpton, and Montaign, had all reported into the squadron before we, the second cadre, appeared and were all experienced C-47 pilots. They were to become our flight leaders. The first initials of the last names of my group all began with the letter "D," with one exception: Day, Delong, Dinmore, Davis, Decelles, Dixon, and Orville Wray. The next group arrived a month later and they became our co-pilots, not because we were more able but because we happened to arrive a month earlier. Of the pilots in my group, Eddie Day and Orville Wray were to become my closest friends.

Orvie Wray was the great "swordsman" of the 349th Troop Carrier Group, if not the entire Air Force. With the ladies, he was indefatigable and almost insatiable, without even trying. He couldn't help himself. He just had that magical, indefinable appeal to women. He wasn't tall, dark, and handsome but, rather, of medium build and pleasant but not remarkable countenance. It didn't matter. Some of his exploits were truly epic and he was, of course, the envy of all.

Two or three weeks before we were scheduled to return home (a month or so after VE Day), Orvie and I, after an all night binge at the Officers Club, suddenly realized that we hadn't yet seen Paris. Accordingly, we combined my half bottle of Johnny Walker Red and his half bottle of John Jamison, put on our trench coats, and took off for the "city of lights" on his motor cycle. How and where he had appropriated the machine was unclear. We arrived in the city about mid-morning and then realized how tired we were. We spent the next couple of hours trying to find a hotel so that we could rest and get cleaned up. We forgot that without official leave papers, we couldn't get proper "approved" hotel rooms. There were plenty of unauthorized hotels, but those rooms all came with a girl. We were too exhausted for that sort of thing, even Orvie, so we spent another hour or so trying to find a movie so that we could at least sit comfortably and try to get some sleep. We finally found one that I've never forgotten, *Till We Meet Again*, with George Brent and Merle Oberon, (a re-make of an earlier film, *One Way Passage*, with William Powell and Kay Frances). In our state, sleepless and hung over, watching dubbed-in French from that handsome Irish face had a surreal, almost nightmare quality. Emerging from the movie after a little rest we began enjoying the sights and sound of the Champs Elysees. Toward evening we found ourselves in a posh night club, the *Lido*, enjoying a good dinner which was interrupted by applause coming from the back of the dining room. Bob Hope and his pal Jerry Colonna had been recognized and the GIs were urging them up onto the stage. He complied and put on a very funny impromptu show for about fifteen minutes then returned to finish his dinner. What a great and unselfish entertainer he was. After dinner we did find ourselves "unauthorized" hotels, and the next morning we somehow found each other and the motorcycle and returned to Airstrip A-73. Nothing was said about our AWOL, but with the war over everything was a good deal more relaxed.

Ed Day was a freckle-faced, rugged, red-head born and bred in Brooklyn. He was given to effortlessly inventing rhyming couplets. A typical greeting might be "morning Glory, what's the story." In two years I never saw him out of sorts or ill-tempered. He gave me my first insight as to what it meant to be a New Yorker or, more accurately, a Brooklynite. In Brooklyn, the social structure, the social unit, was the block. One's school, friends, and life centered in a fairly restricted area. He told me once, as absolute truth, that he not only had never been to the Statue of Liberty but that he had never seen it! It wasn't until I got to know Eddie that I learned that the image of the worldly, sophisticated New Yorker is often a myth and that New Yorkers can be the most provincial people in the world, believing that little of interest goes on west of the Hudson River and not much of anything happens between Chicago and San Francisco.

Some of the non-rated non-flying men in the group became good friends as well. Ed Archer, our communications officer, had been a pharmacist in civilian life and we had much in common, especially when we talked about politics. Willy Frankel was the weather officer at Pope Field but "hung out" with our squadron more than with the other three in the group. Willy was the prototypical fast-talking street-smart, Manhattanite. He was a successful young Wall Street stock broker when he "got patriotic," put his career on hold, and, in his late thirties, joined the Air Force. Willy was very smart and knew a lot about many things. I was trying to learn how to play bridge, and he gave me a lot of helpful clues. He was a tournament player and, among other things, never sorted his hand into suits, an act he said could give players (of his caliber) valuable information. The secret of bridge was in the bidding and, when the dummy went down, Willy knew where ninety-five percent of the cards were. After the bidding, play was almost automatic. He never gambled with us knowing that it would be unfair.

On one of our flights to New York, Willy took me into the visitor's gallery of the New York Stock Exchange (he knew all the security people by their first names) advising me, half in jest, to be careful to whom and how I waved to anyone on the floor lest I suddenly owned a hundred shares of U.S. Steel. On that trip he also introduced me to the wonders of lox and bagels prepared properly at his favorite lunch place—Fleetwood's. Just to be in his company was a treat. He had a kind of Groucho Marxian sense of humor. He told me how to get a free meal if you were hungry and broke: just stand at the window of a good restaurant and pick your nose; they'd have you inside and fed in ten minutes. We didn't keep in touch after the war but I'm certain he must have had a successful career.

Leo "Doc" Kelly, our flight surgeon, interested me especially when talking about medicine and may have done more to ignite my interest in the medical profession than I realized at the time. Doc was an amiable, big bear of a man from New Jersey whose responsibilities attending three or four hundred healthy young men left him plenty of free time. Doc always knew where to get graphic movies at a place in Newark for our stag parties and I remember a few "training missions" to that town for that sole purpose.

The only person in the group I tended to avoid was a taciturn young pilot named Davis. He was the strong/silent type and a half a head taller than me, so I couldn't get too frisky with him. My aversion turned to dislike when his one comment after the news of President Roosevelt's death was announced in April 1945 was, "good."

Most of our flying at Alliance was to familiarize ourselves with the flight characteristics of the C-47. It was a joy to fly, had no idiosyncrasies, and was as forgiving and stable as any plane ever built—even in the hands of inexperienced pilots. Our routine missions over the flatlands of Nebraska were not too interesting, so we invented games to make things more interesting—like herding cows.

In the life of every pilot there are episodes that change one's feelings of invincibility. In my case it took not one but three. The first occurred when, to relieve boredom, I was herding cows at very low altitude and suddenly noted something very large whiz by my window. It was a huge steel tower supporting six or eight high-tension lines, which I had just flown under!

The second "thought adjustment" episode occurred on a flight into Philadelphia. My clearance had been "contact," which meant that I was not authorized to fly on instruments and that I had to maintain visual contact with the ground. The weather was deteriorating rapidly so I steadily lost altitude until suddenly I was "socked in." I was directly over the Philadelphia Navy Yard and could not see a thing. At that precise moment I saw a large crane flash by my window slightly above me. I pushed the throttles forward and the control columns back as hard as I dared, prayed, and headed for the heavens. How close I came to disaster I'll never know.

A third and final brainless episode involved a flight out of Greensboro, North Carolina, on a cold, wet, winter's night. With fifty passengers in the back of my C-46, I had reached about five thousand feet when both engines began to misfire and I began to lose altitude. As I tried to think of everything that could be causing the problem my crew chief, Chuck Agar, standing between the pilot and co-pilot seats pointed at the carburetor heat controls, which I had forgotten to turn on during our pre-take-off check list. The carburetor heat controls, when "on," prevent ice from forming in the carburetor. When ice forms in the carburetor the fuel flow is blocked. The three lessons I learned were: don't herd cows in an airplane, don't file contact clearance in uncertain weather, have a crew chief smarter than you are!

For the next fourteen months at Ft. Bragg, from about February 1944 to March 1945, we trained elements of the 82nd and 101st Airborne Divisions as they prepared for their critical role in the European invasion. I admired these young warriors but never envied them and never, under any circumstances or for any reason, was I tempted to join them by stepping out of a perfectly good airplane. It always seemed pointless to me to practice something that had to be right the first time. Double glider tows pulling two ungainly CG 4-A gliders was a little tricky at times. Gliders slow the C-47 down to very near its stall speed of about 83 mph. At this speed the controls became extremely "mushy."

Almost routinely, the platoon leader of any stick of paratroopers asked who was to be their pilot. When a beardless youth (me) was pointed out, they invariable let it be known that it would be safer to jump out of the airplane than to land with me. We dropped thousands of those troops in the year at Bragg and I never saw a "chute" fail. The real hazards in training missions were carbines, helmets, and other pieces of loose equipment falling on the troops already on the ground, and the fear, on night missions, of being dropped inadvertently into water. Shedding a wet harness was almost impossible.

As we trained the airborne divisions, we developed a real affection for the C-47 and its replacement, the C-46 Commando. The C-46 was twice as big, carried more than twice the payload, and was twice as powerful as the C-47. It was powered by two remarkable engines, the largest radial engines built up to that time—the Pratt-Whitney 2000 hp R-2800s. Like all Curtis aircraft, it was said to have been built to take off, fly, and land in a three-point attitude. This wasn't quite true but nearly so. One had to exceed one's assigned altitude by a few hundred feet then dive down to get the airplane on the "step." The early models were difficult to fly in formation, especially in turbulence, but this was corrected in later models.

We dropped paratroopers and towed gliders all over Georgia, North Carolina, Alabama, and Mississippi, "invaded" Long Island twice, and probably became the most proficient troop carrier group in the Air Force. But what we did not get was the thing uppermost in our minds—orders for overseas duty.

About the first of June 1944, we got orders for a secret mission. Excitement ran high until we realized the mission was to fly hundreds of troops to Panama. Why this was important we never learned, but not being in on D-Day and the invasion was totally frustrating.

Three weeks after our adventure in Panama, I again found myself on leave in Southern California and again was unsuccessful at getting to Honolulu. But this leave was to be significantly different than any other. Aunt Mary Margaret was in the interior decorating business with Harriet Shellenberger in their very successful studio on the Sunset Strip. Harriet's niece, Eileen, was their office assistant, and because she and I were nearly the same age, my aunt suggested we meet. That was how I met the green-eyed, raven-haired beauty with whom I was to share my life.

Eileen Frances Quinn was born in Denver in 1924 but moved to Phoenix at age two. Her father worked for the Phoenix Power and Light Company and had worked up to executive level before his untimely death just before the war. At our first meeting, I was, in a word, smitten, and I was amazed to find that my feelings were reciprocated. We became unofficially engaged that June and then officially the following December. We decided to postpone marriage until the end of the war was at least in sight. We knew that Germany was on its last legs, but Japan was another matter. Also, by the fall, it was a certainty that the 349th Troop Carrier group was headed for Europe.

Although we were so much in love and wanted nothing more than to be together, interrupting Eileen's career for some sort of apartment in Fayetteville, North Carolina, hardly seemed a fair exchange. Returning to Pope Field alone that summer was not easy, and it was even more difficult the next Christmas. But for us, absence did make the heart grow fonder. Thankfully, as the training routine during the fall of 1944 grew steadily more serious, my job was made more tolerable by frequent letters from Eileen.

Finally, in February 1945, as had been rumored for weeks, we received orders to the European Theater of Operations and left Pope Field in March 1945. Our trip overseas was via the southern route from Miami to Jamaica, British Guyana, Natal, across the South Atlantic to Ascension Island, north to Liberia, Morocco, and finally to our base in England, Barkston Heath, near the village of Grantham.

The 349th was assigned to the Ninth Air Force and later to a composite group called the First Allied Airborne Army. The European War was almost over, and our one mission that could be called combat support was flying a British brigade of airborne infantry to secure the enormous Luftwaffe/Wermacht/German Naval complex at Stavanger, Norway. We didn't expect any armed resistance from the Germans and there was none. They had had enough war by that time.

The mission to Stavanger proved more interesting than in any sense dangerous. The British Commander, a Colonel who had seen hazardous duty throughout the war and was worshiped by his men, received a formal surrender by the German Commander, and although the British troops landed with loaded weapons, no shots were fired.

Landing our sixty fully-loaded C-46s in a forty-mile-an-hour cross wind on a neglected airstrip went according to plan but required careful airmanship. Later that night, an unusually severe storm blew in off the North Sea, and my plane was damaged when the rudder lock failed; this damaged not only the alignment but also the rudder itself. As replacement parts were flown up from England, the four of us (me, my co-pilot Gill Griffen, our crew chief Chuck Agar, and our radioman Izzy Taflin) spent ten days in Stavanger waiting for parts and then repairing our damaged plane.

During that time, we received plenty of "Five-in-One" rations (one carton would feed one man for five days or five men for one day) from England. Coincidentally, we struck up a friendship with a Norwegian family who lived on the perimeter of the airfield. In each carton of Five-in-Ones, there were five or ten little packets of cigarettes, so we traded with the Norwegians, our cigarettes for their fresh eggs and milk. They were an interesting and cordial group, and I remember their eldest daughter in particular. She was about fifteen, very pretty, and fluent in five languages: her native language, Swedish, German, French, and English. Yet, she was not considered especially precocious! Before we parted company, her father asked me if there was any way I could take her back to England when I returned so that she could be with distant relatives. I was tempted but, of course, was prohibited from doing so.

I also remember meeting a group of Russian POWs in Stavanger. They made it clear, however, that were they to be released, they would kill their German captors. The British CO obviated that threat by keeping them confined in the prison camp to avoid unnecessary bloodshed. The Russians

were particularly impressed by our model 1911 Colt '45 pistols, and liked
the nearly one-half-inch muzzles of the weapon. The sturdy old '45 was
designed to stop a man running full tilt and blow him backwards; with a
half-inch slug and a muzzle velocity of about seven hundred ft/sec, it literally could! The Russians loved that concept.

Prior to Norway, in April of 1945 while in England, I had been given
the opportunity to check-out in a four-engine aircraft, the C-109, a converted B-24 designed to carry gasoline rather than bombs in the bomb
bay. The theory was that General George S. Patton, in his lightning thrust
across southern France, was outrunning his fuel supply and needed to be
re-supplied by air. Our one mission in May 1945 was scrubbed on the
flight line, minutes before takeoff. The colorful general had not only se-
cured our drop zone but also was fifty miles beyond it. More frustration!

After moving to Airstrip A-73, in May 1945, midway between Paris
and Amiens, France, we got word that we would soon be heading home.
We were probably the last group sent to Europe and one of the first to return. After a one-month leave, we were to regroup at Castle Air Force Base
in Salina, California, to prepare for deployment to the Asia-Pacific Theatre
of Operations, and, we thought, probably to Okinawa.

The 349th left France in mid-July 1945 and flew home the northern
route: Scotland, Iceland, Greenland, Labrador, and, finally, Massachusetts.
Within forty-eight hours we were on our way by train to Los Angeles and
from there we would begin our thirty-day leave. Since Eileen and I had
planned to be married as soon as I got home, I headed for Phoenix.

Eileen's sister, Mary, had been engaged to an Air Force fighter pilot,
Warren Schwab, for over a year. Warren had been shot down flying his
P-51 in the summer of 1944 and had been a prisoner of war for nearly a
year at Stalag II. He had not been too badly treated, but because of the
chaos in Nazi Germany the last year of the war, he had very little more
than potatoes to eat. (After the war, it was years before he could even look

at one again.) He had been liberated by the Russians and nearly killed by a combination of vodka and kindness.

Warren and I each arrived in Phoenix within two weeks of one another. He and Mary, like Eileen and I, planned to wed as soon as we got home, so Eileen, Mary, and my future mother-in-law, Marguerite Quinn, had made all the plans for a double wedding. It was then I learned how simple a wedding can be for the groom. About all that was required of me was that I buy a ring and show up for the ceremony. (I was to learn much more about all this twenty or so years later, when I was the father of the bride.)

All the parties, dinners, luncheons, and receptions were the bride's responsibilities, which was fine with me. On August 4, 1945, we were wed at St. Francis Church with Father Cosgrove officiating. He was an amiable, middle-aged priest who was, at times, a little confused about who was to say what and when to whom. If he had performed other double weddings, there couldn't have been too many. Except for the brutal heat in Phoenix during August, all went well. Marguerite, the world's greatest mother-in-law, had planned events perfectly, and everyone seemed to have a good time. Marguerite was a rare and wonderful person; she was wise, loving, and generous. In all the years that followed, through college, med school, internship, and residency, through stressful and happy times, no one could have been more supportive. Even when Eileen and I had a disagreement, she invariably took my part. For the twenty years she was with us after our marriage, she was a treasured friend.

After the wedding, we left for our honeymoon in Los Angeles and San Francisco and a round of parties with family and friends. Eileen had never seen San Francisco, so showing her "my" town was great fun. On the fourteenth of August, as we were leaving the hotel for dinner, the news of the final surrender of Japan was announced, and San Franciscans went a little mad. I think San Francisco was as dangerous a place to be that night as any night I had spent during the war. There was vandalism and rioting; there were women who took off their clothes to frolic in public fountains;

cable cars were overturned and set afire. Many shop owners had open bars in their stores. It was wild and crazy but exhilarating. Suddenly, after six years, the bloodiest and most destructive war in history was over.

When the 349th reassembled in Salinas, about the first of September 1945, there was uncertainty about where and what our next mission would be. Deployment to the Asia-Pacific Theater seemed unlikely. Within two weeks we were again transferred to the Air Force base in Merced, California, and, yet again, three weeks later, back to Bergstrom Field in Austin, Texas. There were still young pilots being fed into the system, so our mission was to instruct them as they transitioned into C-46s. It was easy duty, so we, as newlyweds, had a pleasant time in an attractive university town.

Our group commander, Colonel Len Barrow, made a pitch for us all to consider staying in the Air Force, but it lacked conviction. I had serious doubt that without a formal education, my only skill, driving an airplane, would carry me very far. Walt Hurd, now a lieutenant colonel and group operations officer, had an entrée with Philippine Air Lines and talked to several of us about joining him and having a career in civil aviation. But again, I thought my lack of education would sooner or later be a problem. So, with regret because I loved to fly so much, I decided to return to civilian life when the opportunity presented itself. It came sooner than I expected. At that time, there was a point system that prioritized people electing to be demobilized. Because my home of record was Hawaii, all of my service, including all of my time in the continental United States (CONUS), was considered overseas time, which doubled the point value. Accordingly, early in November 1945, Eileen and I departed Austin for March Field, California, where I was discharged from active duty. The idea of another war or any reason to be recalled to active duty was out of the question, so I elected to stay in the inactive reserves. It was a decision that, years later, proved to be very practical.

My parents had arrived in California a few weeks earlier for a well-deserved vacation. After three and a half years, our reunion was quite emotional. It was also a pleasure to introduce my bride to them. I remember that at the first sight of my parents, I was a little shocked. They seemed to have aged and grown smaller. Four years of war and the constant worry of two sons at risk (John was in the Pacific with the 7th Fleet while I was in Europe) had taken their toll. But in all other respects, they seemed unchanged, as was the usual round of parties with family and friends.

By late November, we were able to book passage home to Hawaii on the *Lurline*. This flagship of the Matson line was still configured as a troop ship, so many of the luxuries of the past were absent. It was a fairly rough passage, and from the first morning at sea, Eileen was violently seasick and probably cursed the day she married someone from Hawaii. Finally, after five days of misery, she was able to totter on deck just as we rounded Diamond Head and caught our first glimpse of the green valleys above the city of Honolulu. By the time we docked, she was still quite wobbly and dehydrated but was beginning to enjoy all the new sights and sounds.

For the next few weeks, until after the first of the year, of 1946, we had a carefree time living with my parents in the house on Ferdinand Avenue in Manoa Valley, exploring the Islands, surfing at Makapuu, and partying with Punahou friends. The time passed very quickly, and it was not until January that I had to start thinking about the future.

Reflections

I do not remember feeling hate or a desire to kill Germans or Japanese during the war. I simply knew that I was well trained, well equipped, could accomplish any mission for which I had been trained, and that victory was inevitable. During the war I saw a great deal of destruction but no casualties, except Holocaust survivors, nor did I lose any close friends. After Stavanger, Norway, the only time I saw an enemy soldier was on a trip to Halle, Germany, near Leipzig, to visit a friend in the Seventh Armored Division. We were walking down the street when two young men wearing what was left of their Wermacht uniforms approached from the opposite direction. As we drew abreast, they didn't just give way, they stepped into the gutter and gave little bows. I thought this obsequious gesture by two former supermen was contemptible, and I have never forgotten it.

So, after the most devastating war in history, I had escaped unscathed. I never felt any guilt that I was spared when so many good men had been killed or injured, I just felt enormously grateful and lucky. I was shot at only once that I know of, and it annoyed me. However, unlike Winston Churchill, I didn't find it "exhilarating" not to have been hit. I have known many men who faced combat on the ground and in the air, and those who saw the most, talked about it the least. I never heard one of them echo Churchill's fatuous remark.

I have been asked my most imperishable memories of the war. There are several. On Victory in Europe night, May 8, 1945, I was in Nottingham, England, and I retain an image of the faces of the children looking in absolute wonderment at a city fully lit at night. They had never seen anything like it. Another memory is the total destruction of many German cities. Flying over Aachen, one could not find an intact roof, except the one over the great Cathedral. There were tank tracks and rubble, but no roads. Another was the appearance of Holocaust survivors and the ammoniacal stench of starvation. One of our missions in July of 1945 was to fly hundreds of these pathetic, starved survivors from Brussels to Paris, and these were the strongest of the victims. They had been cleaned, fed, and clothed, but they just starred, zombie-like, at a world they could hardly comprehend. Remembering them, it enrages me to hear so-called revisionists contend that the Holocaust never happened. Another memory is the courage and forbearance of the British people. I recall a great gaping hole in central London with a sign proclaiming "Smyth & Sons temporarily out of business."

Finally, I remember the warmth of our reception as the liberating force in Stavanger, Norway, and attending the first free religious service in six years. The incredible emotion and beauty of the singing from the congregation is, to this day, unforgettable.

III
1946-1953

Christmas and New Year celebrations of 1945 were joyful and, although John was still on duty in the Navy, the stress of war was over for my parents. Showing Eileen the activities we enjoyed growing up in Hawaii and introducing her to all my friends were great fun. We two and our friends all had common experiences that, though differing in detail, made us *en rapport*. When not hiking, surfing, spear fishing, or partying, Eileen and I helped my father in his various businesses: Pacific Indies, an import-export house; a bus franchise at Pearl Harbor; and the automobile lot, Federal Motors. However, it didn't take long for me to realize that I had neither an aptitude for nor interest in the world of business. It was tactfully suggested that I consider some sort of academic training with courses at the University of Hawaii.

At the University, I met the first of two people during a momentous year who essentially shaped my destiny for the next forty-five years. As a preliminary to registration, I was assigned to Dr. Bilger, Chairman of the Chemistry Department, as my faculty advisor. We talked for some time, and at the end of our meeting he suggested that I consider enrolling at the University with the same major I had originally started at Berkeley in 1942—pre-med. He also suggested that since I had been through a war and was now married, I might approach academics with more maturity and purpose. He assured me that my poor grades in the past would not compromise a fresh start. I don't remember more than two conversations with Dr. Bilger, yet his counsel and understanding profoundly affected my life. Initially, I enrolled in a biology course, a history course, and an English course for the spring semester. Eileen joined me and enrolled in an art history course.

Getting back into the habit of studying was easier than I thought it would be, and, obviously, Eileen's support was critical. By the end of the semester, I was committed to fulltime college work. By the next semester, in the fall of 1946, I signed up for a more ambitious program of sixteen credit hours. Soon, with all the reading, I began experiencing eye strain and problems focusing. After consultation and examination with Dr. Corboy, an ex-Navy flight surgeon, we began chatting and he asked me if I had been in the service during the war. When I told him I had been in the Air Force and a pilot, he couldn't believe it. He said, "With eyes like that, you never would have flown for the Navy." It was then I remembered that toward the end of my flying career, I was experiencing some difficulty seeing instruments at night. The astigmatism had caught up with me, confirming that my decision to leave the military had been correct. Much as I still missed flying, I had no choice but to accept the inevitable.

Throughout the spring of 1946, my mother was experiencing health problems more worrisome than chronic upper respiratory infections. There was a kind of malaise bordering on depression. In May, she underwent a tonsillectomy, which seemed to help. In retrospect, however, I believe some of her problems were psychosomatic and the result of four years of tension and stress from having two sons in harm's way. Of course, these were obvious concerns and common to all parents with sons on active duty, but for my mother, there were also the intermittent worries as my father's business affairs were alternately good and bad, and, on top of that, her intolerance of the subtropical climate. As I progressed in my medical training, I looked for scientific studies on the relationship of psychological stress to somatic illness. It wasn't until years later, after the Vietnam War, that the concept of post-traumatic stress disorder (PTSD) reached public awareness. For parents, wives, and even children after World War II, and very likely previous wars, it also existed. People on the home front bore up well during the war but suffered all sorts of problems months or even years later.

In June 1946, I met Oscar Thorup, the second person who was to profoundly affect my life. Oscar had married a classmate of mine at Punahou,

Barbara Turnbull, and had returned to the Islands after graduating from the University of Virginia Medical School in order to intern at Queen's Hospital in Honolulu. We became life-long friends, and I remain in touch with Barby to this day. We were about the same age, both of us were newlywed, and we shared a community of interests. Oscar was brilliant and enthusiastic about almost everything, and the four of us, when I could get away from studies and he had a rare day off, had wonderful times in each other's company. We would cram as much into one day as possible—typically we'd begin at dawn with a round of golf at Oahu Country Club followed by a picnic on the beach with surfing or spear fishing; after that, perhaps a bowling match, dinner, and then either a movie or bridge. Ah! to be young, healthy, and not know the meaning of fatigue.

Later that summer, Oscar invited me to make rounds twice with attending physicians at Queen's, and on one occasion I was able to watch a surgical procedure by Dr. Cloward, who was a member of the Harvey Cushing Society and the first board-certified neurosurgeon in Hawaii. From that moment on, I had few doubts about what I wanted to do with the rest of my life. The whole aura of the operating room and the discipline of the assistant surgeons, anesthesiologists, and nurses was fascinating. Furthermore, as Oscar told me more about the University of Virginia and the unique genius of its founder, Thomas Jefferson, the more interesting the school sounded.

In October 1946, after living with my parents for almost a year, Eileen and I finally got our own apartment. Living with them was pleasant and easy and the house was quite large enough for four, but there comes a time when every young couple needs to be on their own. The opportunity came when two young Honolulu architects, Allan Johnson and Tommy Perkins, bought and converted King Kalākaua's summer palace at the foot of Diamond Head into an apartment condominium. We got a studio apartment with a bath and kitchenette. It was small, but it was ours, and we loved being on our own. The location was spectacular. At low tide we could walk out on the coral washed by the sea for fifty yards or more, and at high tide we could snorkel or spearfish. New Year's Eve of 1946, we had a memorable dinner party with Barby Thorup, my parents, and old friends from California, Bob and Sybil Schuyler. There was perhaps one more bottle of champagne than necessary, but with the fireworks at Waikiki, our own apartment, and old friends, it was a beautiful way to ring out the old year and greet 1947. It was to be our last New Year's Eve in Hawaii.

In 1946, there was no medical school in Hawaii, and because of the competition of thousands of returning veterans, getting into graduate school anywhere was becoming increasingly difficult. It soon became obvious that I would stand a better chance of getting into medical school if I were first an undergraduate at that school. I wrote inquiries to several prestigious schools—McGill, Michigan, Johns Hopkins, and, of course, the University of Virginia. For one reason after another (e.g., McGill required two years of Latin), the choice narrowed down to Virginia. I began pressing my case to the dean of admissions, Dean Ferguson. Once again Oscar's advice proved valuable. Because the dean was known to look forward to socializing on weekends, and said yes to virtually everyone on Friday and no to virtually everyone on Monday, Oscar advised that I time my letters accordingly. In any event, in an "if you must come, then come" kind of letter from the dean, which arrived June 8, 1947, I was admitted to the fall term. By working hard at the University of Hawaii, I had accumulated forty-five semester hours, with decent grades, in a year-and-a-half.

The spring semester of 1947 at Hawaii passed rapidly, and my time there was memorable because of an inspiring teacher, Dr. Frederick Mann. Dr. Mann was on a teaching sabbatical from Oxford University and made the subject of inorganic chemistry so fascinating I could hardly wait to get home to review that day's lecture and prepare for the next. To be unprepared for such a teacher was unthinkable. Great teachers like Dr. Mann are rare; they are never forgotten, and students are perpetually in their debt.

As soon as the semester ended, we began making preparations for the next chapter in our lives—Charlottesville and the University of Virginia.

Since my total wartime service equaled thirty-four months, and I was entitled to another twelve months as authorized by the legislation of the G.I. Bill of Rights (The Servicemen's Readjustment Act of 1944), I had a total of forty-six months of active service credit. This meant that my benefits under the G.I. Bill entitled me to five academic years of study and would cover the cost of tuition and books, as well as a stipend of about one-hundred-four dollars a month. That, with a little help from my father, was enough to carry us through my remaining college years and almost half of medical school.

After a nine-hour flight, we arrived in San Francisco, spent one night at the Fairmont, and then took the train to Phoenix. In preparation for our trip east, we bought our first car, a Dodge coup, with a bench seat in front, no rear seat, and a huge trunk. It was a used car but held up well for the next two years. We left Phoenix on the first of September, and four days later we arrived in Front Royal, Virginia. Our first night in the Old Dominion was at a charming bed and breakfast inn. About ten the following morning we arrived in Charlottesville, drove west about five miles to the little village of Ivy and from there, another mile up a winding picturesque road to our home for the next six years, Chinquapin Hill.

Again the Thorups had helped us, this time by helping us find a place to live. Barby's parents were old friends of another retired military couple, Colonel and Mrs. White, whose son, Allan, had married Cecily Baker. Cecily's parents, Monica and Jeff Baker, owned Chinquapin Hill and had a garage available for rent. We arrived at Chinquapin a day earlier than expected, and our first look at the garage was a shock. It was dismal—raw cinder block walls, ghastly paper curtains, a rickety iron bed, an ancient Morris chair, and a table filled with supers from Monica's bee hives, dripping with honey. At this point, after Monica had stepped out, Eileen's courage failed her for a little while. But after a few tears, the two of us pitched in, with Monica's help, to make the place habitable the first night. That, not counting the sea-sickness on the way to Hawaii, was probably the low point in our marriage.

Monica Baker was quite a remarkable person whom we grew to love during the next six years and for the many years of her life after we left Virginia. She and Jeff could not have been more different. Jeff was from a long line of distinguished educators in Vermont. He was tall, thin, and reminiscent of the actor James Stewart. He was also one of the kindest and most decent men I have ever known. He was a partner in an established brokerage firm in Detroit, Baker-Simons & Co. He disliked Detroit, and Monica couldn't stand the place, so they spent most of their time in Virginia. Monica was British to the core, but the fact that she was an American citizen by marriage didn't upset her greatly. She was of the landed gentry in Britain and had been presented at court as a young woman. Jeff's approach to business, as well as to life in general, was academic and compatible with his heritage. He managed his business affairs capably, but his primary interests were in an organization called One World, the United Nations, and anything written by Robert Benchley, whom he loved to read aloud to anyone who would listen. Jeff was unbelievably inept around the house and kitchen, even making a cup of tea was a challenge, but he was well informed, a moderate middle-of-the-road Republican, and incapable of meanness, guile, or cruelty. Monica was forthright, capable, dynamic, a knowledgeable horticulturist, and a loyal and generous friend devoted to her church and good works in the parish. She was a good cook in the English tradition but did not fully subscribe to the germ theory of disease. Having been raised with servants, cleaning the kitchen, for instance, was not a high-priority item. Her health was more robust than Jeff's, but she was subject to attacks of asthma that were sometimes incapacitating.

After the initial shock of seeing what was to become our home, we went to work building an apartment. Our first consultant carpenter was a local character, Ben Furneyhough, a rustic who could easily have been cast in a Ma and Pa Kettle movie. Ben knew the basics of carpentry and built in a small kitchen, a large closet, and a bookcase upon which I hung a hinged dining room table. Later in the year, when my parents came for their first visit, we had painted the place, got rid of the paper curtains, and with the rugs they bought us, the apartment had become quite comfortable. It served us well for six years.

The fall term at the University soon demanded my full attention and energy. I was determined to graduate in June 1949, so I signed up for a formidable workload—eighteen semester hours. Though some of the courses were easy, the total workload was not. Physics, because I had never taken calculus, was particularly difficult; but Eileen typed all my laboratory results, producing a folder that was a thing of beauty. As we immersed ourselves in the romantic history of the University and learned more about the genius of the man who founded it, we came to appreciate what the school offered beyond mere academics.

My mother and father came to visit us for a few days following their first visit to New York in over twenty years. They were impressed with the beauty of the Virginia countryside, the University, and their brief visit to Williamsburg. Half a mile from our village of Ivy, on the road to Chinquapin, there was an old farmhouse with a concrete monument in front bearing a plate noting that it was the birthplace of Meriwether Lewis. Depending on the accuracy of my Great-Aunt Edith, I am distantly related to Meriwether. Meriwether Lewis's father was the brother of my great-great-great grandfather, we think. If true, it would make me about the fifteenth cousin of the great explorer.

By Christmas of 1947, we were squared away in our apartment, and a week later spent the first of many New Year's Eves with Monica and Jeff. Every New Year's Eve followed the same format: sherry at five, followed by a dinner of roast beef, Yorkshire pudding, and plum duff (with coins, thimbles, and other surprises embedded) for desert. After dinner, we would adjourn to the living room, turn on the shortwave to hear Big Ben chime midnight in London, seven o'clock in Virginia, and, after hugs and kisses, the New Year having begun, we were free to say goodnight.

In 1947, the Grounds (*never* "campus") of the University were generally acknowledged to be the most beautiful of any college in the country, if

not the world. The neoclassical architecture created a symmetry and definition that was, and remains, unique. The five thousand undergraduates
were almost exclusively men. Coats and ties were *de rigueur*, and first-year
students were expected to wear hats, which were to be tipped to upper-
classmen and, of course, faculty. There was no other form of hazing. The
spirit of Thomas Jefferson was a living presence. One walked on The Lawn
with a degree of decorum because "the heart of the University lay buried
there"; academic achievement was commendable but it wasn't necessarily
the most important measure of a man.

Social life revolved around fraternity functions, sporting events, and
the big dance weekends: Openers, Mid-Winters, Little Easters, and Easters. I didn't try to re-affiliate with the Zeta Psi fraternity because Zetes
at Virginia tended to be wealthy young bachelors from Richmond, and I
was married and we were on a strict budget. To be a member of the college community was enough. Fraternity life, unlike that at the University
of California, was very democratic. Just about any man who wanted to be
in a fraternity could be, but even if not, there was no snobbery. There was
drinking, probably too much, but it was never an excuse for rude behavior
or arm waving. There was a favorite watering hole called Carol's Tea Room;
however, no one knew who Carol was, tea was not served, and there was
never any room. Women were treated with respect because "pursuing a
woman to her tears" was considered boorish. The secret societies, especially
the most secret of all, the 7 Society, were shrouded in mystery and romanticism. But the very heart and soul of the University was the Honor System, which was administered entirely by the students. It was very simple:
cheating, lying, or stealing was not tolerated and any student found doing
so was advised to leave the University immediately.

People who do not understand the freedom that this code imparts may
wink and smirk at such naïveté, but that is their limitation. One could take
examinations outside on a lawn, or in the library an arm's length away from
all the answers to test questions, or anywhere. But once one signed a pledge

that all the work in the blue book was one's own, it was not questioned. I'm sure there have been Virginia graduates who cheated on examinations, but I don't know any. The point is that they have to live with their own consciences. For those of us who stood by the Honor System, there is greater peace of mind in getting a C on one's own than an A by cheating. The integrity that adherence to this ethic engendered hit home when, after my second year of medical school, I went up to Washington, DC, to take Part I of the National Medical Boards at George Washington University. It was a proctored exam, with people walking up and down to see if anyone was peeking at the work of others. Oddly, the fact that they were doing so made one feel like a cheater.

Because Eileen and I lived five miles from Grounds and were on a limited budget, we did not become too involved in the social scene. We were just grinding away, as were most veterans of the war, in the hopes of getting grades good enough to get into graduate school. Nonetheless, having become friends with Oscar's brother, Kent, who was a member of the Alpha Tau Omega fraternity, we were often invited to their functions. On the dance weekends, it was the custom, or possibly a requirement, to have chaperones at the fraternities. Eileen and I were often asked to chaperone because we enjoyed entering into the festivities, and we went home early.

Over time, I learned that the spirit of the University had begun to change after the war because of the influx of hardworking former servicemen. In my many conversations with various people, I came to understand that before the war, academics were considered an interesting diversion between parties. However, both before and after the war, adherence to the Jeffersonian principal "to pledge eternal hostility to any form of tyranny over the mind of man," has never changed. But the University has continued to evolve since I was in attendance. By the end of the twentieth century, the school had tripled in enrollment since I began attending and has steadily improved in stature. But the basic tenants remain the same: to prepare graduates for a lifetime of useful and honorable work.

In February 1948, my motivation to do the best I could at my studies was further enhanced by the happy news that Eileen was pregnant for the first time and that the baby was due the following September. It seems funny to admit now, but we had actually undergone infertility studies to find out if there were any problems since we had been married for so many years. Many years later, at a medical school class reunion, the physician we had consulted, Dr. Norman Thornton, asked if we had ever had more children. When I told him we had six, he was greatly amused.

Oscar had forewarned me that for an undergrad hoping to enter the medical school at the University, the one pre-medical course the admissions committee attached great importance to was organic chemistry. Accordingly, I decided to devote an entire summer to it. It was a good decision. The course was taught by Professor Berger, a slightly built, dignified professor of German background. He was precise, knowledgeable, and the author of our textbook. His German accent somehow enhanced his superb lectures. There were two lectures and two laboratories daily for seven weeks. His morning lecture began at eight o'clock and at nine, even if he was in mid-sentence, he stopped and then continued the sentence at the beginning of the one o'clock lecture. His first remark to us on the first day of class was, "Gentlemen, if you can learn to count to four, you will pass this course." He was, of course, correct.

Anyone who has taken organic chemistry will remember that the laboratory work involves the use of glass coils, condensers, and retorts. In hot humid weather, like Virginia in August, water formed on all the cold apparatus, and it was a constant battle to keep the water from running into places it was not wanted. Extensive use of paper towels is one of my clearest memories of the labs. I also developed the habit of making up my own quizzes and making them so complicated that I didn't think Dr. Berger would dare ask anything so difficult. I would routinely see about half my problems on his next test. The hard work paid off and probably helped my application to medical school the next year—just as Oscar had predicted.

Eileen's pregnancy progressed smoothly, and my mother arrived in August to be on hand for the birth of her first granddaughter. After a long, tiring, but uncomplicated labor, Margaret Clayton arrived late on a stormy afternoon, September 29, 1948.

Once home at Chinquapin Hill, everything proceeded smoothly, for about a week. Then Margaret developed colic. I can say from first-hand experience, colic in the newborn can make life a veritable hell on earth for the most attentive new parent. For weeks, the same sequence of events occurred: each day, all was well until after supper when, just as I was getting to my studies, she started crying, even screaming, and this continued for the next four or five hours. Our apartment was one room with but two doors, one led into the clothes closet and the other into the bathroom, so any attempt at studying was impossible. When Margaret, out of exhaustion, finally went to sleep about midnight, it was too late and I was in no frame of mind to get any work done. Ever since that first six weeks, I must admit that I have had an iota of understanding, a scintilla of sympathy for people who have homicidal thoughts when in the throes of serious sleep deprivation brought on by a colicky infant. I must have been taking easy courses that semester because somehow my grades held up. After the first week of November, Margaret improved and it was clear sailing thereafter.

Cecily and Allan White had moved out of the apartment above us and a young law student, his wife, and baby moved in. Colin and Jackie Campbell had much in common with us, with the exception of politics, and we became good friends. The presidential election of 1948, Thomas E. Dewey versus Harry S. Truman, was memorable. I have made mistakes in my life and done things I'm not too proud of, but on Election Day, November 2, 1948, I did the only thing I am truly ashamed to have done. I voted Republican. I never did it again. The only thing I can say in my defense is that I was working hard, missing a lot of sleep, and not thinking clearly. The press had convinced me that Truman had no chance to win, and I remember thinking that the country could ill-afford a divided Congress and executive branch. So, stupid as it sounds, I voted to make the inevitable unanimous.

On election night, Colin had arranged a small victory party to toast Dewey's certain victory. At seven o'clock, we went upstairs for drinks just as the first returns were coming in. An hour later the slight edge to the president hadn't changed and there was, for the first time, a look of concern in Colin's face. By ten o'clock, there was a look of panic and disbelief. By midnight, Colin was in total despair when Truman's victory was announced.

In the summer of 1948, we came to know Monica's brother and sister-in-law, Pat and Sally Deakin. They had a small piece of land, perhaps ten acres, about two miles from Chinquapin Hill. The land was poor due to decades of tobacco farming in the nineteenth century, but Pat, by hard work, managed a living by growing wheat and livestock. Pat had been trained as an estate agent in England before the war, but because there were few estates after the war that could use his talents, he came to the United Stated in the hope of doing better. Sally had been trained at the prestigious school of midwifery in Edinburgh, Scotland. They were wonderful, warmhearted people and we had many pleasant evenings in their small but cozy farmhouse. After final exams, I helped Pat by working in the fields to bring in his wheat crop. There was no better way to shake off "finalitis," that vague dissatisfaction and feeling that one could have and should have done better, than hard physical labor in the fields. And never did a cold bottle of beer after work taste better.

Pat and Sally had not yet had children, so when Eileen came home with Margaret, Sally was of immeasurable support with our new baby and, even after the colic abated, helped us two young and inexperienced parents. Several years after we left Virginia, Pat and Sally, who had returned to England in the early 1950s, conceived their first child. Sally was then in her mid-forties, so it was a near miracle, and their child, Donald, became the focus of their lives. When he was eighteen, Donald, on his way to Liverpool one stormy day to get his passport for his first trip to the United States, was killed in a senseless automobile accident. By all accounts, he was a young man of great potential. He was a graduate of Eton and had all the prerequisites for a distinguished career. We never saw Pat and Sally again after we left Virginia but we corresponded for years. Monica told us later that Donald's death was so devastating that the Deakins were never quite the same again.

After the 1948 holiday season, the race to the finish line of my last college year was on. Much of the pressure was relieved when, weeks earlier than expected, I received the letter advising me that I was accepted into medical school. I knew my grades were good enough, but the competition was so intense I had refused to become too optimistic. There were over fifteen hundred applications for the entering class and only fifteen seats of a class of seventy-five were available for out-of-state applicants. Though I had completed two years of undergraduate work at the University, I was still considered out-of-state because the University ruled that one had to be an in-state resident at least one year before matriculation. I never knew why I was lucky enough to be accepted; there were hundreds as well qualified as I. It may have been that I was from Hawaii and that the geographical diversity appealed to the admissions committee; I know of no other graduate of the medical school from Hawaii up to that time.

Letters from home bore the good news that my wartime squadron commander, Walt Hurd, and his wife, Ann, had established their home in Honolulu. By 1949, Walt had become the senior pilot for Philippine Air Lines. His transpacific flights from the South Pacific to the mainland put him in Honolulu as often as either San Francisco or Manila. He had phoned my parents shortly after they had settled and the two couples soon became friends. Walt had a wide breadth of interests, a superior intellect, and could discuss any number of subjects. Ann was an experienced school teacher and, like Walt, had a multitude of interests. Together they made an unusually interesting couple who had great appeal to my parents.

In May, I was stunned to receive a letter advising me that I had been elected into Phi Beta Kappa. I never knew who put me up for the honor,

especially because a month or two earlier I had made a loose-lipped remark to the effect that "I never met a Phi Beta who wasn't sort of a nerd."
My family never let me forget that smart-aleck remark. The dinner at the
induction ceremony was held in the Rotunda. It was a dignified, formal,
and impressive event, and I was struck by the number of faculty members
I admired who were on hand.

Graduation for my undergraduate degree was held June 13, 1949. I
remember clearly the thrill of the academic procession from the Rotunda
down The Lawn to Cabell Hall, with the Philadelphia Symphony led by
Bruno Walter playing the *Academic Festival Overture*, Eileen sitting with
Margaret, who was on her best behavior, and the beauty of a perfect late
spring day in Charlottesville. Following graduation, Monica gave us a
lovely lunch at Chinquapin with many friends from our little village of Ivy.

Two weeks later, we, with Kent Thorup, headed west to spend the summer in Phoenix. The G.I. Bill stipend stopped when school was not in
session, so the first priority was to get some sort of job. In the summer of
1949, there was a recession in Phoenix and jobs were scarce, unless one
wanted to pick cantaloupes in 110-degree heat. After searching the want
ads, Kent and I were interviewed by the sales manager of the Lindsey
Water Softener Company and were offered a commission-only job selling
their product. The plan was for us to contact the doctors and the lawyers,
since I was about to enter medical school and Kent had been accepted at
the law school. This plan turned out to be spectacularly unsuccessful. So,
we began selling door to door, trying to demonstrate the advantages of
soft water to bored housewives. Day after day, or more accurately, morning
after morning, we pounded the pavement and tried to peddle our product with absolutely no success. By mid-day, exhausted and dehydrated, we
would repair to Dick's Tavern on Central Avenue. The idea of going out
again into an even hotter afternoon was intolerable, so we found ourselves
spending more and more time at Dick's establishment. We were on the
verge of panic and the only thing that saved me from suicide was the oc-

casional check from my generous father and, I think, Marguerite slipping Eileen an occasional ten or twenty dollars on the quiet. The entire summer was depressing beyond belief and it was years before we were able to find it funny. By the end of summer, we had sold one water softener—to a person who should not have bought one. He was a cardiologist who told us, as he was signing the sales contract, that it was ill-advised for a person like himself with high blood pressure and a bad heart to buy anything that put more sodium in his drinking water. Kent and I split our thirty-six dollar commission and celebrated by having an extra beer at Dick's.

Kent and I had learned that if we had to depend on selling anything for a living, we would probably starve, so by the end of August we were eager to head back to Virginia. On September fourth, the day that Eileen and I had been working toward for so long, medical school would begin. I remember that as I walked up the stairs of the medical school the first day, I felt intimidated, excited, and eager to get on with my chosen career.

Reflections

The question of racism at a university in the South a decade or more before Martin Luther King nags at one's conscience, especially if one professes to be a liberal humanist. Before Dr. King made the country aware of the gross inequities of segregation, the custom was accepted without much thought; it had been going on for a long, long time. In Charlottesville in the late 1940s and early 1950s, students had very little contact with black people at anything approaching the same social level. At the time, blacks were the working class and filled more or less menial jobs—waiters, household helpers, janitors, and the like. There were no black undergraduates at the University of Virginia at the time I was there; and there never had been. I did not know of any militant white people who even discussed this state of affairs. Denial of equitable civil liberties was a non-issue. However, I do not recall ever seeing "Whites Only" signs on any public place or anywhere at the University.

I am not ashamed of the memory of this lack of sophistication. How can one be ashamed of something about which one is not aware? For one who says that lack of awareness is in itself shameful and no excuse, so be it. Let him walk in the shoes of those of us whose total energy, time, and intellect for four years was committed to qualifying for graduate school, and then committing to four more years of advanced studies. It is at least understandable, if not forgivable, that there was little time to ruminate over societal ills. I have always been perplexed by headlines of "students taking to the streets to protest" this or that cause. How could they afford that much time away from their studies? (Studies, incidentally, that would give them the knowledge to espouse what was or was not truly important.) However, after Dr. King and other heroes of the civil rights movement made us aware of the evils of segregation, to then refuse to understand would have been unconscionable.

In defense of my peers, most of whom were raised in the South, I do not recall a single episode of overt racial bigotry, or slurs, or even jokes demeaning black people. In my third year at the University, we played a football game against Harvard. On the Harvard team there was a talented black player. It was the first time a black athlete *ever* appeared on a southern college gridiron. There were a few rumors about demonstrations and protests but nothing came of them. We beat the Harvard team by about five touchdowns, which may have further defused any unpleasantness. During my six years at the University, I met only one unabashed, avowed racist, and he was considered a little odd. From a practical point of view, in medical school, indigent black people made up a critically important part of our clinic population. Without exception, they were understanding of our lack of experience and were patient and appreciative of our ministrations. Our education would have been far poorer without them.

Me diving at Punahou

Punahou campus in 1938

Me, Dad, Mother, and John at Koko Head, 1939

Mother, 1941

Yale and Bobby Lewis, 1943

My plane, "Niner Easy," photo taken by my wingman over France, 1945

Me and John, 1944

Pilots of the 314th Troop Carrier Squadron, June 6, 1944.

Eileen's sister, Mary, and Warren Schwab and Eileen and Me
at our double wedding, 1945

Me and Eileen arriving in Honolulu, 1945

Oscar and Barby Thorup

Post-wedding portrait, 1946

Eileen and Margaret at Chinquapin Hill, VA, 1949

University of Virginia School of Medicine, 1949

Eileen's mother, Marguerite Quinn
The world's greatest mother-in-law

Medical School

The first day our class assembled, September 4, 1949, there was an orientation meeting. Certain customs of the past and an overview of what lay ahead were presented. Soon after, we paired off and received our first ten-day assignment: a complete, disarticulated human skeleton—our "box of bones." That was the day I met Bill Lilly, my laboratory partner for the next four years and lifelong friend. Bill was born in West Virginia but graduated from Washington and Lee University before medical school. Bill was a slow talker but had a very retentive mind. I was different on both counts, so we seemed to complement each other.

Our first assignment, osteology, covered the first 250 pages of *Gray's Anatomy*. In ten days we were to learn every facet, protuberance, foramen, and groove of every bone in the body; then we were to have an oral exam. I couldn't believe it. Learning that vast amount of material in the time allotted seemed an impossibility. Everyone spent about a week on the skull and two or three days on everything else. On exam day, we presented ourselves to our examiners in groups of four. Bill went first and was asked to discuss the skull! He knew the material as well as anyone, but to make a coherent, organized presentation in ten minutes would have been impossible. I was next and was asked to discuss a small rib. If there was one set of bones I had hardly considered, it was the ribs. I remembered having heard that one could identify the first rib by dropping it, for it was the only rib of the twelve that landed on three points. Beyond that, virtually all the ribs were the same and there wasn't very much to talk about. I think I must have dropped that rib twenty times in the next ten minutes, mumbling things about the "head" and "tubercle." Somehow we all passed the exam.

The Monday morning after the osteology exam, we were introduced to our cadavers—four students to each specimen. I recall a solemn warning that any foolishness or tricks or even gross disrespect outside the anatomy lab could result in immediate expulsion from school. Such things had happened in the past but not for many years.

For the next four months, I saw little of Eileen and Margaret. I worked all day, occasionally getting home for dinner, then went back to the lab for a few more hours of work before getting home, reeking of the stench of formaldehyde and glycerin, and collapsing in bed. Sometimes I would take a Sunday off. Medical school puts a strain on the most solid marriage, and that first semester may have been the worst. To go through medical school married, one better marry the right woman. As for me, I doubt that I would have had the tenacity and mental discipline to have made it through four tough years without the steady, uncomplaining presence of Eileen. When one says "we" made it through medical school, it is the literal truth.

The first year of medical school at Virginia in 1949 consisted of four subjects: anatomy and histology/embryology during the first semester and biochemistry and physiology the second. It was the equivalent of memorizing the New York City telephone book.

The vast amount of material in biochemistry and physiology was presented by two memorable teachers: Dr. Alfred Chanutin and Dr. Sidney Britton. Dr. Chanutin, professor of biochemistry, was, by reputation, terrifying. If he took a dislike to a student, for whatever reason, that unlucky fellow was not likely to graduate. Oscar had forewarned me of his strong personality. "Dr. Chan" was from a Russian-Jewish background and had grown up in the toughest part of New York City. He had achieved prominence in the world of academic medicine from very humble beginnings. Along the way he had also been a champion golden gloves boxer, as one unhappy student found out after challenging Dr. Chan physically. During the war he obviously had deep feelings about the horrors of the Holocaust in Nazi Germany, and he appointed himself a committee of one, according to Oscar, to see to it that no one who wasn't committed to his studies was going to pass biochemistry. Conversely, he looked kindly on veterans of the war. He didn't make the subject matter easy, no one could, but I did gather that the atmosphere in his classroom was a good deal more relaxed that it had been during the war years. Dr. Chan was a superb lecturer and teacher.

Dr. Sidney Britton, professor of physiology, was altogether different; in fact, some thought he was from a different planet. He was a splendid teacher but a little eccentric. He once published a paper, picked up by *Time* magazine, suggesting that human sperm might be used in apes to breed a subhuman species that could be trained to do menial labor. Whether or not he was truly serious is questionable, but I remember him bringing in a basket full of fan/hate mail after the article was published. It was hard to believe the venom, primarily from religious fundamentalists, that the article generated. Death threats were the least offensive messages.

Somehow our class made it through the first year without anyone failing; but the work seemed so overwhelming there were times when I had doubts about my ability to make a success of a career in medicine. The old saying at Virginia was that in the first year of medical school, one was scared to death and in the second, one was bored to death. In the third and fourth year, when we began hands-on clinical work, all that went before was appreciated and the work began to be fun.

At Christmas 1949, we had our first houseguest, our dear friend Norman Wright, who we had first met in Hawaii when we returned after the war. Though born and raised in Pennsylvania, he had attended the University of Alabama and had come to Hawaii in the late 1930s to teach English at the University of Hawaii. He soon became involved in the Honolulu Community Theater (HCT) and gave up teaching to become the publisher's representative for the New York firm of Snyder & Company.

Norm was a talented actor and appeared in some of HCT's most successful productions as diverse as *King Lear*, the lead in *Death of a Salesman*, and opposite Judith Anderson in *Media*. He also appeared in several movies and television plays filmed on location in Hawaii. He had many friends in the theater, most notably the great English actor, playwright, and wit, Robert Morley. In the mid-1950s, Norm seriously considered leaving Honolulu to try for a career on the New York stage but ultimately decided against it. He had the talent but knew as well as anyone that success on

Broadway requires more than just talent—timing and pure luck are equally important. Plus, he loved his job with Snyder, which made it necessary for him to travel all over the world. Annually he would travel to the Orient, India, Europe, London, and the major cities in the United States.

Norm had the most unique gift for friendship of anyone I ever knew. His relationship with my parents was almost like that of a son and, to me, for fifty years, almost like that of a brother. He was a gourmet cook, nervous but excellent, a superb mimic, and uproariously funny. Our dear friends and neighbors, Bob and Margie Walsh, laughed so hard at Norm's pantomime of Queen Victoria on the "throne" (costumed with a tiny doily on his head while balancing a large salt shaker upon it) I feared Bob would have a stroke. Another of Norm's singular accomplishments was his ability to write perfect "mirror image" sentences. Without hesitation he could write any sentence and then re-write it in a fashion which, when held up to a mirror, was a perfect duplicate of the original. I asked him how he had learned this remarkable feat and he said he had never "learned" it. It was just something he had always been able to do from an early age and couldn't remember a time when he could *not* do it.

In his younger days, Norm had a truly remarkable tolerance for liquor and, no matter how much he drank, never showed any effect; similarly, he was never ill, no matter how much, what, or where he ate. Always a heavy smoker, he developed lung cancer in his mid-sixties, underwent a pneumonectomy, and survived another eighteen years without a recurrence. He died in 1997, at the age of eighty, from kidney failure. Norm was the only person who was our houseguest in every home we had (save one) from Chinquapin Hill to our final retirement home in Colorado. At his death, he left the bulk of his considerable estate evenly divided between my children and John's. Though sometimes years would pass between his visits, we always eagerly awaited not only his visits but also his wonderful letters.

Soon after the end of the first year of medical school, and after my annual stint helping Pat Deakin get in his wheat crop, we left Chinquapin

for Phoenix and then a summer vacation in Honolulu—our first trip home
in three years. My father had arranged for us to have the private compartment in the back of the huge Boeing "Stratocruiser," the civilian version
of the military KC-97. Margaret was a great little traveler and seemed as
excited as we were as we rounded Diamond Head and got our first view of
Manoa Valley. Walt and Ann Hurd, having planned a vacation in California, gave us their apartment for six weeks. It was perfect for us, and we had
great fun entertaining family and friends. John's first two children, Prenty
and Nancy, were the perfect age for Margaret, and the three of them had
a wonderful time playing in the ocean, going to the zoo, hiking, and picnicking. It was a delightful summer, but it was to be our last in the Islands
for twenty years.

In mid-August, Eileen's school chum, Debbie Best, came to Honolulu
for her summer vacation. Among other talents, Debbie was a superb Tex-
Mex cook and it was at our apartment, for a Mexican dinner, that Deb
and Norm first met. Norm had been a confirmed bachelor, but they hit it
off at once and their friendship soon turned into a romance. Three years
later, when I was interning at St. Joseph's Hospital in Phoenix, they were
married and I was Norm's best man. Their marriage was a happy one for
forty-three years, until Deb's death in 1996, a year before Norm's.

We left Honolulu the last day of August 1950, and I was a little surprised to realize that I was as anxious to get back to work as I had been to
get away two months earlier. The second year of medical school at Virginia
was, as advertised, difficult and sometimes deadly boring. Dr. Bray's clinical diagnosis class was a case in point. Promptly at 1:00 p.m., after lunch
on a warm fall day, we would assemble in class; the shades would be drawn,
the slide projector turned on, and a monocyte four feet across would be
projected on the screen. For the next hour, Dr. Bray would lecture with his
gentle Virginia accent and tell us more about the monocyte than any person could possibly want to know. No one, of course, was still awake at the
end of the hour. Dr. Bray was a tall courtly gentleman and he never seemed

to mind what was going on, he'd become used to it over the years, but he did not appreciate pencils and books dropping on the floor.

And so on it went: pharmacology, laboratory diagnosis, pathology, etc. At one point the subject matter was so soporific I considered asking for a recall to active duty, as the Korean War was much in the news. Taking my chances in a war seemed preferable to being bored to death. However, I realized that even if I could have flown again, it would upset too many people who had sacrificed too much to get us as far as we had progressed.

At Christmas, the Campbells invited us to Jackie's father's beautiful home on the eastern shore of Maryland, at Lynnhaven Bay. General Thompson, a third generation West Pointer, was a distinguished soldier and, as a young man, a horse cavalry officer. His tales of watching the cavalry in the Olympic equestrian events of the 1920s were fascinating. He was especially impressed with the riders from Ireland who, though they did not always win the steeplechase events, got the most out of their mounts. But of even greater interest was meeting his mother-in-law, Mrs. Cameron, who was in her nineties and quite frail physically but unimpaired mentally. She usually dined in her room but, if feeling strong enough, enjoyed nothing more than joining the young people for conversation after dinner. As a teenage Army bride, she remembered dancing with General George Armstrong Custer at Fort Leavenworth in the 1870s. She said every young woman on the post was in love with the dashing general.

The following morning, we went out into the bay in General Thompson's skiff to harvest oysters from his private oyster bed. We brought in a full bushel basket and had oysters cooked every possible way—baked, fried, and roasted—but nothing was better than the ones we shucked and ate raw right out of the bay, ice cold and just slightly salted from seawater.

The last weeks of the second year of medical school were, for me, a time of soul-searching, self-analysis, and introspection. Because the second year was so utterly boring, there were times when I seriously doubted my commitment to become a good doctor. Furthermore, I had never been baptized, which, though it never bothered me, seemed to concern others. For that reason, and the fact that I thought spiritual counseling would help my self-doubts about pursuing medicine, I began taking instructions from Father Moore at Holy Comforter Catholic Church in Charlottesville. Father Moore was a fine man and one I always felt comfortable talking to. I learned the basic teachings, rituals, and beliefs of the Church. After both of us decided that I understood enough, I was baptized and confirmed. Then I made a big mistake. I made what is called a good confession. I let it all hang out, believing that after absolution and penance I would have peace of mind and be spiritually uplifted. It didn't work that way. I felt humiliated, embarrassed, and a damned fool. I never confessed or received the sacraments again, though I did keep going to mass with Eileen for many years.

When the second year came mercifully to an end, Bill Lilly and I decided to operate a boy's summer camp at the Blue Ridge Swimming Pool. The pool, owned by Monica and Jeff, was a tenth of a mile down the road from Chinquapin Hill. Though it passed all the required health regulations, the water was full of silt and so murky that one could not see the bottom of the pool. It was almost a hundred meters long and thirty feet wide. Our campers, about twenty youngsters, would arrive at nine-thirty in the morning, swim and play until noon, have a lunch of sandwiches they brought and Kool-Aid that we made, and go home mid-afternoon. It was a little nerve-wracking keeping track of all the kids, some of whom did not swim well, in a pool with cloudy water. But we didn't lose anybody, and financially it was a qualified success. It was, at least, a healthy break from classrooms and laboratories.

By the beginning of the third year of medical school, the G.I. Bill had played out and the cost of tuition, books, and monthly stipend had to be assumed by my father. Eileen's talents as a seamstress for friends in Ivy further supplemented our income. Though we didn't have much, we had enough for the essentials and an occasional luxury. A party was a six-pack of beer and a potluck picnic. All of our medical and law school friends were in the same situation, so we always had fun.

At the time, I was not fully aware of how bad the economy in Honolulu had become. My parents had sold the big house on Ferdinand Avenue in upper Manoa in February 1950 and were building a "small big house" (big rooms but not too many of them) at Wailupe Peninsula. In the interim, and while we visited home the summer of 1950, they rented an apartment at Ala Wai Gardens. They were glad to be rid of the big house and for a time enjoyed the simplicity of apartment living. But building their new home was a slow, frustrating business, and it took almost a year. The Hawaiian work ethic, non-availability of certain materials in the Islands, and constant strikes were contributing factors. My father's business affairs occasionally fared well but were more often mediocre to poor. I was aware of the sacrifices they were making on my behalf and vowed to make it up to them someday.

Manoa Valley is verdant and beautiful because of a great deal of rain, but the high humidity seemed to aggravate my mother's chronic upper respiratory infections and bronchitis. My parents hoped the weather at Wailupe, with less rain, would help. It didn't. It was lower, windier, and hotter, and within a year they moved back to Manoa, a few blocks from the old house. More important, the old dichotomy persisted—mother loved her home and many dear friends but never liked the weather and the small town atmosphere of Honolulu. In 1952, with a business in the doldrums and little reason for optimism, they decided they would probably move back to California permanently within a year.

To understand the business climate in Honolulu, a short review of its history is relevant. Honolulu, though in an exotic locale, was beset with the unattractive characteristics of any small city. It was provincial and insular. The society was four-tiered. There were the *kamaainas* (old timers headed by descendants of the missionaries), the military, the remaining Hawaiians, and everyone else. Native Hawaiians were hardly a factor as they were disappearing by intermarriage, and their culture was being manipulated by the tourist industry into shows they thought tourists would find authentic.

Two centuries earlier, when Hawaii was discovered, there were an estimated three hundred thousand natives, and each Island was ruled by a local chief. In 1792, after ten years of war, King Kamehameha I united the Islands under his rule, but with the coming of missionaries and Europeans and the introduction of their diseases, particularly measles, the population was reduced. By 1850, not more than seventy thousand natives remained. Hawaii's last monarch, Queen Liliuokalani, was removed from the throne in 1894, in a bloodless coup led by nine Americans, two Britons, two Germans, and supported by the United States Navy. The excuse that she was removed because she "had exceeded her constitutional authority" was a charade. She was removed because the men who led the revolution wanted the land and the wealth that went with it. The usurpers proclaimed the Islands a republic and, in 1900, petitioned the United States Congress to establish it as a territory. The descendents of these men became known as The Big Five, and they controlled the Hawaiian economy until after World War II.

Beginning in the late 1930s, labor leaders on the west coast, seeking power and being indifferent to the havoc they caused businessmen, nearly ruined the Island economy through the power of the maritime strike. It took until the 1960s for the stranglehold the Big Five had on Hawaii's economy to break. Big labor, the war, statehood in 1959, tourism, the jet age, and vast amount of money from Japan invested in Island real estate all combined to change Hawaii permanently and irrevocably.

The status of the pre-war military was clouded by resentment of the native Hawaiians stemming from the infamous Massey trial. Massey, a naval officer, shot and killed two Hawaiians he thought had attacked his wife. They hadn't. But Clarence Darrow, retained by Massey, managed an acquittal. Following the war, however, the impact of the Defense Department payroll on the Island economy as well as the appreciation for the role of the Navy in saving Hawaii dispelled any lingering ill will.

After our summer as camp counselors in 1951, Eileen and I eagerly awaited the beginning of my third year of medical school and my first experience with the hands-on treatment of patients. The didactic work was less intense but was still a major part of our curriculum. Dealing with patients was often a nervous business, but the indigent black and white populations were appreciative and patient with our lack of experience. Some were virtually professional patients and would often guide us by asking the right questions and suggesting the correct part of the chest to listen to or the correct quadrant of the abdomen to palpate.

The country people I met had a unique *patois* and had colorful names for a variety of illnesses: "white risens" were boils; "dew poison" I never understood. But one I never forgot was "save my mighty Jesus"; when I asked my patient how he had felt, he told me of a high fever, a terrible stiff neck and an incapacitating headache—the classic signs of spinal meningitis; thus, his name was not too far off the mark.

One awful case I will never forget was that of a strapping young country girl who had stepped on a rake a week earlier. One of the tines had punctured her foot. The country doctor had prescribed the right medicine, tetanus antitoxin, but her fundamentalist pastor forbade any form of "shots." Just after she entered the emergency room, ill but conscious, she convulsed for the first time. The convulsions continued every few minutes for almost a week in spite of massive doses of antitoxin, the primitive country pastor's edict to the contrary notwithstanding. She never lost consciousness and died of exhaustion and kidney failure. "Lockjaw" is not a death I would wish on anyone. It was the first time I ever saw a patient die—in spite of heroic treatment.

There were many unforgettable days that year, a year that passed so quickly it was hard to believe. The most difficult parts of the third and fourth years were the case presentations to the faculty and, of course, to one's peers. One was responsible for every aspect of one's case, from initial contact to final resolution, and the preparation had to be thorough. But, it was almost never thorough enough. The case had to be known and understood forward and backward. In addition, one had to be prepared for many "what else could it be?" type questions. In spite of one's best efforts, humiliation and a display of ignorance were the rule. Occasionally, but rarely, one would have a stroke of luck and answer a question brilliantly. It was a great teaching method and proved invaluable in the years ahead.

The third year also marked the beginning of the end of innocence. Up to that time, one's normal reaction to pain and suffering was subjective and empathetic, but after that year, perhaps unfortunately, one became somewhat jaded and more objective. The old adage "whenever something is learned, something is lost" became understandable. In moments of crisis, objectivity and detachment are essential for the physician.

During the summer of 1952, after driving Eileen and Margaret to Phoenix, I returned to the East Coast for a clinical externship at the Walter Reed Army Medical Center in Washington, D.C. I was assigned as I had hoped I would be, to the Obstetrical Service. The standards of practice at Walter Reed were of the highest quality and, save for the awful heat of Washington in August, it was a valuable learning experience. After my externship, I returned to Phoenix and packed up our little four-door Plymouth the way we had always done—cardboard boxes on the floor in the rear, level with the seat, and Margaret's crib mattress over that. By today's standards, lacking seat belts, it probably was not a safe way to travel, but it gave Margaret room to roll around, nap, and play.

Back in school, the fourth year required more clinical work and proportionately fewer lectures. It was during my two-month rotation on Obstetrics that I became sure that this was the specialty that interested me most. The chairman of the department was Dr. Norman Thornton. He epitomized the kind of doctor I wanted to become. He was knowledgeable,

a superb clinician, a gifted surgeon and teacher, and a friend to all struggling medical students. I had first known him in 1948, when he attended
Eileen during her first pregnancy, and never forgot the total confidence
that he inspired.

For my first obstetrical case, I was assigned to attend a very large black
lady in her tenth pregnancy. Once assigned a labor patient, the student was
expected to remain in close attendance at all times until delivery. For six
hours I did not leave her side and scrupulously monitored every twinge of
discomfort and the baby's heart beat. There was no progress in labor and
no detectable contractions. In the seventh hour, she turned to me and said,
"Doctor the baby's a-comin." There were still no contractions until three or
four minutes later when a prolonged tetanic contraction lasting two minutes occurred and the baby appeared—in the labor bed. Untoward events
like precipitous deliveries were not supposed to happen, and even though
the baby and mother were fine, a report explaining the circumstances had
to be written. After turning in my report, I'm sure I heard laughter from
Dr. Thornton's office.

In the spring, I applied for a rotating internship at St. Joseph's Hospital in Phoenix as my first choice and was duly "matched." Our last year
of school was almost relaxed compared to what had gone before. Barring
some totally unforeseen event, graduation and the M.D. degree were near
certainties. I was aware that a rotating internship at a private open-staff
hospital did not carry the same prestige that a straight internship at a
teaching hospital did, but I had to think of certain practicalities. Prestigious internships often paid no stipend at all and I couldn't afford that
with a wife, baby, and yet another baby due in August. The princely sum of
ninety dollars a month was well above the average for interns at that time
and was enough for us to live on. As a staff member, there would be no
hospital bill for the new baby nor, of course, a charge from the attending
physician.

Graduation from medical school, including the academic procession
down The Lawn from the Rotunda to Cabell Hall, was even more impres-

sive than it had been four years before. This time we wore the hoods lined with green over our academic gowns. I don't remember formally taking the Hippocratic Oath during graduation week but we were encouraged to study it. Throughout my career, the Oath has always served as *the* ethical guide in the practice of medicine. I went to mass to give thanks for being permitted to embark on the career I had always dreamed of pursuing.

A few days after a lovely farewell party given us by Vivian Clapp at her exquisite home, Acorn Cottage, we bade an emotional farewell to Jeff and Monica and to all our other dear friends at Chinquapin Hill and Ivy and headed west.

In retrospect, though Chinquapin was six or seven miles from the University and the commute was sometimes tiresome, it was quiet, beautiful, and nestled near pine woods. There were no distractions, no traffic, and the air was clean. There was no better place to walk in the evenings to clear one's mind after a busy day at school. For us, it was the perfect place to live in order to accomplish what we had to during the momentous years of 1947-1953.

Reflections

I have often wondered what it is that makes one want to be a physician; what is the one characteristic that is common to almost all practitioners? I am convinced of several things that it is not. During medical school, I only knew one person who unabashedly admitted that he was motivated by a desire to make money. I only knew one other, a Christian missionary's son, who was motivated by the love of his fellow man. No one ever spoke of prestige as a motivating factor. So if not materialism, humanitarianism, or power, what then? I think it is simple curiosity—curiosity about how the human organism reacts to an infinite variety of illnesses, stress, injuries, and disease. Even the desire to alleviate pain and suffering is secondary to curiosity. It is insatiable curiosity that gets the grubby medical student, the harassed intern or resident, and the busy practitioner out of bed each morning to face new challenges.

Lastly, the rewards of a career in medicine, the things that Hippocrates said make physicians "respected by all men," are as true today as they were twenty-five centuries ago. It is still wrong to willfully deviate from accepted medical standards in treatment, to knowingly cause a death, to give a woman an instrument to self-induce an abortion, and to divulge privileged communication. As a code of ethics, the Oath can hardly be improved upon, modern knowledge and new technology notwithstanding.

IV
1953-1962

My Internship began at 8:00 a.m., July 1, 1953, at St. Joseph's Hospital at the old location in Phoenix, Arizona, at 6th and Van Buren Street. We moved to the new (and present) site on Thomas Road two months later. My first rotation, however, was in the emergency room at Maricopa County Hospital. As I presented myself for duty, there were three patients who needed immediate attention. The first was an elderly man with a deep scalp laceration bleeding profusely, the next was a middle-aged man suffering an apparent heart attack, and the third was a young woman in the midst of a severe asthma attack. I had no idea who to attend first or exactly what to do. To give myself a little time to think, I decided to stop the bleeding first then evaluate the others. The charge nurse, who was far more experienced than I, suggested starting an IV on the asthma patient and oxygen and an EKG on the heart patient. These sounded like good ideas and by the time I closed the laceration, the other patients were more or less stabilized. It was not the first time, and certainly not the last, that a nurse bailed me out of a tight situation.

Asthma in Phoenix was common and virtually a daily occurrence. It became a point of pride for the house staff members that if we could treat asthma sufferers with enough aminophylline and epinephrine in the emergency room we would be able to send them home without having to admit them to the hospital. Heat stroke was another common problem, especially among the itinerant field workers and the homeless. The only fatality I saw in the ER that first month was an aged Latino who was brought in with a temperature so high it was off the scale of a thermometer and he failed to respond to ice baths, fans, and IV fluids.

By the first of August, I was back at St. Joseph's just in time for the arrival of our second baby, Richard Clayton II. The delivery, unlike Margaret's, was so fast that there was almost no time for anesthesia and, though painful, was uncomplicated.

The new St. Joseph's opened early in September 1953, and it was exciting to be part of the first house staff in a sparkling, state-of-the-art facility. When the rotation schedule for the twelve interns was published, I started to make plans to trade my time so that I could be off the services that didn't interest me and on the ones that did—particularly obstetrics and gynecology. Obstetrics became a very busy service almost at once and was soon to average over three-hundred deliveries a month.

The standard of care at an open-staff private hospital was quite different from that of a teaching hospital and varied from excellent to poor. Working with the obvious experts became the goal and dodging being assigned to the patients of the "hacks" became a sort of game. There was a core of well-trained, board-certified internists, surgeons, pediatricians, and obstetricians. There was also, unfortunately, a large group of practitioners who were unskilled but were favored by the administration because they admitted their patients only to St. Joseph's. Finally, there were many general practitioners of variable competence. One infamous general practitioner, who had been on the staff for years, did surgery which was self-taught and for which he had had no formal training. I assisted him once on a vaginal hysterectomy on an obese, thirty-five-year-old virgin. It was a nightmare experience. A thirty minute operation turned into a three hour ordeal requiring multiple blood transfusions. He used the wrong instruments on a poorly selected patient and obviously knew little of pelvic anatomy.

The hazards that laypersons faced when attended by doctors who had a misplaced confidence in their ability was a lesson I never forgot. Years later, when risk management and quality control became vital concerns, the things I remembered seeing as an intern became invaluable. The malpractice crisis of the 1960s and beyond was, more often than not, due to the ministrations of incompetent physicians and was compounded by a certain amount of greed among plaintiffs' attorneys. The slogan that "the general practitioner's practice should end at the hospital door" may be too harsh, but that "it should end at the operating room door" might not be. In the 1950s, the quality of the practitioner's work, except in the most flagrant examples of incompetence, was pretty much ignored.

My pediatrics rotation was enjoyable because of several extremely well-trained attending physicians, but I learned that I would never be able to practice that specialty—attending fatally ill children was more than I could handle emotionally, and the proper objectivity and detachment was, for me, impossible.

As far as I was concerned, the busy obstetrical service at St. Joseph's was marvelous. As attending physicians grew to know me, they allowed me greater latitude not only with clinic patients but with private patients as well. It was a busy service and I achieved a record of sorts when I delivered ten patients in one twenty-hour shift.

In the spring of 1954, I had an unexpected two-week holiday when I contracted mumps. I was never very ill and, frankly, enjoyed catching up on my reading and time with Eileen, Margaret, and Clayt. It must have been a bad season for mumps in Phoenix that year. One very prominent and respected internist became ill and suffered every possible major complication from an illness that is usually considered benign. He was bedridden for months with the complications of orchitis, pancreatitis, and meningitis.

Also during the spring of 1954, I began writing letters to various hospitals—applying for residency training in obstetrics. I received an encouraging letter from the University of California Medical Center in San Francisco and was very happy to be accepted into their program. Coincidentally, during this same time period, I also applied to the Air Force for a return to active duty as a medical officer in an Air Force sponsored residency program. My application to the Air Force was also approved, which was good news because it meant that I would receive higher pay than regular first-year residents.

Another reason I was looking forward to my impending move back to the San Francisco area was that after eighteen years in Hawaii, my parents had returned to the mainland permanently in December 1953, and after weeks of looking at places to settle from Santa Rosa to Sebastopol, they finally decided on San Francisco. We enjoyed a happy family reunion when Eileen and I, with Margaret and Clayt, returned to begin my term as a junior assistant resident at California in July of 1954.

Residency

My Residency training began at the University of California Hospital at 8:00 a.m., July 1, 1954, and I delivered my first baby an hour and a half later. It was the beginning of the most intense, exhausting, and exhilarating three years of my life. It also put me in association with some of the finest minds in the specialty of obstetrics and gynecology. Our professor and chairman of the department was Herbert F. Traut, a world-famous gynecologic pathologist. His most famous contribution, and one that might well have been considered for a Nobel Prize, was co-authoring, with Dr. George Papanicolaou, the first paper on exfoliative cytology. The so-called "Pap Smear" evolved from this epochal work. As house officers, whenever we submitted a specimen from the cervix, the specimen was labeled a "P-T smear" and, because Dr. Papanicolaou was the senior author of the paper, never a "T-P smear." The technique of obtaining the smear was very precise and achieved by using a moist cotton-tipped applicator stick and bulb aspiration. Endocervical brushes and spatulas were not used because Dr. Traut considered that such devices collected superficial biopsies rather than truly exfoliated cells.

Dr. Traut was a formidable, powerful personality and disagreeing with him on any level or for any reason took either a very brave or a very foolish person. I still remember many of the points he emphasized in his welcoming address to the new class of residents. We were counseled to observe proper decorum, dress appropriately, appear neat and well-groomed, never to smoke or chew gum in the presence of a patient, and never to argue with a senior nurse. "You can be replaced, they can't," he advised us. He also stressed that mistakes involving patient care would not be tolerated because there was too much expert help available at all times. He reminded us that if we were guilty of some error that adversely affected the health of a patient, no one would say, in effect, *Oh well, don't worry, you tried your best*; nor would fatigue ever be accepted as an excuse. It was a sobering lecture. Physically, he was not a tall man, but he was powerfully built and his persona was as commanding as a four-star general in the military. In fact, the organization of a pyramidal residency training program was not unlike that of a taut military unit: interns were the equivalent of second lieutenants, residents were the captains, chief residents the majors, associate professors the colonels, and professors were the generals.

The fact of married house officers was a post WWII phenomenon and a relatively new one to Dr. Traut and one that he grew accustomed to but probably never really endorsed. His commitment to the specialty had been absolute his entire professional life and he expected the same from all of us. Any free time, when we were not getting caught up on sleep, was to be spent with our families and on no other extracurricular activities. I never saw Dr. Traut display anger or even raise his voice, but his contempt for sloppy or incompetent work was withering. He was as forceful a leader as I have ever known in or out of the military, and to disappoint him in any aspect of our work was too bitter a thought to contemplate.

As I already noted, the structure of the training program was pyramidal. Once accepted, barring gross incompetence, one was pretty much assured of completing the three years necessary to meet the requirements for certification by the American Board. A fourth year of training might be offered to three or four from the pool of ten assistant residents, but the exalted chief resident, the fifth year, was offered only to the *crème de la crème*, who, with few exceptions, went on to careers in academic medicine.

There were, of course, others on the teaching staff besides Dr. Traut, and there was a great deal to be learned from each of them as well. The other full professor was Dr. Earnest Page, prominent because of his work on toxemia in pregnancy. There were also Doctors Earl King, a consummate surgeon, Ned Overstreet, an erudite professional who was to be consulted if one sought to publish, and Ed Hill, an outstanding clinician.

On a day-to-day basis, one learned volumes from the residents one or two years ahead in the program. In my case, I learned as much from Jim Merrill as anyone I ever worked with. His knowledge of every aspect of obstetrics and gynecology, from the practical to the theoretical, was profound and, after his tenure as chief resident, he became a Markel Scholar. Later in his career, Jim became a professor of Obstetrics and Gynecology at the University of Oklahoma Medical School. Jim has remained my mentor and friend from the 1950s to the present.

I grew to appreciate the hierarchy of the Residency program in time but, for me, there were more pressing problems early in the first year. Having been approved for residency training by the Air Force, I naively assumed that I would be on active duty and that pay and allowances would begin on July 1, 1954. But for unexplained reasons, days and weeks went by with no word from Washington. A regular commission required congressional and, ultimately, presidential action. For the first six weeks after July 1, I rented a dingy room on Irving Street two blocks from the hospital. Then at the beginning of August, I rented a garden apartment in Stonestown. Stonestown was a new development on 19th Avenue about three miles from the hospital and consisted of tower apartments and two-story buildings with garden apartments. I assumed, incorrectly, that it could not be too much longer before I was ordered to active duty. When Congress adjourned for the summer recess, and I still had heard nothing, I was forced to borrow money to meet my commitments. Fortunately, Dr. Traut had a fund available for just such contingencies and it saw me through a difficult time. Finally, on the first of October, I received my orders, established a pay record at Hamilton A.F.B., and soon was receiving my first lieutenant's monthly pay and allowances. At something over three hundred dollars a month, I felt positively affluent.

Our apartment at Stonestown consisted of two bedrooms with connecting bath, a living room with a dining area, and a kitchen. We had almost no furniture and spent the early weeks utilizing packing cases. The apartment was just the right size for us and even accommodated another baby a year later. I never forgot Dr. Traut's understanding and generosity. In spite of his formidable presence, he was always kind and, I think, though house staff with families were new to him, he grew to enjoy the role of near father figure.

My parents, having visited many areas in California, finally settled back in San Francisco and rented a furnished apartment in the Sunset District. They were beset by severe financial worries but thoroughly enjoyed being back home, countless good times with the grandchildren, and a host of lifelong friends. It was not until May of 1955, however, that they found an attractive unfurnished apartment at Park Merced, about a mile from Stonestown. They were, at last, able to send for all their household effects and establish a home. Their lives then assumed a pattern that was typical of their last years together—rather bleak and with chronic economic woes interspersed with times of joy and happiness. For the first time in my memory, however, I could tell that there were days when my father acted more fatigued than seemed appropriate. He rested more and seemed less inclined to bounce upstairs two at a time. He still enjoyed an occasional game of golf and entertaining—he was always a warm and attentive host—but I could see subtle changes.

Eileen's third pregnancy was proceeding uneventfully, and on Halloween morning she called me at the hospital, afraid that labor was beginning, and said that she'd just as soon not have a Halloween baby. She was taken promptly to the labor room and even more promptly to the delivery room, where Jim Merrill delivered Ellen Frances before Ed Hill was able to get from his office to the fifteenth floor. As before, both mother and baby were in excellent condition. Once home, Margaret and Clayton were fascinated by, and very proud of, their new little sister.

As for me, the work continued to be engrossing and satisfying but, at times, exhausting. I remember going to work on Friday morning and coming home the following Monday evening, having had no sleep other than cat naps, and collapsing in bed to sleep twelve hours. Except for the six months on pathology, we were "on call" every other night and every other weekend for the first two years. As the gynecology resident on pathology, it was my responsibility to prepare every surgical specimen for microscopic analysis, report my findings, and discuss each one with Dr. Traut. To sit next to that great man morning after morning, listening and learning, was the most rewarding six months of the entire three years. He would critique and discuss every specimen whether it was mundane or complicated. Dr. Traut also jealously guarded his pathology lab and his prerogative to do his own pathology. The other residents in pathology didn't appreciate having to look over our shoulders, but Dr. Traut's prestige was such that there was nothing they could do about it; it obviously worked to our advantage.

The work was not always relentlessly serious; there were lighter moments, occasionally. One occurred when a bona fide princess arrived from India, a Maharani of some obscure state, in an entourage of three Rolls Royces. Her Highness had traveled half way around the world to be delivered of her fifth child by the renowned Dr. Herbert Traut. After several days in residence at the hospital, there were the preliminary signs of labor and she was promptly transported to the labor room. It soon became obvious that she was, in fact, in early labor. The chief resident asked me to supervise Her Highness while he looked for Dr. Traut. He had no sooner left than the labor became intense, so I corralled the intern to stand by while I looked for the resident. In no time, the labor became tumultuous and the intern told a student nurse to attend the patient while he looked for me. Within minutes, Her Highness precipitously delivered the little prince in her labor bed attended only by a student nurse. A few minutes later, Dr. Traut, who had been less than a hundred yards away in the pathology lab all the time—where the paging system did not reach—strolled by. Of course, Her Highness and the baby were perfectly healthy and, happily, no one was upset and soon all the principals began to see the humor in the situation. When the Maharani left the hospital a week later, she gave each of the nurses who had attended her a gold compact and cigarette lighters to each of the house staff.

The second six months of the second year, I rotated to the San Francisco County Hospital. This period also included three months on general surgery. The obstetrical service was split with the residents from Stanford, and promptly at midnight we would switch coverage with them.

The San Francisco County Hospital emergency room was a remarkable experience. On weekends especially, it was incredibly busy with an almost unbelievable parade of patients in various stages of disrepair. Whenever it rained, those of us on duty made every effort to find a couch and get some sleep because we knew that within hours every drunk and bum would be washed out of their hovels under bridges and would show up on one pretext or another in the emergency room. These individuals, who by the 1990s would be called "economically deprived substance abusers," were, by and large, docile and appreciative. The older derelicts evoked a certain sympathy but the young ones, defeated by life in their twenties, were depressing.

For two months, we had a strikingly beautiful intern with us. When some of our patients saw her, after awakening out of anesthesia or an alcoholic stupor, and had been bathed, and placed between clean sheets, and fed hot pork and beans, they were convinced that they had died and were in Heaven with an angel.

Some cases were funny, some gruesome, and some a combination of both. There was the reasonably well-dressed man who entered the ER complaining of "stomach trouble." He did not appear very ill so was asked to sit and was told that he would be attended soon. With the usual madhouse of activity, he was more or less forgotten. A half hour later, he returned to the receptionist and asked if he could be seen because he was "very sore." He was placed on a gurney, his raincoat, which he had been holding over his lower abdomen, removed, his belt buckle loosened, and trousers lowered—revealing an extruded loop of bowel. At sight of this, frantic calls to the laboratory, the blood bank, and the operating room were made. As he was wheeled away, a brief history revealed that he had attempted hari-kari with a small penknife but had lost interest after he had cut himself half way across his abdomen. At surgery, Quent Bonser, the surgical resident, and I opened him with a midline incision from his umbilicus to the symphysis pubis in order to adequately explore all the other organs for possible injury and found…nothing. There was a small bleeder that was easily ligated but no other damage. We irrigated the incision he made and closed it, perfunctorily, with large stay sutures and then meticulously closed the incision we made in layers according to approved technique. In the following weeks, his incision healed per primum with a barely visible hairline scar; ours became infected, dehisced, and took five weeks to heal by secondary intention.

Another was the case of a young man who, in a fit of pique after an argument with his boyfriend, decided to commit suicide—by giving himself a plaster of Paris enema. When I walked into the operating suite, I heard sounds unlike I had ever heard before. It was the clinking sound of a chisel on stone reminiscent of what I think Michelangelo's studio in ancient Florence must have sounded like. Unhappily, the poor creature achieved his original intent and ultimately died.

Another case, though one I did not personally see, was that of a man who entered the ER after having been emasculated by a jealous rival. A homemade device had been applied so that hemorrhage was not an immediate problem. His prized body parts were in a bloody paper bag that he was holding on his lap. At that time there was a population of ravenous wild cats that patrolled the basement of the hospital in search of rats. One of these animals suddenly appeared, scented the bloody bag, leaped up, snatched it, and took off down the hall. With a scream, the patient and an assortment of nurses, interns, and residents gave chase to rescue his prized equipment. It was said that no one in the history of the hospital had ever witnessed such a parade. I do not know if the pursuit was successful but knowing how clever cats are, secreting their "prey," I doubt it. These and other bizarre cases left indelible memories of events at the Mission Emergency Room at the San Francisco County Hospital.

All of my co-residents, both ahead of and behind me in the hierarchy, got along well. Rare personality clashes were almost always due to fatigue. One intern, Sam Abulhaj, a Palestinian, was a pleasant and hardworking colleague. He gave me my first insight as to the nature of the problems in the Middle East that the western world has been grappling with since the end of World War II. Sam and his family had lived on the same land for over a century. His father was influential and held a rank equivalent to that of a governor. When the United Nations mandated the boundaries of the state of Israel, his family was suddenly not only without land but without a country. His brother had actually been jailed briefly for trespassing on what had formerly been his land. I recall thinking that it all seemed quite unfair, but because the Western world was guilt ridden over the horrors of the Holocaust, the fate of the Muslims was greeted by a collective shrug of the shoulders. Palestinians, after all, did not have much to do with the Judeo-Christian ethic. Very few people at the time had any conception of the trouble that would emanate for decades from the region.

By the third year of residency, the call schedule was reduced to being on call every third night and every third weekend. It seemed like a virtual vacation. As the New Year began, I knew that I would soon be getting word where my first duty station would be after June 30, the day my residency ended. The Air Force residency program carried a "year for year plus one" commitment, which meant I owed the Air Force a four-year payback. The first week of April, I received word that I would be sent to Ellington Field in Houston, Texas; but two weeks later this was changed to Harlingen Air Force Base, Texas. Harlingen was a navigator training base and part of the Air Training Command. I would have preferred being nearer a larger city but had no choice in the matter; and I was faced with the difficulty of having to leave my parents in San Francisco.

By the spring of 1957, we had accumulated a little furniture, saved a little money, and were in far better shape financially than we had been in 1954. My parents were comfortably settled in their apartment in Park Merced, and though not entirely free of financial worries, the most severe strains were improved. My father's health, however, was a worry. He began experiencing episodes of severe "indigestion," which he had never had in the past; then came transient chest pains. In the last week of April, we were concerned enough to have him evaluated by a cardiologist, who prescribed a low-fat diet, increased exercise, and ordered an electrocardiogram, which was read as normal. Ten days later, he experienced chest pains that were more severe and persistent. He was hospitalized at the medical center, and by late afternoon he seemed more comfortable. But as I left his room that evening, he asked me to send in the nurse to bring him a blanket because "his feet were cold." In retrospect, I should have been more perceptive—his hands and feet were never cold.

I got to the hospital at seven the next morning and went to see him before starting work and was stopped at the door by the nurse and doctor who told me that he had died fifteen minutes earlier. It was a shock but, I think, not a surprise. I left the hospital and went to Park Merced, gave my mother the sad news, and phoned Eileen. When one loses a parent suddenly, it's a little like kicking out a ladder that one is standing on. An integral part of your life is suddenly gone. There is no preparation. I could not believe that I would never again see him laugh so hard that he was reduced to tears, enjoy his grandchildren, host a party, savor a meal at Fisherman's Warf, glide off a moving cable car (as all San Franciscan's do whether they need to or not), nail a drive straight down a fairway, or dance with my mother—and they were very good together.

The rest of the day I spent trying to console my mother, yet how does one console someone who has lost a life partner of thirty-seven years? I also had to comfort Eileen and the babies. The children were solemn and understood that something very sad had happened. I phoned John and Aunt Mary Margaret and a few friends of my parents in the city. I remember making arrangements at a Catholic funeral home for a mass, but those few days were a blur. My father was buried in a cemetery in Daly City. I visited the place once and never went again. It had absolutely nothing to do with him. Any time I wanted to remember my father's presence, all I had to do was walk into the lobby of the Fairmont Hotel, or drive out to the site of Sutro Baths near the Cliff House, or listen to my mother play the piano in their apartment, or just look out over the city he loved.

This was the way, in what seemed like a fraction of a second, I lost the most generous, steadfast, and supportive friend I ever had. Knowing that his many worries were a thing of the past offered some, but not much, consolation.

Sadly, we were not quite through with family losses. Three weeks after my father's funeral, Aunt Mary Margaret, who had come to the funeral and seemed to be her usual buoyant self, chatting and playing with the children, returned to Los Angeles from a trip to New York and upon exiting the airplane, became acutely ill. She collapsed on the spot and died three days later from fulminating meningococcal meningitis. I hated knowing that we would have to leave my mother in such a state. The only consolation was that she was safe and secure in her apartment and would be comforted by a large group of old friends.

I regarded the future with a mix of conflicting emotions. I wondered if my professional skills would be up to the tasks ahead, I was concerned about my mother's state of mind and how she would cope at the age of 62 with being alone without family nearby for the first time in her life, and yet, I was eager to get on with whatever lay ahead.

We arrived in Harlingen, Texas, the last week of June, 1957, after an uneventful drive and a short visit in Phoenix. The children were good travelers in spite of the heat. Before the days of automobile air conditioners, the only way to keep cool was to suck on ice cubes and drink cold soft drinks. In 1957, Harlingen was a town of about thirty-five thousand people. It is located roughly twenty-five miles northwest of Brownsville, Texas, the southernmost city in the United States, which is directly across the border from Matamoros, Mexico. There were attractive areas in Harlingen at the time, but we were not prepared for the intense heat and humidity. From Valentine's Day to Halloween, at least one room in every home had to have an air conditioner. The few days I spent in equatorial Africa in 1945, were cool by comparison. Wearing my Class A uniform (shirt, tie, and "blouse"), I reported to the hospital commander, Lieutenant Colonel Martin, and was introduced at the weekly staff meeting, and almost passed out from the heat.

Our first priority was housing, and we found a small three-bedroom brick house that was just about to be completed. Taking advantage of the VA loan, we were able to buy it for twelve thousand dollars. Although it was small, we were very happy there for the next three years. It was just off the highway leading to the air base and a short walk from a shopping center and market.

The hospital was a typical "H" frame fifty-bed facility. As a regular Air Force officer and a captain since February 1956, I was senior to all the other physicians except the commander. My predecessor and co-obstetrician was Dr. Arthur Leber, who was from a small village in Poland and a Holocaust survivor. He was interesting and very courageous but poorly trained and had to be closely supervised. Dr. Leber left the military two months after I arrived, and I was then helped on obstetrical call by general medical officers who expressed an interest in the specialty. I was, of course, on first call or back-up call at all times, but the workload and number of deliveries was not too great. Though technically the senior medical officer after the commander, I knew less about the ways of the medical service than any of my colleagues. They knew it and I knew it, so for the first several weeks, I tried to keep a low profile. This was not too difficult until about the fourth month after we arrived, when the hospital commander, a radiologist by training, abruptly resigned to enter private practice.

Suddenly I was the hospital commander, and I knew absolutely nothing about running a hospital. But it proved to be a blessing in disguise. In the two months it took to appoint a new permanent commander, the experience taught me that I wanted nothing to do with hospital administration. I also learned that the way hospital commanders were chosen at that time was a fundamentally flawed process. Essentially, it was just a question of asking someone if they wanted to give it a try. At the time, there was no formal training in hospital administration, budget management, quality control, risk management, or personnel management. Talented, respected, and effective leaders, therefore, appeared by pure luck and were rare. In my experience with nine different hospital commanders, three were outstanding, four were marginal, and two were caricatures. I have always believed that there should be co-commanders at an Air Force hospital—one trained medical service officer and the other a physician with special training in the elements of leadership. But the military has always insisted on one leader as the ultimate authority. Too many hospital commanders are just clinicians, bored with the grind of the practice of medicine, aspiring to higher rank. Unlike the Army medical service, the Air Force has no such thing as a "pure clinician" who achieves flag rank.

In spite of the oppressive heat, Harlingen was a pleasant town with a local citizenry cordial to the military. Going across the border from Brownsville to Matamoros was an interesting experience. For many of the young military people, it was a revelation to see what poverty in a third world country was all about and to learn the dangers of exposing oneself to drugs and various sexually transmitted diseases. Shopping in Matamoros was fun and there were several excellent, moderately-priced restaurants serving the hottest jalapeños I have ever tried to eat. Many people were under the mistaken notion that Matamoros depended on Brownsville to support its economy when, in reality, the opposite was true. Much more money poured into Brownsville from Mexicans buying major appliances and automobiles than the reverse.

Being stationed in Harlingen offered many other diversions, such as trips to the Padre Island beaches, experiencing the world famous white wing dove season, and shopping trips to the many colorful towns along the Lower Rio Grande Valley. But by midsummer, everyone began counting the days until the first "blue-norther" would arrive in the fall to break the relentless summer heat.

In mid-August, our hopes were realized when Eileen learned that our fourth baby would arrive the following February. Eileen's pregnancy proceeded uneventfully, and it was good to know that the most uncomfortable time, the last three months, would be during cooler weather. John Joseph arrived, in a hurry, on February 24, 1958. One of my general medical officers, Dick Peters, attended Eileen. Her labor and delivery were even faster than it had been with Ellen. As with the others, Eileen made an uncomplicated recovery.

My mother had arrived for a visit during Christmas 1957, and it was good for her morale to be with us and the grandchildren. Her life had assumed a rather dull pattern in San Francisco and we talked at length about the future. Ever since my internship, I had planned to join a group of obstetricians in Phoenix when my military obligations were fulfilled. In spite of the heat in Phoenix that she remembered, it was an altogether different place in the 1960s than it was in the 1930s. It was now a small metropolis and air conditioning was universal. She enjoyed all of Eileen's family and, of course, wanted to be near her grandchildren. Christmas Eve 1957 was very gay with a big party at the officers club and a lot of champagne. My mother said she could never remember being kissed by so many colonels.

Through 1958, work at the hospital continued to be busy and I felt increasing confidence in my clinical skills. There wasn't much major gynecological surgery, however, because the female population of the base was so young. Nonetheless, I began collecting and writing up my cases as required for certification by the American Board of Obstetrics and Gynecology two years in the future. At that time one could not even apply for Part I of the examination until three years after Residency.

The winter of 1958 in Harlingen went into the record books as one of the wettest on record. Torrential rains for days and weeks swept the area, and the Rio Grande became a mile wide at one point. There was widespread flooding, but of greater danger was the rattlesnakes that were flooded out of their dens.

The spring of 1959, we inherited Ophelia, whose last name I don't think I ever knew, from another couple who had transferred from the area. Ophelia was a Mexican national, widowed, spoke no English, and was, for Eileen, an absolute treasure. Two days a week she would arrive to clean the house, sometimes tend the garden, and, if she ran out of things to do, wash the car. She was a whirlwind of activity and very thorough. She was trying to learn cosmetology and delighted in manicuring the girls and dressing their hair. Sometimes she stayed late and cooked superb Mexican dinners, and all of this at one dollar an hour!

Another noteworthy event in 1959 was the visit of Dr. Frank Berry. One morning I was called to the base commander's office ASAP. When I reported to him, he tossed a TWX at me, which was an advisory message that Dr. Berry was arriving that afternoon, but that he did not want the usual formalities associated with the arrival of an individual with a rank equivalent to a four-star general. Dr. Berry was the Assistant Secretary of Defense for Health Sciences. Colonel Olive instructed me to meet his plane and act as his escort on base, as well as "find out what'n hell he wanted." I arranged for his quarters on base and met his plane. As he had requested, there was no honor guard or bands playing ruffles and flourishes, but everything else was spit'n'polish.

Dr. Berry was a tall, white-haired, distinguished man, probably in his seventies, and professor emeritus of surgery at Columbia University. In the military medical service, he was best known as the author of the "Berry Plan," which permitted residents in training to complete their specialty work before being subject to the doctor draft. He had no plans for the evening, so after he was squared away in quarters, I invited him to dinner. We knew a superb restaurant just across the border in Nuevo Progresso called Arturo's, a little oasis in the desert. It was quite formal, with waiters in black tie, and had superior food and service. After stopping at home to pick up Eileen and meet the children, whom he genuinely seemed to enjoy, we motored up the valley to Arturo's and, as usual, enjoyed an excellent meal.

It was only after I had returned Dr. Berry to his quarters that it oc-curred to me that taking a high-ranking government official across the border to a foreign country might not have been such a good idea. Suppose something untoward had happened? Dr. Berry said that the purpose of his trip was to meet with Sir Oliver Frank, the British Ambassador who, at that time, was visiting the fabled King Ranch not too far from Harlingen and that he "never had time" to see him in Washington. To justify his per diem, Dr. Berry met with the hospital staff and answered all their ques-tions about the future of the medical corps. That, too, was a success because his fund of knowledge as well as his informality made a great hit with my colleagues. A week later we got a nice thank you note and an invitation to visit him the next time I was in Washington.

In the late summer of 1959, Eileen was again pregnant and the due date for our fifth baby was February 1960. As before, the pregnancy was free of complications and in November, we treated ourselves to a trip to San Antonio to visit all the historic sites, particularly the Alamo, and to enjoy the colorful River Walk. My two favorite cities in Texas have always been San Antonio and Austin. They somehow seem much more real than the new, glitzier places. Just before Christmas, I made a quick trip to San Francisco. My mother appeared well enough but was bored, lonely, and depressed. We talked about the future and the probability of making our home in Phoenix in another year-and-a-half when my military obligations would come to an end.

Our fifth child, Katherine Ann, arrived March 10, 1960, and was delivered by our Air Force consultant, Dr. George Petta, at the Valley Baptist Hospital in Harlingen. Once again, Eileen's delivery was uncomplicated and prompt, although a little more controlled than the previous two.

On April 1, 1960, we were surprised, thrilled, and excited to learn that my next assignment was to be chief of obstetrics at the new United States Air Force Academy hospital, beginning August 1, 1960. No better job could be imagined than to be among the first twelve doctors at the new Academy hospital. I don't know why I was picked for such a marvelous assignment, but I could not escape the notion that our very pleasant evening with Dr. Berry might have had something to do with it. Of course, our tentative plans for Phoenix were deferred. Living in Colorado for three years sounded very appealing, as did having my mother join us, seeing Bobby and Yale Lewis again, and getting away from the long, long oppressive summer heat in the Lower Rio Grande Valley.

The only cause for concern as we approached our departure date from Texas was selling our little house. The real estate market in the Lower Rio Grande Valley in 1960 was in a mild recession. Fortunately, and to our great relief, we sold the house two weeks before we were scheduled to depart. I don't recall selling it at a profit, but to be free of the worry was all that mattered. We also gave away our dachshund puppy, Stormy, perhaps the dumbest and most stubborn animal in dogdom, to unsuspecting neighbors. We left Harlingen just before dawn on June 30, 1960, so that we could make the 750 mile trip to El Paso in one day.

Three hours out, at sunup, we passed through some hill country just as John was waking up. He looked out the window and, never having seen any natural feature over ten feet high, asked, "What's that?" at the sight of a small mountain. We arrived in El Paso after fourteen hours of driving and spent the next three days visiting Eileen's sister Mary and her husband Warren. We arrived in Phoenix on July 5, and spent the next few days visiting Marguerite and the rest of Eileen's family. On July 8, I made a quick trip to San Francisco to look after my mother who was hospitalized for a bronchoscopy. In those days, before the advent of fiber optics, "swallowing the brass pipe" was a miserable, painful process. All the tests for tuberculosis and cancer were negative and she made a fairly prompt recovery.

I returned to Phoenix and we left for Colorado, with a small U-Haul trailer in tow, and arrived in the Pikes Peak area on July 24, 1960. When we saw Pikes Peak and the Front Range of the Rockies, it was love at first sight, and for the next fifty years that love has never changed. I have always loved the restless power of the sea, but the majesty of the Rocky Mountains stirs the soul and, for me, inspires a sense of well-being. I had landed at Lowry Air Force Base in Denver often during the war when I was stationed at Alliance, Nebraska, but Denver, being several miles from the mountains, was not nearly as dramatic as Colorado Springs nestled at the foot of Pikes Peak.

The Academy was spectacular and everything we expected it to be. It was the showplace of the Air Force, with excellent housing, fine schools, and all in a breathtaking setting. The quarters were the best I'd ever seen in the military, and as a new major with a large family, I qualified for a four bedroom, two-bathroom home with more space than we knew what to do with. The only poorly planned room was the dining area, which was so small that it barely accommodated the dining table, let alone the chairs. To supplement our lack of furniture, we simply checked out good quality beds, couches, and chairs from the Service and Supply area, and in no time were comfortably settled.

Our next door neighbors, by a pleasant coincidence, were a young couple from Hawaii, Gordon and Heli Gray. Gordon was in the Punahou class of 1945 and Heli in the class of 1946. Their four children were about the same age as ours, so they were very compatible neighbors and we have remained friends ever since our first meeting.

Morale at the Academy was high and everyone was committed to the mission: to graduate outstanding young men (there were no women at the time) into the Air Force as career officers. It was a most exciting time to be in the Air Force. Everyone, at every level, no matter whether they were support personnel, faculty members, doctors, administrators, or commander was "hand-picked." During the next two years, I came to know some of the brightest, most dedicated, and most interesting people I ever met in the military. We were encouraged to become involved in all cadet activities. Eileen and I became sponsors of Cadet Squadron Eighteen and acted as hosts to groups of cadets, usually four or five, on the rare weekends when they were "off." For the first-year cadets, to be able to come into a home with small children running around, relax, and enjoy a hamburger without any hazing was as much a treat for them as it was for us. Because we were from Hawaii, we usually requested cadets from the Islands. One special young man was (Charles) Lacy Veach, Punahou class of 1962, who later had a distinguished career as an astronaut.

After almost four months attending our patients in the clinic and then sending them to the Fort Carson army hospital for delivery, we moved into our new hospital on November 20, 1960, and I delivered the first baby three days later. The baby was a girl, and I was alleged to have said at her birth that it was "too bad she wasn't a boy for she might have gone to school here." Twenty-three years later, that baby, Cadet Deanna Reeves, did graduate from the Academy and became a career officer.

The rest of the medical staff were all specialists, all well-trained, and were a stimulating group of co-workers. Tommy Armour (the son of the golf immortal) and Gene Weston were the surgeons, and I was soon joined by Ford Oliphant on obstetrics/gynecology. The other specialists were Larry Smith and Jim Lodge, pediatrics; Mark Wegleightner, ear, nose, and throat; Claud Anderson, internal medicine; Bob Anderson and John Kavanaugh, psychiatry; Ralph Cotton, orthopedics; Jerry Lemon, radiology; Wally Haworth, flight medicine; Jack Benson, anesthesiology; and our commander, Dick Fixott, ophthalmology. And there were two general medical officers who later specialized in OB/GYN, Jim Maxwell and

Joe Scott. Jim Lodge was the son-in-law of the Chief of Staff of the Air Force, the legendary General Curtis LeMay. Jim and Jeannie (LeMay) downplayed their unique rolls, of course, but would occasionally host the general, who would arrive, unannounced, for a quiet weekend away from the Pentagon. It was said that LeMay hated Washington and loathed McNamara, the Secretary of Defense. LeMay's idea of a relaxing weekend was to watch an old movie, do crossword puzzles, and enjoy a game of penny ante poker at Jim and Jeannie's quarters.

By late fall 1960, my mother felt that life in San Francisco was losing its appeal and, at our urging, made plans to join us in Colorado. I don't know how she did it, alone and not feeling well, but in mid-December she arrived, and two weeks later she moved into a small two-bedroom apartment near the Golf Acres Shopping Center in Colorado Springs. It was good for her morale to be near us and the grandchildren, and her health seemed to improve in the dry climate. The nine years she lived in that small apartment in Colorado Springs were the longest span of years she ever lived in the same home in her life. For the first several months, she felt well except for the fatigue that was universal until one became used to the altitude. She was perpetually thrilled by the view of snow-capped Pikes Peak from her bedroom window each morning. Gradually she became accustomed to the changeable and often violent weather in the spring—beautiful mornings giving way to thunderstorms in the afternoon.

For me, work at the hospital became increasingly busy and challenging, and sharing the workload with someone as well-trained as Ford Oliphant was a pleasure. In the spring, I was sent to Sandia, New Mexico, for a nuclear weapons seminar, and missed delivering Heli Gray's last baby, who decided to arrive three weeks early. The weapons seminar was a fascinating and sobering experience. The destructive power of such awesome weapons made it obvious that there could never be a winner in a nuclear war. For a week, every lecture, with rare exceptions, was classified "secret" or "top secret," and every member of the audience was warned to keep what they heard in that room, *in* that room. It came as a surprise when I picked up the latest edition of *Time* magazine at the airport on the way home, an edition devoted in its entirety to the topic of nuclear arms, and saw that virtually everything I had heard in the preceding week, with a single exception, was set forth in the magazine. It was quite a revelation and I remember thinking, so much for classified information and *so much for secrets in a world full of nuclear arms.*

In early June, five other escort officers and I were named to accompany one hundred cadets on their "summer enrichment tour" to Europe. It was a memorable three-and-a-half weeks that included stops in Madrid, Rome, Athens, Paris, Wiesbaden, and Berlin. There were many unforgettable moments, like the last night in Madrid when Major General Jack Ryan (later to become Chief of Staff of the Air Force) hosted a ball at the Castellana Hilton. The cadets in dress uniforms, plus a hundred young ladies in lovely ball gowns, created a romantic picture I have never forgotten.

In Rome, we were invited to a public audience at St. Peter's with the most beloved Pope of the twentieth century, Pope John XXIII. We had been briefed the day before that public audiences were joyful, informal affairs and that when the "cadets from the United States Air Force Academy in Colorado" were recognized, it was appropriate to cheer. A hundred cadets can make a lot of noise—and they did. I was close enough to His Holiness to see him do a double take, smile briefly, and wave to the cheering cadets.

In Paris, a lecture by General Lauris Norstad, the commanding officer of all USAF forces in Europe, was one of the most informative I have ever heard. Norstad, who was soft spoken and hardly ever raised his voice, was absolutely riveting. One cadet, in the question and answer period, asked one of those "what if" questions. The General more or less squashed the young man by reminding him that contingency plans were always on a "need to know" basis, that they were secret, and that men "died for that information." At that time, the tactical situation in Berlin was tense. The infamous "wall" went up two weeks later. I remember the stark difference between East and West Berlin. The rubble and burned buildings from World War II were still evident in the east, but the west was bustling with activity and sparkling with many new buildings under construction and little evidence of the destruction of twenty years earlier.

I don't know who planned the logistics for the trip, but it could not have been better, nor could have the conduct of our cadets. From the tour of Franco's Valley of the Fallen, to the public audience with the Pope, to the tour of East Berlin, our country could not have had better ambassadors. Given one hundred healthy young men with half their time free to do with what they would, there was not a single episode or incident that would have brought discredit to their country or the Air Force. It was an unforgettable four weeks. Unfortunately, the air transport requirements of the Vietnam War a few years later ended the summer enrichment program at the Air Force Academy.

In the fall of 1961, I began getting my cases typed and in order and studying for Part I of the American Board examinations. In 1962, I took Part I and came out of the test depressed and certain that I had not done well. However, on February 2, I received word that I had passed and that Part II, the oral exams, would be given at the Edgewater Beach hotel in Chicago in April 1962.

The years 1961-1962 were wonderfully exciting to be in the military service because the heroic flights into space of Alan Shepard and John Glenn served to focus the attention of the country. The popularity of our young president, John F. Kennedy, and his gracious wife, Jacqueline, was universal except, of course, for conservative Republicans. Barry Goldwater was admired because of his honesty, but he continually demonstrated his meager intellect and unsuitability to be the leader of the free world. As a counterpoint to the progressives, the psychopath, General Edwin Walker, and the ravings of the John Birch Society generated headlines that far exceeded their threat to the nation.

In March 1962, I attended a two-week seminar on Obstetrics and Gynecology at the Harvard University Medical School and Boston Lying-In Hospital. During the next fifteen years, I enjoyed that seminar four more times. As a preparation for Part II of the board examinations, it was invaluable. The examinations, no matter how prepared one felt one was, were nerve wracking. Success or failure on the exams was often a function of a bad attitude on the part of the examinee. Bluff, bluster, or cockiness was the kiss of death. The usual questioning would begin with something simple, and then, by probing deeper, the depth of knowledge of the examinee became exposed. Becoming argumentative was extremely ill-advised. The only part of the examination I felt quite comfortable with was the gross and micro-pathology; I am sure that was due to my many hours with Dr. Traut. At the end of the meeting, I spoke with Dr. Thornton (who had not been one of my examiners) and I interpreted his cordiality as a good sign. On the last day of April, I received a letter from the board advising me that I had passed and would soon be receiving my diploma.

During the winter and following spring of 1962, I came to know Dr. Clyde Blake. Dr. Blake was our civilian consultant for OB/GYN problems. His help on difficult cases was often invaluable, and when time permitted, I would operate with him at civilian hospitals in Colorado Springs. Although we did not always agree, I recognized that he was a highly-skilled surgeon and felt that I could learn a great deal from him. When he told me that he and his partner, Keith Kerr, were looking for a third man in the expanding OB/GYN service at the Colorado Springs Medical Center, I began to think seriously of resigning my commission and joining the group. It was a difficult choice because I enjoyed the Air Force and all the people I worked with and I knew that an interesting career lay ahead. Yet as I returned home each evening, I began to feel more and more like the robin returning to the nest to be confronted by five chicks with their mouths open begging for their worm. My income as a major was certainly adequate but, looking to the future, the expense of educating our children and other responsibilities were obvious concerns. I had also heard, indirectly, that my next assignment would probably be to the Air Force Regional Hospital in Wiesbaden, Germany, and, though a choice assignment, moving there with five youngsters would be difficult. A final concern was, of course, my mother, whose health was precarious. I could not leave her alone in Colorado Springs and was not at all sure she could tolerate a move to Europe.

When I received word that I had passed the boards, I, with some reluctance, decided to resign from the Air Force and join Clyde and Keith at the Medical Center in Colorado Springs. But the prospect of immediately doubling my income was not the only reason. In the medical corps at that time, there was no monetary incentive to being board certified, and I was repeatedly denied the opportunity to attend the School of Aviation Medicine, which I had a strong interest in attending. Although there was no mission requirement for an obstetrician/gynecologist to be a flight surgeon, it was still annoying for me, as a former line officer, to be denied the opportunity to expand my horizons. So, with some lingering reservations, I submitted my resignation to take effect October 1, 1962, and we began house hunting in Colorado Springs. We found a place in our price range in mid-August. It was a roomy four-bedroom two-bath house on Eagle View Drive, and it was our home for the next seventeen years. I was officially a civilian again on October 1, 1962. Eileen and all the children, save Clayt, looked forward to a totally new life style.

Within two weeks, the Cuban missile crisis burst upon the world scene and I wondered if I had made a mistake. We now know that the world teetered on the edge of a nuclear holocaust during those thirteen days—October 13 through October 27, 1962. Fortunately, our young president was up to the challenge and chose to ignore the bombast of some of his military leaders. General LeMay was a great warrior but had limited skills in geopolitics and diplomacy. President Kennedy had never fully trusted the opinions of high-ranking military men after being euchred into approving the ill-conceived and ill-planned Bay of Pigs disaster in 1961. Relying on the advice of cooler, more seasoned civilian leaders, he chose the blockade option. With great skill, by assuring the Russians there would be no attack on Cuba if the missiles were withdrawn, he gave the Russians a face-saving way out of the dangerous situation they had created. I remember sitting in my car at a shopping center on the twelfth day of the crisis, listening to news bulletins and wondering if the shops would still be there the next day because surely NORAD, which was headquartered in Colorado Springs, would be a target for nuclear missiles. It was a terrifying moment in history and its resolution represented the high-point of the Kennedy administration. It also marked the end of the influence of the great World War II military leaders on national policy.

Reflections

In the nine years after graduation from medical school, which included one year as an intern in an open-staff Catholic hospital, three years as a resident physician in one of the country's finest teaching hospitals, three years as a staff physician in a small Air Force hospital, and two years as a department chairman in an intermediate-sized Air Force hospital, I was able to begin forming opinions on the nature of the practice of my specialty in a variety of settings.

As an intern I had seen the best and the worst of civilian practice. At that time (1953), there was no emphasis on quality control or risk management and only inconsequential emphasis on peer review. Some practitioners were blatantly incompetent and had achieved prominence "through a graveyard full of mistakes," yet they were tolerated because by admitting all their patients to a particular hospital, the hospital benefited financially. Even though relatively inexperienced, I, and my fellow interns, soon knew who the incompetents were and, as much as we could, avoided attending their patients. There were, of course, other physicians on staff who were well-trained and fully competent and from whom much could be learned.

As a resident physician at a world-famous teaching hospital, the work was exhausting but exhilarating. To be in daily contact for three years with the great teachers and great practitioners of my specialty was a privilege given to relatively few. I thought then and think now that to have the ability and intelligence to teach at that level is the epitome of a career in medicine.

As a physician at military hospitals for five years, I came to realize that the positives of such service vastly outnumbered the negatives. The principal negative at that time (and for many years thereafter) was the odious Medical Officer of the Day (MOD) requirement. The responsibility of the MOD fell on everyone no matter if he was a psychiatrist, pediatrician, flight surgeon, or internist. The MOD was the emergency room physician from the end of duty hours on one day to the beginning of duty hours the next and was the primary physician for everyone who entered the emergency room. Thus, an internist might be the first responder to an automobile accident victim or an obstetrician to a baby with incipient pneumonia or a psychiatrist to an airman with appendicitis.

It is my opinion that the single duty requirement—forcing physicians to attend problems for which they had no aptitude or competence—drove more physicians out of the military medical corps than any other factor. But the positives of practicing medicine in the military were many and included the absence of the threat of malpractice litigation, non-interference by the requirements of insurance companies regarding post-operative or post-partum lengths of stay, a guaranteed adequate salary, a thirty-day vacation annually, the opportunity to experience different cultures in different countries, the requirement of continuing medical education by attending excellent seminars, retirement benefits for career personnel, and the importance of being part of the overall mission of the United States Air Force in a troubled, dangerous world.

V
1962-1979

As we settled into our new home—nearly barren of furniture except for beds, a few chairs, a dining room table, and two small couches we had acquired in Stonestown—Eileen's sixth pregnancy was confirmed. The pregnancy progressed uneventfully until March 1963, when she took a bad fall and severely sprained her knee. For the last two months of her pregnancy, Eileen was in a full-leg cast while the ligaments healed. How she managed with five active children, the chores involved in establishing a new home, and, later, the heat of an early spring, was a minor miracle and a tribute to her fortitude. Margaret was enrolled at East Junior High School and Clayt and Ellen at Divine Redeemer Elementary School.

Eileen went into labor the morning of May 6. As we headed toward the hospital, she remembered she "needed a few things," so we detoured to Kaufman's Department Store downtown. I double parked, expecting her to be out in five minutes. It seemed like half an hour and, knowing her track record of precipitous deliveries, I began to panic while visualizing the headlines in the paper, "Obstetrician's Wife Delivers in Store While He Waits in Car," which would have been terrible publicity for a new young doctor early in his practice. Finally, she reappeared and we sped to St. Frances Hospital. She was admitted and twenty-eight minutes later Elizabeth Marie appeared. Had Clyde Blake not been in the hospital, he never would have made it to the delivery room in time. Fortunately, Eileen's leg cast had been removed two weeks earlier.

The transition from military to civilian practice was not difficult. The staff members at the Colorado Springs Medical Center were well-trained, experienced people who practiced the highest quality of medicine. They were a diverse group, as might be expected, and from the most senior to the youngest, were helpful to the new boy on the block. Clyde Blake was a skilled surgeon, and over the next two years, I learned a great deal from him, especially techniques in vaginal surgery—hysterectomies, repairs, and the like. He had learned a great deal from his mentor, the colorful Kermit Krantz, at the University of Kansas Medical School. Dr. Krantz, in spite of his eccentricities, was as knowledgeable as any living person about pelvic anatomy. Keith Kerr had trained in Boston, and as a student of Hertig, Rock, and other notables, was philosophically more compatible with my training. At California, only Drs. Earl King, Ed Hill, and Jim Merrill were skilled at vaginal surgery, and, unfortunately, I didn't operate with them as often as I would have liked. During my military years, the young age of my patients did not offer many opportunities to become truly skilled at this type of gynecologic surgery.

The first few months of my association with the medical center were not busy and the enforced idleness was a new experience and difficult to get used to. I was allotted new patients in an equitable manner, and when I was on call I was busy. Generally though, building a new practice was a slow process. In surgery, assisting Clyde and Keith as well as the general surgeons, George Lindeman and Wally Kearny, kept me fairly busy. To pass the time, I did what many young physicians starting out have time to do. I wrote a couple of papers for the Rocky Mountain Medical Journal.

Gradually, I came to know the personality quirks and foibles of my colleagues. I recall one incident involving George Lindeman, a man of superb technical ability, which still embarrasses me. During Christmas 1962, at the medical center's annual banquet, Eileen and I were seated with the Lindeman's, whom we hardly knew, at a table for four. No one ever accused George of being garrulous and I, when confronted with taciturnity, tend to babble. To keep the conversational ball rolling, I asked George if he had ever heard of a "bunch of nuts that climb up Pikes Peak every New Year's Eve and set off firecrackers"—the Adaman Club. He said he had. For the rest of the evening, what had passed for conversation before became absolutely nil. A day later I found out that George was the current president of the Adaman Club. Needless to say, we never became close friends. There were others, however, who remained good friends in spite of my leaving the medical center two and a half years later under strained circumstances: the pediatricians John Kanas and Glenn Shoptaugh, who continued to attend my children; and the internists Bob Smith and Roy Dent, whom I was to call upon a few years later for my own health problems.

I was on salary the first year at the medical center, but thereafter, my income was based on productivity. As a result, I never had to become involved in the direct billing of patients for services. In fact, I did not even know what the charges were for obstetrical and gynecological care. The group practice at the medical center was, in effect, a forerunner of what would later be called an HMO. The relationship the physicians of the medical center enjoyed with their fellow practitioners in Colorado Springs was friendly enough on the social level, but we were rarely referred patients by general practitioners because once a patient was referred to our nascent HMO, and thus our staff of specialists, they were never seen again by their original referring physician.

When I joined the medical center, it was in a building that had been converted from a mansion, which was the former home of a past governor of the state. We were clearly outgrowing it, so plans were well advanced to build a modern, larger, three-story building. In the existing building there were only two offices for the OB/GYN service, so I could occupy one of them only when either Keith or Clyde was out. It was not an ideal situation, but we were all optimistic about the new building, which was under construction by the fall of 1963.

I was seeing patients that dreadful day, November 22, 1963, when the news of President Kennedy's assassination came over the wire services and television. Most of my colleagues were conservative Republicans, but even they were shocked at the news, though perhaps not a saddened and depressed as I was. The terrible pageantry of the president's funeral, the courage of Mrs. Kennedy, and, two days later, the grotesque slaying of Lee

Harvey Oswald on live television, mesmerized the entire world. It was days before I could concentrate on work.

The years 1963 and 1964 were increasingly busy as my practice grew. Gynecological surgery was infrequent but I continued to learn a lot assisting the medical center's own general surgeons, Clyde and Keith, as well as other surgeons in Colorado Springs not associated with the medical center.

Through 1964, however, I was becoming increasingly concerned about my mother's emotional and physical health. In spite of her lifelong code of appearing free of care in the presence of others, I knew that such was not the case. There were nagging health problems that a multitude of antibiotics, cough suppressants, antacids, and aspirins helped only temporarily. Her emotional problems were more subtle and were aggravated by ongoing financial worries, a more or less cloistered existence forced upon her by weather extremes in Colorado Springs, and loneliness as old friends faded away through illness, infirmity, or death. Additionally, she was constantly concerned over my brother's inability to find a satisfying career as he went from job to job selling mutual funds, used cars, and appliances at Sears Roebuck, none of which suited his talents or potential. Only a lifelong interest in current events, correspondence, books, daily piano practice, and occasional visits with old friends like Norm, Walt Hurd, the Lewises, and happy hours with the grandchildren kept her from clinical depression.

Eileen's relationship with my mother was always friendly but not loving or intimate. My mother never fully understood the reasons for the distance between them. My mother also thought, mistakenly, that people who were not overtly demonstrative were more or less uncaring, and she could not be convinced otherwise. Conversely, Eileen was not much impressed with demonstrative people who "came on strong." By nature, Eileen was somewhat conservative, so it took time for her to commit to any relationship either positively or negatively. The backgrounds of these two women in my life could not have been more different. My mother never understood the energy, imagination, hard work, and, most particularly, the time it takes a wife and mother to deal with the needs of six active children (who had totally different personalities, ages, and needs), run a household, plan meals, and budget time for a husband whose career demanded so much time away from home while dedicated to the needs of his patients. Very few of my mother's friends had large families, and most of those who had one or two children had the resources to maintain domestic help. I once asked my mother how she thought her life might have been different with six children and a marginal income. The very question seemed to annoy her and she dismissed it as "impossible to answer."

So, for my mother, the days and weeks passed slowly and were a sort of a "sea of loneliness with a few islands of happiness." I was able to help each month with the financial strain, but there was not enough money for many luxuries, and though she would have loved a trip to Honolulu to see John and the other grandchildren, it was out of the question. The best I could do was to act as a sort of sounding board for woes that she could not voice to other people, stop by for lunch once or twice a week, try to boost her morale, and hope for better times.

An appalling letter, written by John's wife, Nini, in August 1964, was a crushing blow to my mother when added to everything else. The letter, full of pop psychiatry and based on little knowledge or study, blamed my mother's "dominating" personality for John's shortcomings, his lack of success in business, and his "passive/aggressiveness." It was a classic case of kicking someone who is down. My mother was mystified and deeply hurt. I read the letter and it angered me. It was, of course, no more accurate than any psychiatric evaluation based on hearsay; but more importantly, it served no useful purpose. It was ill-informed and pointlessly cruel. The letter was a classic example of a little knowledge being a dangerous thing and it led to a painful estrangement that lasted several years. There was finally a rapprochement, but the scars never fully healed.

The only good news in the fall of 1964 was that Barry Goldwater, the favorite of not only the lunatic fringe (the racists, the John Birchers, the militarists, and the crypto-fascists) but also the conservatives in general, was soundly beaten by Lyndon Johnson in the November presidential election. For a time, at least, the right-wing conservatives were silenced. The bad news was that we were being inexorably drawn into the quagmire of Vietnam. My opinion at the time was that checking the spread of communism in Vietnam was the correct national foreign policy for the United States. It was not until the Tet Offensive in 1969 that I realized our country had blundered into a Vietnamese civil war—a war that we could not win. Douglas MacArthur's admonition to "never get involved in a land war in Asia" was correct. Vietnam became a tragic misadventure and the first war that America clearly lost. Along with the American Revolutionary War and the Civil War, the Vietnamese War became one of the most unpopular wars in our history.

The last week of 1964, the physicians of the medical center began moving into our state-of-the-art medical building. Everybody was enthusiastic about our spacious and attractive public areas, the well-planned traffic flow, comfortable physicians' offices, and efficient treatment rooms. Destruction of the old governor's mansion was soon complete, and once the ground was cleared, beautiful landscaping around the front of the building began. We all faced the future with renewed optimism.

It was about this time that I first met Jim Myers. He, and his wife, Teddy, shared a community of interests with Eileen and me that often centered on our children's activities at the Divine Redeemer School and Parish. Jim and I also had similar wartime experiences. During the war, Jim was stationed in Italy and was a navigator in a B-24 squadron in the 12th Air Force; after the war, he went to college and medical school just as I had. Jim and Teddy had a large family, though Jim feigned ignorance about how many children he had—he thought usually eight or nine or ten—who were more or less the same ages as our six. Jim and I often drove together to the monthly Denver OB/GYN Society meetings. In the spring of 1965, we went to the Harvard OB/GYN seminar that I had attended three years earlier. Jim enjoyed Boston, the seminar, and meeting our old friends, Cecily and Russ Armentrout, who had moved from Atlanta to Shrewsbury, Massachusetts. Jim had taken his residency in OB/GYN at the University of Colorado. Though qualified, he never got around to taking the American Board examinations. We did not often work together in the operating or delivery room but enjoyed each other's company, and philosophically we were pretty much in agreement. Jim was a cradle Catholic with a deep and unquestioning belief in his religion. His brother, Rollie, was a priest and, like Jim, a thoroughly likeable man. Jim's faith was not intellectual but simply an integral part of his being. Teddy and Eileen were friends and shared many common concerns and interests.

In the summer of 1965, we took our first family vacation. We met Ann and Walt Hurd and their children at the north rim of the Grand Canyon and exchanged house keys. The Hurds went to our place on Eagle View Drive and we to their beautiful home in Mountain View, California. Our children loved the California experience, especially San Francisco and Golden Gate Park. It was a good trip overall, but I learned an important lesson, which had to be re-learned on a trip to Charlottesville three years later: it is virtually impossible to keep six children of different ages, sexes, hormone levels, and interests happy all the time. Such trips constantly teeter on the edge of disaster.

The initial enthusiasm of working in our new medical building slowly began to erode. The monthly staff meetings became a bore, then a chore, and finally an ordeal. More and more, the meetings degenerated into hours of repressed recriminations, jealousies, and hurt feelings. Most of the time, unfortunately, differences stemmed from who was getting how much of the income pie. There were two partnerships in the group: a realty partnership consisting of the eight members who first formed the group, and a professional partnership. The former had a double source of income— rent from all the partners plus their incomes from professional services based on productivity. But within this structure there were three tiers: the "granddaddies," who formed the group; the long-time associate physicians, who were not part of the original real estate partnership; and newcomers, like me. Conflicts about how income was to be divided arose among all three groups. That their basic disagreements were essentially economic was, to me, disillusioning. I was never interested in medical economics, and to see how these vulgar matters upset men I admired was a surprise. Parenthetically, I can say that in my entire career, I never knew any physician who, if he did not ruin his career by self-indulgence, or drugs, or liquor, or by tragic accident, did not make enough money to live comfortably and even luxuriously. I also noted that some of my colleagues avoided the unpleasantness of staff meetings by simply not attending.

A final assault on my idealism came the latter part of 1965, when it became apparent that Clyde Blake was taking over the care of some of my patients. This breech of medical ethics emanated from one pathological condition, endometriosis, and one treatment for it, the surgical procedure called pre-sacral neurectomy. Endometriosis is a painful but benign condition caused by ectopic flecks of endometrium scattered about the pelvis causing cyclic pain and is often associated with infertility. The cause is unknown and theories of retrograde menstruation vs. simple coelomic metaplasia are concepts that have been theorized for years. Clyde was convinced that by meticulously removing certain nerve tissue in the pelvis (pre-sacral neurectomy) he could not only relieve cyclic pain (often true) but also improve fertility (impossible to document in the literature). Since pelvic pain is the commonest symptom in gynecology, his counsel to many young women had wide appeal and they willingly subjected themselves to major surgery.

Pre-sacral neurectomy is a major operative procedure that is not without risk and involves isolating and removing sensory nerves from the pelvis. Clyde was enthusiastic about the procedure and, as is often the case, enthusiasm tends to cloud one's judgment, and can lead to overuse and, sometimes, questionable patient selection. Results of pre-sacral neurectomy are a function of technique and the amount of time one is willing to devote to the painstaking removal of nerve tissue. It is an easy operation to do incompletely, and since there is no pathological specimen other than normal nerve tissue, results are subjective and difficult to evaluate.

At first I chose to ignore the fact that I was losing patients, but, since I could not compete with a man who had been in practice for many years in Colorado Springs (and whose reputation was sound and well-deserved) nor countenance this violation of medical ethics, or approve of an unproven operative procedure that I not only had not seen nor even heard of before, I had no option but to resign from the medical center, in April 1966.

The foregoing notwithstanding, Clyde remained Eileen's doctor, and in early 1966, at a routine check-up, he noted a pelvic tumor. Initially he thought it to be a large ovarian cyst, but it proved to be a benign uterine tumor of sufficient size to justify hysterectomy. Eileen's recovery from surgery was uncomplicated until three nights after the surgery when, watching Art Carney and Jackie Gleason, she began laughing so hard at those two clowns she undoubtedly broke several subcutaneous stitches.

When I had resigned from the medical center, I was gratified to note that most of my former colleagues were sympathetic to my predicament. There was a brief legal problem based on a restricted practice paragraph in my employment contract that forbade my practicing in El Paso County for a period of time, six months as I recall, after resigning. Through my attorney, this was challenged and resolved without litigation, since Colorado law at the time actually discouraged such "non-compete" clauses for physicians.

Jim Myers and I had talked about joining in practice from the time I realized I would have to leave the medical center. In May 1965, we became partners and I joined him in his office, a little house on Union Boulevard near Platte Avenue. Jim and I never had a formal written instrument of partnership—just a handshake—nor did we ever have a serious disagreement. It was a partnership that lasted thirteen years, and I have nothing but good memories of our association. Later, when we moved into our new offices on Union Boulevard near Palmer Park, we had a brief association with a third physician, Dr. Cliff Sherwood, but it was unsatisfactory and we parted on good terms within a year.

The years 1965 through 1968 were increasingly busy years as Jim and I settled into our practice. The first few months were a little tight financially, but it was soon clear sailing and remained so over the many years we were together. It was the first time I ever had to think about fees and what to charge for my services. Medical insurance was not universal at this time and, consequently, we found ourselves writing off a fair amount of business. Our fees were compatible with what was usual and customary for the time, but charging for services was, to me, always a little embarrassing. Interestingly, up to that time, charging a fellow physician or any of his immediate family was unthinkable. In a sense it was a violation of the spirit of the Hippocratic Oath. Furthermore, professionally, there is no greater compliment than being a physician's physician. I recall the first time I ever charged a fellow physician's wife for a surgical procedure, and it was only at his insistence. He pointed out that not charging an amount equal to his medical insurance coverage was just foolhardy. I finally did charge the physician for services but always regretted doing so.

The notion of what was and was not ethical in the 1960s has undergone considerable change since then. I recall a spirited debate at an El Paso County medical meeting during this time when it was argued that sending out yearly reminders to patients to come in for a check-up and Pap smear was a form of advertising, hence unethical. No reputable physician ever advertised in the lay press or television or any public medium. Advertising was a custom limited to chiropractors, naturopaths, phrenologists, and other irregular practitioners and cultists.

The days of "Robin Hood medicine" (i.e., not charging the poor and overcharging the wealthy), were long gone; but there was dissatisfaction with the low fee schedule and paperwork required for welfare patients. In reality, welfare constituted a minor part of one's practice; in our case, less than ten percent. There was also chronic grumbling among the physicians about the ever increasing amount of time one had to spend on hospital committees, which was a by-product of the increasing emphasis on quality control and risk management. Finally, there was passionate resentment over escalating malpractice premiums which once had been a few hundred dollars a year but were now costing thousands. Most practitioners were confused about what constituted "informed consent," and how to document it was not at all clear. No one thought that dwelling on the hazards and potential complications of a course of treatment was reassuring to an already apprehensive patient. But the legal climate was such that we had no choice.

Aside from my medical practice, during the latter part of the decade, the ever-increasing commitment to more and more troops to Vietnam was worrisome, and the number of casualties was sickening. The Johnson administration seemed inept and unable to bring the war to a successful conclusion. To those of us who had served in World War II, it was hard to understand why the greatest war machine on earth could win battle after battle, maintain a casualty ratio of fifty-to-one against a peasant army, and still find itself unable to win the war. At last the peace movement at home began to escalate. Initially, I remember being disgusted with the peaceniks and appalled at their noisy demonstrations. I equated the war in Vietnam with the spirit of World War II and did not comprehend the error of my thinking, or lack of critical thinking, until 1969. I had forgotten Thomas Jefferson's comment in a letter to John Adams in which he said, "A nation united can never be defeated." Ho Chi Min understood this better than our national leaders.

In March 1968, President Johnson stunned the nation by announcing he would not be a candidate for the presidency in the November elections. The consensus was that he was simply worn out by the course of the war and what it was doing to the country. A month later, the nation was shocked by the assassination of Martin Luther King, Jr., and sixty days after that, the shooting of Robert Kennedy. All these depressing events turned the political situation upside down. Suddenly, Hubert Humphrey became the obvious Democratic candidate and the despicable Richard Nixon the most likely Republican. After all that had been accomplished by the Democrats in the preceding three and a half decades (save for the Eisenhower years) it seemed likely that Nixon could gain the White House largely because of an unpopular and mismanaged war. Of all the tragedies that had befallen the nation in 1968, the worst occurred on Election Day, November 5, 1968, when a paranoid, foul-mouthed, anti-Semite became the nation's thirty-seventh president. The fact that he was also brilliant made his assumption to the office doubly dangerous. It was no real surprise that his presidency later ended in disaster.

My mother's health continued to decline, and in spite of moments of happiness, her life had become increasingly circumscribed. On the morning of November 20, 1968, I called before coming to her apartment for lunch and noted that she sounded very strange and confused. When I got to her apartment, she was disoriented and obviously ill. Fearing that she had had a stroke, I called an ambulance and took her to Penrose Hospital. After several days and various tests, a stroke was ruled out. She remained physically unimpaired, but when discharged, it was clear that she could not continue to live alone.

We moved Kathy and Liz to the basement so that my mother could have their bedroom. During the next two and a half months, her mental state rapidly deteriorated, and by late February, she presented a nursing problem with which Eileen could no longer cope. By March, there was no other choice but to move her to a nursing home for proper care. Except for a rapidly progressing dementia, and ultimately the loss of motor control, there was no specific diagnosis. She finally became unresponsive, unable to eat, and unable to recognize me, Eileen, or the children. On May 15, 1969, she passed into a coma and expired. Because she had been plagued by her many health problems for so long, I felt a post mortem examination was essential. The findings showed a minimal amount of bronchiectasis, but no other lung problems, and, surprisingly, Creutzfeldt-Jakob disease (CJD), a transmissible spongiform encephalopathy, an extremely rare condition which I had never heard of. (Thirty years later, the so-called "mad cow disease," an unrelated variant of CJD, began to be written about in the lay press.) After her death, we had a brief memorial service and her ashes were sent to California to be buried with my father in Daly City.

And so a unique and memorable person was gone. I could not help but think that she would have found the sobriquet "mad cow disease" (though technically inaccurate) hilarious. My mother was not an easy person to know well. She had high standards and was never satisfied with anything second rate, not in art, nor music, nor literature, nor, especially, people. The last few years of her life were not happy. She found herself in a cul-de-sac with insoluble problems. There was not enough money to travel, nor did she have the stamina to do so. She had never learned to drive a car so getting from place to place was by public transportation or by walking, which was always subject to the uncertainties of Colorado weather. She enjoyed people but was loathe to present herself as anything other than free of care. One by one, lifelong friends had faded away. Even the piano, a sustaining interest all of her life, lost its appeal due to lack of energy and a cranky neighbor who let it be known that she didn't enjoy listening to someone practice. Except to me, it was impossible for her to unburden herself—not even in her diary. I often thought that in another time, in another place, and with enough money, she might have had a salon peopled with bright young artists, writers, and musicians. It probably would have been in Paris, a city she was homesick for all her life—but never saw. She did not dwell on her mistakes or waste time on self-pity but did realize she had been foolishly extravagant with money and had wasted her undoubted literary and musical talents. Yet, even in her lowest moments, her morale was always invigorated by buying "fripperies" that she neither needed nor could afford. She was complex, funny, and sometimes unreasonable yet, until near the end of her life, stimulating to talk to and well-informed.

Tucked away in her diary I found the following two pieces (and I don't know if they were written by her or someone else) that could serve as appropriate epitaphs:

> My road has been long. I have learned much, loved much, felt much and I have been loved so today I know not everything, but a good deal.

> And even the light of the sun will fade at last
> And the leaves will fall and the birds will hasten away
> And I will be left in the snow of a flowerless day
> To think of the glories of Spring
> And the joys of a youth long past.

During the last months of 1969, Eileen and I spent a good deal of time settling my mother's affairs and deciding what possessions to keep, sell, store, or give to charity. There was no insurance or estate. I talked to John and he said there was nothing he wanted—no books, silver, furniture, or even jewelry. Suddenly we had more furniture than we knew what to do with and decided to keep only those things that had been in the family for some time. I missed my bi-weekly lunches and talks with my mother but realized that her passing was a release from a life that she was no longer truly enjoying. The children, as children are, were self-absorbed and although they missed "Grammy" were not terribly saddened. As for the time she stayed with us in a demented state, it did not seem to have left any scars on their young psyches.

One by one, the children followed pretty much the same patterns through school in the 1960s and 1970s. The girls, except for Elizabeth, went to Divine Redeemer after kindergarten, then to Benet Hill for high school. Liz had a reading problem in the first grade and was subject to an embarrassing experience by being made an example of in front of her classmates by an ignorant nun who knew nothing of reading problems. Humiliation was not an uncommon form of discipline in parochial schools at the time. We transferred her to a public school, held her back one year, and placed her under the supervision of a teacher who had special training in children with reading problems. The boys went through Divine Redeemer, East Junior High, and Wasson High School.

As the children grew and matured through the pre-teen and teen years, Eileen and I recognized our blessings as they dodged the miss-steps that so many of their generation had to deal with. None ever had a problem with drugs; all had a healthy interest in sports, music, and the arts. Their friends, with rare exceptions, were outgoing, attractive young people. I have always believed that my generation, even with the hazards of World War II, had an easier time than did our children. The choices that my generation faced were clear and obvious while our children's generation faced choices that were much more complex and uncertain. The only war they had to think about—Vietnam—was unpopular and divisive. I don't recall any of Clayt's or John's friends being eager to get involved in the Vietnam War, as my generation had been in World War II.

Margaret graduated from Benet Hill in 1966 as a member of the school's first graduating class. After a year at the University of Colorado's Cragmore campus, she began her career in the dental profession, first as a receptionist, then a dental assistant, and finally as an office manager in a group dental practice.

Clayt graduated from Wasson in 1971, spent a year with the Ross Auction house in Colorado Springs learning a good deal about the value of antiques, and then started college. He first entered Western State in Gunnison, and then transferred to the University of Northern Colorado in Greeley. His interest in the area of sports was perhaps greater than his ability but he loved being part of the team, and he enjoyed track, football, and, later, cricket! In high school he was an average student, but he did much better when challenged at the university level.

Ellen's interest in ballet, which began at the age of five with Madame von Gregory at the Air Force Academy, never wavered for the next thirty years. Her talent and work ethic were remarkable. At Benet Hill she ran afoul of a psychologically disturbed nun who was convinced that an interest in ballet was the work of the devil. Accordingly, she transferred to Wasson in her junior year but was then accepted at the Academy of the Washington Ballet in Washington, DC, for her senior year.

John's athletic talent focused on skiing. Through high school at Wasson he was a member of the Broadmoor Ski Team, and, after graduation, he spent a year with the Vail Ski Team hoping to garner enough FIS points (Federation International de Ski) to be considered for the U.S. Olympic development squad. Unfortunately, the winter of 1967-1968 was a disaster for fledgling competitive skiers. Lack of snow forced the cancellation of one race after another, especially in his best event, downhill, so his dreams of an Olympic tryout evaporated.

Kathy, the most dedicated student of all, spent three years at Benet Hill and one at Wasson (her junior year) graduating with the best academic record of all her siblings. She also enjoyed ballet and appeared with her sisters in two of Norman Cornick's Christmas *Nutcracker* performances. Benet Hill had no varsity sports, so Kathy and a few of her friends became cheerleaders at the Fountain Valley Boys School. Her interest in science and subsequent career as an educator was inspired by a gifted teacher of physics at Benet Hill.

Elizabeth enjoyed school and all her friends but was not particularly interested in academics. She enjoyed track and field, but whatever ability she had was muted by a total disinterest in competition. She never enjoyed winning or, more accurately, besting her friends in foot races or any other form of competition—the exact opposite of John's intense competitive spirit. With her striking good looks, it really didn't matter too much.

At age eight, she broke both her legs skiing at Crested Butte and spent the best six weeks of her young life being carried from place to place by her brothers and helped by all her friends. Neither fracture was serious, a "greenstick" on one side and a non-displaced compression on the other, but six weeks of casts may have delayed epiphyseal closure and accounted for her long legs and height.

My mother once wrote that it was her opinion that "people do not change very much. We overcome faults but the essential *us* remains the same." From her diaries and letters I culled adjectives and phrases she used to describe the personalities and characters of our children as she saw them growing up and maturing during the 1960s. I thought she was remarkably prescient.

> Margy: fun loving, fair student, impractical, messy as a youngster changing to very neat with maturity, a people person, extravagant;
> Clayt: sensitive, athletic, empathetic, handsome, average student, hard worker, loyal, enjoys reading and books;
> Ellen: bright, artistic, hard working, committed, sometimes intolerant, professional, intensely loyal to a few, appreciative of quality;
> John: bright, impish, athletic, learns his way, likes music, talented, good mimic, funny, avoids intimacy, competitive;
> Kathy: studious, non-judgmental, bright, stoic, loyal, empathetic, hard working, beautiful, sweet natured;
> Lizzy: intuitive, fair student, beautiful, has a "way" with small children, fashion aware, concern for family, not competitive.

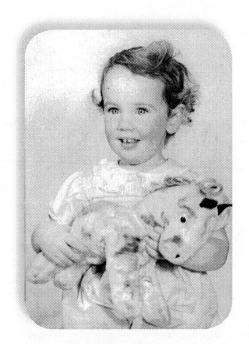

Margy at age one

Margy in high school

Margy writing home from Europe

Julie Gustafson at age 17

Clayt in Stonestown, age 3

Clayt in high school

Sherry, Nick, Clayt, Claytie, Jeni

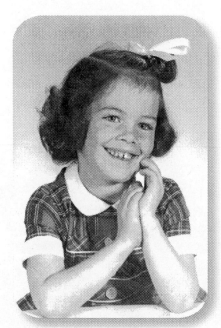

Ellen at age 5

Ellen in high school

David Struthers
Ryan   Ellen
Katherine   Jonathan
Emma and Nelson

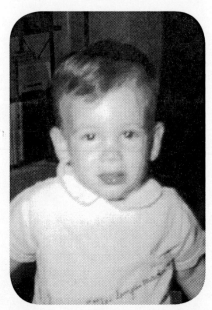

John, in Harlingen, age one

John in high school

John in Hawaii

Kathy at age four

Kathy in high school

Kathy and Annette Sulzman

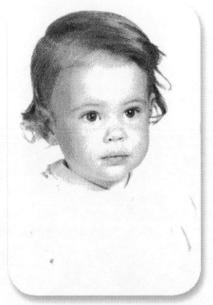

Lizzy at age one

Lizzy in high school

Grant Porter, Brad, Liz, Matt

Our family, Christmas 1995
Me, Clayt, John, Eileen, Liz, Margaret, Kathy, Ellen

In the summer of 1971, Eileen and I, along with Bobby and Yale Lewis and all of our children, rented beach houses a few doors apart at Lanikai, Hawaii, and enjoyed an unforgettable month in the Islands. It was our first trip "home" in almost twenty years. We rented Elia Long's house (I had known Elia thirty years earlier at Punahou) and it was a perfect size for us. There were four bedrooms, two baths, a large living room/dining room, and an ample kitchen. The house was on the beach twenty feet from the ocean. The children were fascinated by being that close to the water as well as by all the other activities they and their cousins—Peter, Roger, and Nancy—thought of to do. There were endless games of volley ball, snorkeling at Waimea and Hanauma Bays, body surfing at Makapuu, hiking in Nuuanu's Jackass Ginger and bathing in the "queens bathtub," great meals both at home and in Honolulu, ti leaf sliding, evenings with Norm and Deb, and a hundred other activities. It was the greatest family vacation we ever spent, and forty years later the memories are still vivid.

Two months after we returned home, at a picnic at Glenn and Joey Shoptaugh's, I was playing ping-pong when I was suddenly stricken with an excruciating abdominal pain. I had never experienced anything so severe. With help, I made it to the car, and with Clayt driving, headed to Penrose hospital. The trip, at the speeds Clayt reached, was the most dangerous part of the whole experience. At the emergency room, the first person I saw was Roy Dent and I was never so glad to see anyone in my life. He did a brief physical exam, ordered an EKG and cardiac enzymes, some Demerol, and admitted me to the intensive care unit. From this point on I became aware, for the first time in my life, of the peculiarities of the healthcare delivery system from the patients point of view. It is an experience all physicians, particularly surgeons, should have at least once in their careers.

As was customary at Penrose, and probably most Catholic hospitals, anyone admitted to intensive care was given the "last rights." By the time the earnest and well-intentioned young priest had finished, about an hour after I received Demerol, I was feeling fine and had no pain at all. Glancing up at the EKG monitor, I could see the little green line moving up and down and left to right in a regular fashion, so I knew death was not imminent; but even if it were, I was spiritually cleansed and "ready." At this point a very pretty and very well-endowed blond nurse appeared with towels, soap, and warm water to give me a bath. I didn't feel I needed one having showered earlier in the day, but routine was routine. As she started, I noted a disquieting stirring in my loins and, rather than embarrass either of us, I told her I could finish the ritual and dismissed her. Obviously my newly acquired spiritual purity went right out the window.

A little later Roy came by to tell me that the EKG looked normal but the cardiac enzymes were not yet available. Feeling perfectly well by this time, I asked the nurse to send someone down to the record room to bring up my unfinished charts so that I could be doing something useful. She went to the nursing station, whispered to the charge nurse, who soon returned with a tranquilizer pill but no charts. Presumably she thought I was not quite rational.

After Eileen came by and found me feeling perfectly well, I noticed another peculiarity of hospital care. Personnel began talking in a kind of baby talk. Bodily functions were referred to as "number one" or "number two" and there were other quirky expressions. I suppose this was meant to be reassuring, friendly, or supportive. The next day after X-rays revealed the nature of my problem—several large gall stones. I was transferred out of intensive care to a private room and at this point noted subtle changes. Nursing care became more perfunctory and I had the feeling that I was thought of as a bit of a malingerer. I had time to reflect and wonder why I hadn't understood the nature of my problem in the preceding months. I had diagnosed gall bladder disease a hundred times in "fair, fat, fifty-year-old females" but it simply never occurred to me, without a family history of gall bladder disease, that my episodes of indigestion were relevant. Being blinded by the obvious is not rare among physicians.

I was discharged within seventy-two hours with instructions to stay on a high-protein diet for the next few weeks in preparation for surgery. So while the family ate hamburger, I had to struggle along on tenderloin and fillet mignon. Six weeks later, Dick Thompson did the gall bladder surgery and I made a prompt recovery. Nothing about the operation or my recovery from it was as painful as the original attack had been. Two weeks after surgery, I played golf and shot the best front nine in my life—two over par.

For the next two years, the nation watched as President Nixon procrastinated while he was obviously planning an end to the Vietnam War that would gain him maximum political advantage in the 1972 campaign. Finally, the tragedy that was Vietnam ended with the United States being beaten in war for the first time in its history. We then had to witness the disgraceful way our returning soldiers were treated. Nixon tried to choreograph a hero's welcome for the men who had been prisoners of war for years, but he fooled no one, and for him to try and look like the savior of those brave men was nauseating to watch. The one foreign policy of the Nixon presidency that won universal approval was the beginning of a rapprochement with China. However, even that was dulled by the knowledge that if a Democrat president had tried the same thing, Nixon would have been the first to call it another example of Democrats being "soft on communism."

Soon after the Nixon victory in the 1972 elections, the Watergate scandal progressed to its inevitable conclusion. Some have likened Nixon's fall to a Greek tragedy, but I think not. To see a man destroyed by his own demons is just part of the story. The other part is that to be a classic tragedy, the man must be of heroic or noble stature—Nixon was hardly that. He was basically a little man, highly intelligent but with no grand vision for the nation, just personal ambition. He was clever but driven by political expediency. After his presidency, he devoted himself to two decades of self-justification. Gloating over any man's destruction, even a villain, is counterproductive. But in Nixon's case, self-destruction was predictable.

It is difficult for me to date precisely when the practice of obstet-rics and gynecology began to undergo fundamental changes. Perhaps it is easier to identify the reasons why. I think there are at least five: advances in technology, the feminist movement, the legalization of abortion, the malpractice crisis, and the hopeless conservatism of the American Medical Association.

The astounding advances in technology, diagnostic tools, and treat-ment modalities are too many and too technical to enumerate in their entirety. But to name just a few: the use of colposcopy and laparoscopy, the development of highly precise imaging techniques, electronic fetal monitoring, advances in the science of genetics, the development of ever more effective antibiotics, our understanding of fluid and blood replace-ment, advances in the study of prenatal nutrition, intensive care of very low-birth-weight premature infants, safer and more effective anesthetics, and advancement of techniques for anesthesia. In the 1950s, a three-year residency in a teaching hospital was adequate to teach the neophyte ob-stetrician/gynecologist what might be called the general practice of his specialty. By the year 2000, a minimum of one more year of formal training was required for the sub-specialties of adolescent OB/GYN, geriatric gy-necology, radical gynecologic surgery, and new techniques in the treatment of infertility.

In obstetrics, the feminist movement and the natural childbirth vogue became important in the daily practice of the specialty; I made a concerted effort to adapt to the change. The days of paternalism, the "don't you wor-ry about technical things you don't understand because I will take good care of you" approach, were rapidly disappearing. The infallibility of the physician was being challenged. I think I had some success because I was "accepted" by some of the more militant feminists in Colorado Springs. I endorsed the concept of natural childbirth because it is obvious that ninety percent of women have always been able to deliver "naturally." The human race survived even before the advent of the American College of Obstet-

rics and Gynecology. But, as with every vogue, uninformed extremism had
to be tempered with common sense.

I recall a few young women who, having read one or two articles in
The Ladies Home Journal about the emotional fulfillment and joy of natural childbirth, presented a laundry list of things they wanted done or not
done incidental to their care. In most cases I listened with nonjudgmental
politeness, I hoped, and I ignored anything ill-advised or frivolous. During
the course of labor and delivery, if the patient remained adamant about not
receiving pain medication, it made my job easier, and as long as there was
no reason to intervene, I didn't. However, electronic fetal monitoring was
becoming commonplace and ever more technical, so if anything occurred
that indicated a hazard to the baby, I did what was appropriate without
regard to the patient's list of do's and don'ts.

There were a few lighter moments for those of us who were acceptable
to the feminists. I was once invited to attend a meeting at a sorority house
at Colorado College. I think I was invited to answer any technical questions that might have arisen in the presentation to the sorority ladies on
how to do their own Pap smears with a cumbersome and complicated set-
up of mirrors and speculums. The contrast between the feminist lecturers
(politically liberal, bra-less, with unshaven legs and armpits) and the young
daughters of the establishment (politically conservative, well-groomed, and
taught from infancy to be very careful about how they touched themselves
"down there") was almost surreal. The lecturers were frank, forthright, and
aggressively immodest. The lecturees were polite and tried their best not to
be shocked and counted the minutes until they could start serving coffee
and cookies at the end of the presentation. It was a scene that a clever
writer and director could have made hilarious in a movie.

After *Roe v. Wade* and the legalization of abortion, an entirely new set
of questions arose about the ethics of the procedure. Initially, I was against
the new law but soon had to admit that abortions (a procedure that had
been done for thousands of years in virtually every culture) were better

done in a hospital setting than in the proverbial back alley. However, I remained opposed to the procedure done for frivolous reasons, for example, that the baby's due date would conflict with vacation plans or that the baby wasn't the right sex. Abortion is always a tragedy. President Clinton had it exactly right when he said abortion should be safe, legal, and rare—with an emphasis on the latter. I am both pro-choice and pro-life. Extreme positions on either side of complex issues are usually wrong. For example, no sane person would argue against abortion in a case I remember well where a mentally handicapped (very low intelligence) girl of sixteen was pregnant by her equally mentally handicapped fifteen-year-old brother. But I have never understood how a reputable physician could charge for doing an abortion. And physicians who make a living doing little else are pariahs. As for the so-called partial birth abortions, an expression I do not understand, nor have I ever seen in the literature, I can only say that in my experience, having delivered between six and seven thousand babies in every conceivable hospital setting—military, civilian, Catholic, non-Catholic, large, small, teaching, and non-teaching—I have *never* seen an elective destructive operation performed on a term or near-term infant. And I would challenge anyone to present a case where there was no other option.

The threat of malpractice litigation continued to escalate and markedly affect clinical judgment. Before 1950, cesarean deliveries typically amounted to six or seven percent in the hands of specialists. A rate significantly higher than that was usually a sign of incompetence. Forceps deliveries, particularly low- and outlet-forceps, were common and mid-forceps were not considered especially risky. Breech deliveries, when they occurred in first pregnancies, were a common reason for cesarean delivery. But in multiparous patients, hence with "proven" pelvises, cesarean delivery was uncommon. When I was last in practice in the mid-1980s and supervised residents in their second and third year of training, cesarean section rates were twenty percent and higher. I talked to residents who not only had never done mid-forceps deliveries, but they had never seen one. Non-oper-

ative breech deliveries were rare. I am sure the trend was the result of malpractice cases stemming from less than perfect results. Clever plaintiff's
attorneys began convincing juries that a less than perfect result was *prima
facie* evidence of malpractice. Physicians were presumed to be at fault and
had to prove that they were not, which was a reversal of the time-honored
presumed-innocent pillar of our judicial system. Because contingency fees
were legal in the United States, unlike Canada and other countries of the
western world, the monetary incentive for attorneys was obvious. For all
these reasons, and others, the practice of obstetrics and gynecology underwent basic changes. The emphasis switched from clinical acumen to
facility in the use of technology, from a physician's considered judgment to
patient's demands, and from a physician's training and experience to what
the courts countenanced and the insurance companies dictated. It is now
quite a different world than the one I grew up in, and yet it is a fact that
fetal/maternal morbidity and mortality are as much improved in the last
five decades as they were in the first five decades of the twentieth century.

Finally, the role of the American Medical Association in the past seventy years must be considered. The AMA has always been relentlessly conservative and incapable of either understanding change or stepping forward with creative ideas. The organization has opposed every progressive
societal initiative since the 1930s. It fought social security, the concept of
medical insurance, Medicare, Medicaid, and health maintenance organizations. It was reluctant to even admit there *was* such a thing as malpractice.
Because it dismisses virtually all progressive initiatives out of hand as "socialism," or steps toward it, the organization is conceived of as a bad joke
by many physicians. It was the reason I simply stopped paying dues many
years ago. I could no longer support an organization so out of touch with
contemporary reality. The AMA has always liked to brag how the medical care delivery system in the United States is the best in the world and
doesn't seem to understand that, to the extent this is true, what is perceived

as socialism is precisely the reason why we have an ever improving quality of medical care. This cause and effect relationship simply eludes the AMA. The nostalgic memory of fee for service practice, involving only the doctor and the patient, is, for better or worse, a thing of the past.

After we returned from Hawaii the summer of 1971, Ellen began the next important chapter in her life—moving to Washington, DC, and a hoped-for career as a dancer. It was not easy to say good-bye to our beloved sixteen year old as she boarded the airplane. She seemed so young and naïve, and yet she had always been more able than most teenagers to differentiate the important from the unimportant, organize her time, and set her priorities. She was to be met at National Airport so her physical safety was not a concern, but even so, it was difficult to see her off. I was reminded of the old saying that with sons, parents hope for their future, with daughters, they pray. Suddenly our household was down to three children instead of six. Margaret was on her own; Clayt was at college; Ellen was in Washington.

My medical practice was flourishing and for the first time in our lives we began to experience a level of affluence. For recreation we enjoyed memberships at the Broadmoor Golf Club and the Woodmoor Country Club. Both the boys enjoyed golf as much as I. John had a shade more natural talent, but Clayt had the better temperament for the game. We were able to take annual trips to Boston or New York or San Francisco for medical meetings. We enjoyed good health, and our dear little friend, Masako Brown, came weekly to help Eileen with the household chores. For ten years we never had a more loyal or pleasant helper, and I think never in all those years did Masako ever forget one of the children's birthdays or Christmas. We had a pleasant circle of friends for golf, parties, and bridge, as well as many visitors—the Hurds, Oscar, Norm, Guppy, and the nephews from Honolulu. It was a time that we were free of worries, and even the international and domestic scenes were tranquil.

In the summer of 1973, Jim and I moved into our new offices in a modern building on Union Boulevard near the corner of Palmer Park. It was an office layout that we had designed ourselves and had far more room than the little house on Platte Avenue. Our consultation offices were well lit, the reception room was large, and the two treatment rooms for each of us enabled us to see more patients far more efficiently. There was a small area we designated as a laboratory in which we were able to do routine antenatal blood counts and urinalyses. Most of our patients chose Penrose Hospital, and, less often, Memorial Hospital. St. Frances Hospital was inconvenient and though the new St. Frances was a big improvement over the antiquated old one, rounds at three different hospitals every morning were too time consuming. The proximity of Penrose and Memorial to our office was the deciding factor for us to limit the hospitals we used to two instead of three.

From the earliest days of our partnership, Jim and I counted ourselves lucky to have so many pleasant co-workers. Initially Jim's mother, Lu, was our receptionist/file clerk and Mary Kenny our nurse assistant. Mary was fun to be around. She was very efficient and a great favorite of our children. On a few occasions, she babysat when Eileen and I were able to get away on trips. Mary had an unending supply of jokes and our children loved her.

Later, when we moved into our new offices, and Lu had passed away, our dedicated crew was June Padden, Shirley Walters, and Sherry North as receptionist, file clerk, and bookkeeper respectively. Our nurse assistant, Debbie Switzer, was a whirlwind of efficiency, preparing patients in four different treatment rooms for two doctors and chaperoning all exams. How she did it without ever appearing flustered is still, in my memory, a little short of miraculous. On weekends, Debbie Morley was our receptionist/assistant. Debbie, who had been a classmate of Margaret's at Benet Hill, was another special person whose sweetness, empathy, and caring personality consistently won praise from our patients. In an office as busy as ours, with a constant variety of personalities among our patients, I can't recall a serious confrontation between our co-workers or between our staff and our patients. If they occurred at all, they were resolved quickly without permanent ill will. These women all made incalculable contributions to the success Jim and I enjoyed, and though Jim's and my paths diverged in 1979, I have never forgotten the loyalty and dedication of our staff.

Early in 1974, Ellen returned from the Academy of the Washington Ballet disillusioned and somewhat depressed having learned what the real world of professional dance was all about. The balletomane who enjoys the beauty of classical ballet, the music, the choreography, the sets, the costumes, and the talent of the performers hasn't the faintest idea of the sacrifices, commitment, and pain it has taken to present what they so much enjoy. Ellen had the work ethic and the talent, but perhaps not the perfect, anorectic "Balanchine body" for classical ballet. She knew that, but when she had to deal with the disloyalty, jealousy, and ruthless ambition of some of her classmates, it was too much for her to tolerate. She also realized that it was not a healthy environment. There were far too many anorectic, psychologically disturbed young women who would make any sacrifice to get one step ahead of their peers. There were too many injuries, often improperly treated or ignored, to the lower back, the ligaments, tendons, and bones, which, in later life, could lead to serious disability. In any group of ten thousand starry-eyed youngsters who dream of dancing the lead in Swan Lake, about ninety percent will quit after a few years of classes. Of the remaining thousand, perhaps a hundred will dance in a *corps de ballet* or a good company, and of those, perhaps twenty will become a prima ballerina. The others will study, sacrifice, endure pain and poverty, and never appear on any stage. Ellen's disappointments were soon eased when she re-entered a far healthier lifestyle of college and, ultimately, marriage and motherhood. While sorting out her priorities, she resumed her formal education at the Colorado Springs campus of the University of Colorado, continued dancing at Colorado College, and occasionally helped out as a receptionist at our office.

Margaret stayed busy learning the dental care delivery system as receptionist and dental assistant. Along the way, she met some interesting characters and often regaled us with some of their idiosyncrasies. Her interest in the profession evolved into a career that sustained her for decades. In 1974, she met Jim Gustafson and a friendship developed into a romance and marriage. Jim, at that time, was an assistant manager at the Broadmoor Golf Club. They were wed in a pretty ceremony at the Briarhurst Manor Estate in Manitou Springs in the spring of 1975. Jim stayed at the Broadmoor for several months but eventually tired of the attitude of his employers—that one was so lucky to be there that adequate pay was unnecessary—and resolved to move back to his home state of Florida where business opportunities were better.

Clayt's odyssey through college began at Western State in Gunnison in 1972. After one year at Western State, he transferred to the University of Northern Colorado for one year and then dropped out in order to work for two years. He eventually returned to get his bachelor's degree in 1978. In 1976, he went with a student tour group to the Soviet Union and got his first exposure to life in a totalitarian state. With the intense heat of a Russian summer and a diet of potatoes and little else, he quickly lost ten pounds. He also lost his passport at a ballet performance in Moscow. In a panic, he reported the loss to the American Embassy the next morning. It had already been turned in by a cleaning woman who was probably more terrified at having the (forbidden) document than was Clayt at having lost it. He later told me of an incident that, to an American, was highly instructive. A social evening for the young Americans to meet their Russian counterparts had been arranged by Intourist. In the course of the evening, Clayt met a young Russian couple who, after an exchange of gifts, invited him to their apartment. On entering, the first thing the young Russian host did was turn on the radio, very loud. This was done quite matter-of-factly as he explained to Clayt that everyone simply assumed their homes were bugged by the KGB and it was the only way they could talk openly and frankly.

In 1975, Clayt met Sherry McCoy in Greeley. Sherry was a young widow whose first husband had died tragically in his twenties of a dissecting aneurism. Their friendship progressed to a love affair and marriage in 1979.

John entered the University of Colorado at Boulder in 1977, but after an undistinguished first year he dropped out to coach skiing for one year. He returned to Boulder the summer of 1979, and after completing a summer session successfully, was allowed to re-enter the University. He graduated three years later. Inspired by several outstanding teachers, he considered staying on in graduate school, but the economic realities of life dawned and he left academia to enter the ski industry. His career for the next twenty-five years, "selling toys to rich kids" as he put it, was and remains very successful.

Kathy graduated fifth in her class from Benet Hill in 1978 and was accepted at the University of Colorado that fall. Though very bright and an excellent student, she wasn't prepared for the demands of a large university. The transition from a small catholic girl's school to the lifestyle of a co-educational mega university overwhelmed her. Her grades the first semester were so poor that she was suspended. But by working hard and earning top grades at a local community college, she was readmitted at Boulder in 1979. Like her brother, she learned from the embarrassment what was required at the university level and graduated with distinguished grades in 1982, and began her career in education—first as a science teacher, then director of an International Baccalaureate program, and, later, as a high school principal.

By 1976, and even more so in 1977, I found that I was getting bored with private practice. I felt that I was falling behind professionally and seemed to be doing the same things and saying the same things to the same people day after day. There simply were not enough challenges. Reading the green journal and the gray journal every month and attending a two-week meeting once a year was not enough to keep up-to-date on the many remarkable technological advances in my specialty. Furthermore, I felt that I was not, for someone in his mid-fifties, maintaining an adequate physical fitness regimen. I also knew that my thirty-year pack-a-day cigarette habit had to be dealt with. Accordingly, I made three resolutions: first, to upgrade my expertise in my specialty; second, to begin a physical training regimen; third, to quit smoking.

In the fall of 1977, I took a pre-test for recertification by the American Boards. The results were so embarrassingly bad that I began to study in earnest a *précis* of the specialty published by the boards. On Christmas Eve 1977, I smoked my last cigarette and found that I was immune from the alleged difficulties of quitting cold turkey. The increased exercise, primarily running, was working, and I began to feel better, especially in the mornings. In April 1978, I took the recertification exam and passed.

I was aware that the University of California hospital offered a year of advanced training to former residents and considered doing that when, coincidentally, I began getting letters from the Air Force inquiring if I would be interested in returning to active duty in the medical corps. Obstetricians/Gynecologists were urgently needed. Combining my years as a line officer in the war and eight more as a medical officer, as well as eight years in the reserves, I had completed eleven years of active duty. I would only need nine more years of active duty to be eligible for retirement. I began to give it serious consideration. Eileen was not opposed to the idea, though it obviously meant a total change in lifestyle and a little less income, but not much less, considering retirement benefits. I met with a young recruiter and the more I talked with him, the more intriguing the idea became. Working with younger people, practicing without the threat of malpractice litigation, not having to worry about the requirements of the insurance industry, traveling, and the obvious benefits of a comfortable retirement, were all powerful inducements. As for the children, all except Elizabeth were on their own and either married or in college.

Furthermore, I was growing increasingly disenchanted with Colorado Springs as a place to spend the rest of my professional life and retirement. As a liberal Democrat, I had very few like-minded friends with whom I could discuss current events. Most were middle of the road conservatives, and there was also an unhealthy group of arch right-wingers. The city itself left much to be desired. It was not an attractive city, although it is in a spectacular setting. Colorado Springs, except for the areas of the Broadmoor and Little London (north on Nevada, Tejon, Cascade, and Wood Avenues), was without character or definition. Every approach to the city from the east, south, and north was tacky and dominated by cheap motels and used car lots. Entry from the west, through Manitou Springs, was not much better. At the turn of the century, Manitou Springs had been a popular spa but had become so run down that it couldn't even be called shabby-gentile. But worst of all was the political environment, which was a coalition of right-wing fanatics, libertarians, and Christian fundamentalists. Every initiative aimed at civic improvement was labeled "socialism" by the cabal if it involved the expenditure of public money. The largest newspaper in the city, *The Gazette Telegraph*, was a bad joke. The city was a relic of the nineteenth century and exhibited neither pride nor a vision for the future.

So by the summer of 1977, Margaret and Jim had moved to Florida, and Clayt was living in Greeley. Ellen had met and ultimately fell in love with David Struthers, and they were married in a beautiful ceremony outdoors at David's alma mater, Colorado College, in May 1977. John and Kathy were in Boulder, and only Elizabeth was still at home. I was, of course, worried about how she would adapt to military life, react to leaving all her childhood friends, and leave the only home she had ever known. When I told her of our plans, it was not surprising that she was visibly unhappy.

I had to tell Jim of my decisions and the reasons for them. If he was surprised, he didn't seem to show it, and I think he realized, perhaps even before I did, that I had become dissatisfied with my situation. He wished me well and we dissolved our partnership without rancor or ill will. I know

I never had a better relationship with any colleague before or after our association.

In August of 1978, we had our last vacation as civilians. With Norm setting the itinerary, Eileen and I went to England with the Wrights to celebrate their twenty-fifth wedding anniversary. Norm was not only a student of English literature but also of English history. After many trips, he knew London about as well as any American could. He arranged the itinerary for the entire trip and it was a spectacular success. In London, we stayed at Brown's Hotel a block off Piccadilly on Dover Street. It was the ultimate in luxury, not too large but exquisitely appointed. High tea at Brown's was an unforgettable experience. Norm's great friend, Robert Morley, the English actor, author, and wit, had given Norm a list of outstanding restaurants, so we dined well and found that the notion that English cooking is poor is a myth. Every aspect of the trip was planned to perfection, from our first dinner at Tiddy Dolls, to Windsor Castle by canal boat, to the awesome Westminster Abbey, to the trip down the Thames to Greenwich and the Maritime Museum, to touring Winston Churchill's wartime headquarters at Whitehall, to a day at the newly completed London Museum, to shopping at Fortnum and Mason's and along Jermyn Street. The finale was a train trip to Scotland on the *Flying Scott*. There can be no more beautiful sight than Edinburgh Castle alight at night on a soft summer evening.

By the time we returned home, and after much thought, I was convinced that re-entering the military was what I wanted to do. Because expertise in my specialty was urgently needed, I realized that I had a little leverage in the choice of a first assignment. The hospital at Holloman Air Force Base in Alamogordo, New Mexico, was the nearest to Colorado, but before making an irrevocable commitment, I thought it prudent to look at the place. It was a good idea because when I saw it, it seemed the most depressing outpost I had ever seen. Everything was brown and dusty and flat. The only hotel in town was a decrepit motel that smelled of the deodorant cakes deposited in men's urinals. The best restaurant was an aging McDonalds. I drove to the air base hospital and introduced myself to the hospital commander, who was soon to be reassigned, and his first question to me was whether I might like to be the new commander. My impression of the place was poor, and when I returned to Colorado Springs I told my recruiter "no way," and that I would serve almost anywhere but Holloman. I also told him that before I was sworn in, I wanted to be assured that I would first be assigned to the School of Aviation Medicine at Brooks Air Force Base in San Antonio, Texas. My short-lived leverage worked. I was guaranteed the latter and was offered Vandenberg Air Force Base as my first duty assignment. Vandenberg was, at least, in California, near the ocean, and green. With these matters settled, I was sworn in on November 20, 1978, the day before my 55th birthday, and soon received orders for Sheppard Air Force Base in Wichita Falls, Texas, for in-processing and indoctrination, with a reporting date of February 2, 1979.

Before leaving Colorado Springs, there was a final, sad responsibility I had to face. Our beautiful black Labrador, Cindy, given to us by Gordy Riegal as a six week old puppy in 1962, had deteriorated significantly and I knew I had to do something I didn't want to do at all. She had been our joyful companion at countless parties and picnics, and a vigilant protector of the family for 16 years. But she was incontinent, almost immobilized by arthritis, unable to walk up and down stairs, and hardly able to eat. I pondered for several days whether to tell all the children what had to be done so that they could come by and say farewell, or simply do it and confront them with a *fait accompli*. For better or worse, I chose the latter, and, telling only Eileen, I took Cindy to the veterinarian for the last time. I have wondered ever since if I made the right choice.

In the two months between being sworn in and my reporting date in early February, there were many details about closing a practice that had to be attended to. In the announcement that I had sent to all active patients, I told them that their medical records would be available for at least six months by simply asking for them. I transported them in the file cabinets to our home and, later, to the home of one of our receptionists and finally to a storage company. They remained available for twenty years and a great many were asked for. I consulted two attorneys, the state medical board, and the AMA for guidelines on how long they should be kept. The consensus was that twenty years was reasonable. Finally, in 1999, there having been no requests for many years, I had them incinerated by the storage company.

Our last Christmas on Eagle View Drive was nostalgic, but we were so busy getting the house in shape for sale or rental, there was little time to be sad. The amount of things one accumulates in seventeen years is mind-boggling. We gave a great many things to Good Will as well as to friends and neighbors. In many ways, the military routine of transfers about every three years is very cathartic; one doesn't have time to accumulate too much. So, over the next nine years, we managed to downsize quite effectively. Our library was fairly large and we learned that keeping books is impractical. They weigh a lot and take up too much room; yet eliminating them is like discarding old friends.

Any misgivings I had about once again adapting to military life didn't last long after reporting to Sheppard Air Force Base on February 1, 1979, for indoctrination. The act of driving onto the base was as comfortable as putting on an old pair of gloves. But there were a few gaffes the first week. The first night on base, I went to the club for dinner and noted the "special" that night was something I had never heard of, Mongolian Barbeque. It was served cafeteria style and I was the only one in line as I started putting the various foods on my plate—thin sliced pork and beef, vegetables and bamboo shoots, and fried noodles. Loaded down with this smorgasbord of goodies, I started the meal with a vigorous appetite. Soon, two younger men joined me at the table, looked at my plate, at me, and back at my plate, and then one said, "Don't you like to cook that stuff, Colonel?" I had no idea how Mongolian Barbeque was supposed to be treated, but rather than look dumber than I was, I mumbled something to the effect that, "I always ate it that way." They looked bemused but I don't think I fooled them a bit.

After I had been fitted for a complete wardrobe, from fatigues to mess dress, I made application for a "uniform allowance," since all the clothes were of a different cut, material, and color than they had been twenty-five years earlier. Unfortunately, a long-in-service NCO "zebra," with about seven stripes on both sleeves, and who had my service record before him, advised me that there was no provision for a second uniform allowance. I would not, of course, argue the point. He was correct, as are most senior master sergeants most of the time. No uniform allowance for me.

After completing the course at Sheppard, I headed back to Colorado Springs for a few days before leaving again for the School of Aviation Medicine at Brooks Air Force Base. I had received several thick volumes of study material to be read before beginning the course work at Brooks. I had skimmed over them, but because I knew a good deal about the theory of flight and something of its physiologic effects, I didn't study them with any degree of thoroughness. To my surprise, we were tested on all the material at the end of the first week of instruction. Somehow I had missed that important information. The test was far more difficult than I had imagined it would be, and though I passed it, I'm sure it was a near thing. The rest of the course for the next six weeks was quite fascinating. I recall an especially entertaining lecture by a well-known audiologist of the effect on hearing after long exposure to high-decibel noise. It explained why most of us who flew reciprocating multiengine aircraft in World War II were often partially deaf. I wore earphones most of the time but usually not over my right ear—so that I could talk to my co-pilot—and for that reason I have only about half the normal acuity in the right ear. Most of the course was extremely interesting and Brooks Field was much more like a college campus than an Air Force base. The ambiance at Brooks Field was one of academia—no marching about, military formations, bands, airplanes, etc. etc., just classes, textbooks, quizzes, lectures, and exams. At the end of the course, Eileen came for graduation before we headed back to Colorado Springs.

A few days later, I loaded up my MGB and headed west for Vandenberg, and what promised to be the most rewarding nine years of our lives. We were to meet new people and experience new cultures that would never have been possible if I had chosen to remain in private practice. The choice we made was the right one and I never had cause to regret it. I was surprised to note that many of my colleagues were not only supportive of the decision we made but even a little envious.

VI
1979-1988

Driving onto the base at Vandenberg, I had that old familiar feeling of coming home, as I always did when arriving at any Air Force base. After reporting to the hospital commander, I was introduced to my sponsor, Tom Cock. Tom and I had much in common. He had been a navigator in B-24s in the 12th Air Force in Italy during the war. And, like me, he had gone to medical school and then, later, specialized in pediatrics. He and his wife, Aria, could not have been more cordial, especially when Eileen and Liz arrived in June 1979. Also on the day I arrived, Tom introduced me to Ted Marvis, another World War II Air Force veteran. Ted had been a special weapons officer in a bomb wing of the 8th Air Force. After the war and medical school, Ted and his wife Phyllis had settled in San Diego and built a large general medicine practice and, like me, Ted had also re-entered the Air Force. Both Tom and Ted were colonels; Tom was Chief of Hospital Services; Ted was Chief of Outpatient Services. The three of us became great friends and remained so for the next thirty years.

Ted invited me to dinner that first night at their beautiful home alongside the seventh fairway at the Lompoc Country Club. Ted filled me in on the personnel at the hospital, the mission at Vandenberg, and points of interest in the Lompoc area. He also provided his considerable expertise on the pros and cons of buying a home off base versus the advantages of living on base. I decided on the latter, mainly because of the proximity of base housing to the hospital.

Not having delivered a baby or done any surgery for the better part of six months, I was a little apprehensive, but within a couple of days, I was back in the groove and felt very comfortable. My office and exam rooms in the clinic were large and well-planned, and the clinic staff all seemed friendly and eager to help.

I had been at Vandenberg for three weeks when I was sent to Wurtsmith Air Force Base in the lower peninsula of Michigan for temporary duty to help a young obstetrician who had been on continuous duty without help, a leave, or even a night off for six months. Wurtsmith was a Strategic Air Command base housing a B-52 wing with "cocked" nuclear bomb carrying aircraft, so the ambiance of the place was a good deal more serious than the relatively relaxed atmosphere at Vandenberg. There were places on the base no one went without proper clearance, lest one find oneself spread-eagled on the ground with snarling dogs ready to attack and very serious security people pointing loaded guns at one's head—and they were not playing games. Wurtsmith was, therefore, a base typical of one-third of the nuclear triad. The other two-thirds were the silo-based intercontinental ballistic missiles and the United States Navy Polaris submarine fleet. It was this nuclear deterrent and the patient, unglamorous professionalism and dedication to duty of the airmen and sailors responsible for the most frightful weapons ever conceived by the mind of man that won the cold war, not the political speeches about "mutually assured destruction." Nothing uttered verbally could compare with the somber reality of a Strategic Air Command flight line.

On my return to Vandenberg, I chose a three bedroom house on Aspen Drive (which seemed appropriate for a Coloradan) and made plans to greet Eileen and Liz when they arrived in June. The house appeared large enough, but when our household effects arrived, we were overwhelmed. We had so many cartons of books filling the living room that we had no room for the furniture. My first chore was to build storage racks in the garage just to house them. Finally, after three weeks of improvising, we settled in. It was crowded but comfortable for the next three years. The total change in lifestyle was difficult for Liz—for about three days. Soon she found friends, and when she discovered that Lompoc had a McDonalds, life went on. Later, when school started, she made many new friends and discovered new interests. She became a cheerleader at Cabrillo High

School, started dating her first real beau, and our worries about her adapting to the new environment soon vanished.

Vandenberg was a Strategic Air Command base, and its mission was unique and interesting. Nuclear missiles were selected at random from various bases in the country, their nuclear warheads removed, and the disarmed weapons shipped to Vandenberg to be launched down range to Kwajalein Atoll in the Marshall Islands. In this manner, the war readiness of the missile fleet was assured. In addition, construction of the space shuttle launch complex and construction of a 15,000 foot runway to land the shuttle at Vandenberg was well underway. The project's cost was in the billions of dollars, but, to my knowledge, it has never been used. The theory was that Cape Canaveral was to be used to insert the shuttle into equatorial orbit and Vandenberg was to be used for polar orbits. However, guidance systems technology became so improved that polar orbits, or their equivalent, could be accomplished from Canaveral. Another high-priority, classified mission at Vandenberg was the development of the MX missile system, which was never discussed.

Work at the hospital was busy but not overwhelming, and when I was joined by another well-trained obstetrician, Dr. Pura Bandalon, there was time for tennis, golf, and picnicking at the beach, as well as familiarizing ourselves with the interesting towns along the south central California coast from Morro Bay to Santa Barbara. Trips to the beach were always fun, but swimming was forbidden—too many people had been lost in the violent surf and treacherous offshore drifts.

In the late summer of 1979, John and Nini came to the mainland for an *aloha* trip to San Francisco. John had been diagnosed with lung cancer, and in spite of surgery and radiation therapy, there had been a recurrence, so the prognosis was poor. We met in the city and returned to some of our favorite haunts—the Fairmont, the City of Paris and the White House, Tommy's Joynt on Van Ness, and a memorable day with cousin Penn Arnett in Marin County. We visited two or three wineries and cheeseries,

Petaluma, and a last lunch at Negri's in Occidental. Though his spirit was good, it was obvious that his energy level was low. By the end of the year, his condition was rapidly deteriorating and no further treatment was offered. I took an emergency leave to say good-bye, and by that time he was too weak to do more than listen to classical music. He did not appear to be suffering much pain, just total exhaustion. Within a month after my visit, John passed away and his ashes were cast into the sea at Makapuu, where we had enjoyed countless hours of surfing as youngsters.

In the summer and fall of 1980, the country watched as Ronald Reagan became the frontrunner and eventual Republican nominee to run against Jimmy Carter for the presidency. Regan had been a popular, if undistinguished, two-time governor of California and became the favorite of the conservative wing of his party. As a competent actor, he could effectively deliver any speech that was handed to him. Thus he became known as the "great communicator" and did pretty much what he was told to do by the Republican movers and shakers. He was likeable, amiable, and, as a former leading man, attractive. Originally an idealistic New Deal Democrat in his post-college pre-Hollywood days, Reagan was the only president who, in his younger days, ever flirted with the idea of joining the Communist Party. On election night, the country watched as a Hollywood personality with modest intellectual gifts triumphed over a highly intelligent, workaholic, former nuclear engineer. President Carter may not have demonstrated great leadership skills, but he deserved better than he got. It was depressing, but the people had spoken.

My own misgivings about President Reagan's grasp of the dangers facing the free world were realized when three things took place: (1) the country got involved in a comic opera adventure in Granada, (2) two hundred forty Marines were slaughtered in Lebanon, and (3) the Iran-Contra fiasco became public knowledge. As usual, the country got what it deserved when the limitations of the "Teflon president" were exposed. Every time Republicans give President Reagan credit for "winning the cold war," my thoughts go back to the flight line at Wurtsmith. The triad of the Strategic Air Command, the Polaris submarine fleet, and the nuclear missile force won the cold war, not a politician saying, "Mr. Gorbachev, tear down that wall."

One of the more amusing missions assigned to the personnel at Vandenberg when Ronald Reagan was president was the so-called Presidential Support Team, of which I was a member. Every time the president was scheduled to arrive at his ranch, Rancho del Cielo, in the hills above Gaviota, we were mobilized to cover the landing of Marine One at the heliport. The convoy consisted of a jeep full of armed marines, a car full of secret service people, a fire engine loaded with hundreds of gallons of water, an ambulance with corpsmen and a doctor, and another jeep full of marines. The fire engine never made it to the top of the hill without having to stop at least once to cool an overheated engine. Arriving at the heliport, we would stand by, then after the landing, go home. Why I, an obstetrician, was chosen wasn't clear. I can't think of a specialist less likely to be of much help in an emergency, but such is the power of the presidency. This caravan was also mobilized for the arrival of visiting heads of state and a select few other VIPs.

We saw Walt and Ann Hurd often during the years at Vandenberg. At that time, they were living in Tarzana, California, near Walt's office at Lockheed headquarters. By 1980, Walt had become the executive in charge of quality control at that vast company and was gaining an international reputation in his career field. In the summer of 1980, I suggested that he be the guest speaker at a hospital sponsored Dining-In. It was arranged and I had the pleasure of introducing my old friend, who was now a Brigadier General in the Air Force Reserve, to the guests. He gave a most interesting talk on the probable future of space exploration and highlighted it with color slides created by artists at Lockheed. Of all the Dining-In presentations I attended over the years, Walt's was one of the most informative.

Walt was always interested in science and his knowledge of a multitude of subjects was extraordinary. I recall trying to draw him out on the technology of the most advanced aircraft of the day, the SR-71 Blackbird. As chief of quality assurance at Lockheed, there was little he did not know about the astonishing technology of that aircraft; unfortunately, most of it was highly classified. But what he could talk about was simply awesome. On a side note, our next door neighbor at Vandenberg was Colonel Ed Payne, who had won a Distinguished Flying Cross by flying in a Blackbird on a record-breaking trip from the East Coast of the United States to England in something less than two hours.

In the spring of 1981, the commanding general at Vandenberg let it be known that senior field-grade officers were encouraged to attend the seminar program of the Air War College. As a physician, the usual pre-requisite military schools of Squadron Officers School and the Command and Staff College could be waived, and direct application would be approved, so I jumped at the chance. For the next year, I read the weekly pamphlets from Maxwell Field, each containing ten to a dozen articles, and attended discussions with our seminar group of about eighteen students. Twice each semester, multiple choice, machine-graded examinations were taken, and at the end of each semester, a formal written report of about five thousand words was submitted to the faculty.

At the outset, I had little appreciation of what I was about to undertake. The seminars were difficult and time consuming, although very interesting. I had assumed the reading material would be boring, full of Pentagonese, and with acronyms and initialisms masquerading as thought; but I could not have been more wrong. Almost without exception, the articles were well written, original, and insightful. There was a refreshing lack of jargon and orthodoxy. At the end of the first semester, and having passed both tests, I submitted my first report. When it was returned, having been corrected by someone who really knew what he was doing, I was appalled at how amateurish and badly written it was. There were no less than ten spelling errors, two or three incomplete sentences, conclusions drawn from nonexistent documentation, an inadequate bibliography, and a few other mistakes. It passed but it was hardly a distinguished piece of work. The final report, which I wrote half a year later, was better. I passed the course, and in retrospect, though it was humbling, it was one of the best experiences of my military career.

In the spring of 1982, I was appointed chief of aerospace medicine at the hospital and, as such, was ordered to flying status. It was great fun flying with my friends and neighbors, Mark Gibson and Joe Draham, in Huey helicopters. I had never flown in "choppers" before and it was interesting to learn their capabilities and historical development. For instance, the aircraft commander sits in the right seat in a helicopter, as opposed to the left seat in a conventional aircraft, allegedly because Igor Sikorsky (the inventor of the helicopter) was left handed. Also, flying low and relatively slow and waving to the children on the ground was an experience we couldn't enjoy when flying multiengine transports. On my last helicopter flight, we flew a patient with threatened premature labor from Vandenberg to the Letterman Army Hospital in San Francisco because the newborn nursery at Vandenberg was not a Level 4 ICU. Because it was a priority air evacuation mission, all other aircraft on our route had to give us wide birth; I was impressed as they peeled away from our flight path. When we landed at Letterman, we were met by an ambulance and the patient was whisked away. We learned later that she was successfully delivered a half hour after our arrival.

During our three years at Vandenberg, Ted and Phyllis Marvis regaled us with their experiences in Wiesbaden, Germany, and insisted that if we didn't request it as our next duty station, we'd regret not doing so. They had lived in a suburb of Wiesbaden, Hochheim, about twenty minutes from the hospital, for three years. A multi-talented man, Ted had a knack for languages and spoke German passably and French expertly. In addition to their strong recommendations, Tom and Aria Cock had already been assigned to Wiesbaden, so it didn't take too much urging for us to request Wiesbaden as our next post. Fortunately, there was an opening for a new OB/GYN Chief of Service in July 1982, so when it was offered, I accepted.

Overall, we enjoyed our three years at Vandenberg. There were a few negatives—principally two weak commanders. The first was inept and the other a blatant careerist whose primary concern was a good Officer Efficiency Report by the commanding general. His concern for all subordinates, regardless of rank or grade, was nil. I followed his career with some interest for many years and was not surprised to see that his primary objective, to reach flag rank, was never realized.

After receiving orders to Wiesbaden, I had one more requirement: the Combat Casualty Care Course (C-4) at San Antonio. The final two days of the course were of special interest—forty-eight hours of survival training. It was not to be compared to the very rugged two-week training required of combat crews going overseas, but for someone my age, it was rugged enough. In just forty-eight hours, I learned how lack of adequate food and rest, dehydration, and a hostile environment can create mind games and make one irritable and impatient with the perceived inadequacies of others. It was enough to make me marvel at the fortitude of the heroic Vietnam POWs, who endured infinitely worse deprivations for years. To survive such an ordeal, one must have either profound religious faith, ultimate faith in one's country, complete faith in one's compatriots, or some combination of all three.

We cleared the base the last week of June 1982, and headed for Los Angeles for the flight to Frankfurt and new experiences in Europe, although I had some misgivings about spending three years in Germany. Except for the field trip with the cadets in 1962, I had not seen Germany since the war and wondered what our reception would be like.

As it turned out, the three years we spent in Germany were the most enjoyable and interesting of our last nine years in the Air Force. Two thousand years ago, Wiesbaden was on the frontier of the Roman Empire's northernmost incursion into Europe. Wiesbaden's thermal baths have made it a famous spa for centuries. Today, with its beautiful Kurpark, Kurhaus, and Stadstheater, where we enjoyed many symphonies and ballets, there may not be a more elegant city in all of Germany. Along Wilhelm-strasse, Wiesbaden's Fifth Avenue, there were stores and shops with the finest quality merchandise. There were superb restaurants all over town serving foods of every possible ethnicity—Chinese, Mexican, Greek, and Italian—and although some meals were better than others, I cannot re-member ever having a bad meal. Every Saturday, the Marktplatz was filled with vendors selling the best breads and produce one could imagine. The local people were genuinely pleasant and seemed to like Americans. They were tolerant, amused, and helpful with our attempts to speak German. There was great civic pride, and if there was a criminal element or seedy part of town, we never saw it.

It was such a lovely city that had it not been for missing our children and grand children, we might have settled there permanently. We found much in the European lifestyle that Americans could adopt to their ad-vantage. In that culture, there is a reverence for nature and for the arts and a calmer pace that, once experienced, is not forgotten. From our home in Aukamm, one of the two military housing areas, we could walk through the Kurpark to downtown Wiesbaden in less than an hour. The park was always immaculate, yet I don't remember seeing maintenance people at work to keep it so. There were no candy wrappers, empty plastic bottles, gum, or cigarette butts—ever. I think the local people had a hand in keep-ing it pristine out of pride as well as a love of beauty.

The famous Weinfest in mid-August, with the finest wines from the Rheingau, which certainly are among the finest in the world and are often from small, family-owned vineyards known primarily to the locals, was, with its incredible diversity of foods, the highlight of the year. Pre-hol-iday shopping from mid-November to Christmas was another memora-ble experience, with innumerable little booths, *Imbiss Stubes*, selling hot *Karttofelpuffer*, cold *Apfelmus*, and hot *Glühwein*. If that didn't put one in

the holiday spirit, nothing could. The profusion of flowers, year round, is
another treasured memory.

   As we approached Frankfurt, after seven hours of flying from New
York, I remember feeling a bit apprehensive about what life might be like
living in Germany. It was the last time I was to be concerned. We were
met by Tom and Aria Cock, who drove us to their home in Aukamm. Our
future home was just a few doors from theirs. As we drove into town, I noticed German workers on their mid-morning break enjoying their customary beer. At nine-thirty in the morning, this struck me as being eminently
civilized and I knew that I was going to enjoy the German work ethic.
They obviously had their priorities in order.

   Our home's floor plan was a mirror image of the Cock's. They had
thoughtfully sent us a floor plan so that we could know what furniture
and bookcases to ship. The houses were sturdily built of concrete and cin-
derblock. On the ground floor there was an ample living room and dining
room, a small kitchen (with no dishwasher or garbage disposal), and a
small study that we were to use as a TV room. On the second floor there
were three bedrooms and two baths, and in the basement, another apartment with bedroom, bath, and sitting room. It was more than ample for us
and accommodated many guests during our years there.

   On the day we arrived, we had no sooner unpacked than we were off on
our first weekend of sightseeing in Alsace-Lorraine. From Strasbourg we
went south to the village of Illhaeusern, then another three kilometers to
the Hotel La Clairière, where we met the Marvises who were on a month's
vacation revisiting Europe for the first time in four years. The Clairière was
small, with perhaps a dozen rooms, but charming and beautifully maintained. It did not have a dining room but did offer breakfast—and what a
breakfast! There was fresh fruit and orange juice, excellent coffee, the most
delectable croissants with fresh country butter, and an assortment of little
pots of jams and jellies.

But the special treat that night was dinner at *L'Auberge de l'Ill*, two kilometers from the hotel. At that time in all of France there were twenty-one or so three-star restaurants. *L'Auberge* was one of them. I've been lucky enough to have had dinner in some great restaurants in great restaurant cities from Hawaii to Europe, but if I had to pick the best of all, it would be *L'Auberge de l'Ill*. The food was superb, the service could not have been better, and the ambiance was perfection. To sit on that beautiful terrace of the chateau by the bank of the glass-smooth Ill River, sipping Kir Royale before dinner, was an unforgettable experience. Once seated at the table we reviewed the wine list, which was as complete as any in France. One could easily spend hundreds of francs on a bottle of wine; we trusted the sommelier to pick one or two moderately priced wines of excellent quality. There was nothing pretentious about the place, just perfection in every detail. The waiters were discrete and so efficient that we were not aware of their presence as they served the several courses. And, as is true of every great restaurant, the place was well lit, the table settings—china and silver—immaculate and beautiful. We were to enjoy *L'Auberge* two more times during our time in Germany, once with our son John and once with Norm and Deb. The quality of the place never varied. Norm, who was a gourmand and knew great restaurants in most of the major cities of the world, agreed that he had never had a more delightful dining experience.

The next morning, after enjoying our *petit déjeuner* at the hotel, we left for our first visit to the little city of Ribeauvillé, one of Tom and Aria's favorite cities in Alsace. We revisited that picturesque town many times and grew to love it too. In fact, Alsace became our favorite "getaway" place for a day or a weekend. There were also many other villages between Strasbourg and Colmar that we discovered, enjoyed, and never forgot.

Back home in Wiesbaden, after our weekend in Alsace, I had to deal with jet lag for the first time in my life. Not only was it embarrassing to literally fall asleep in the middle of dinner, but since my first priority was to prepare for the USAFEUR (United States Air Force Europe) drivers license examination, trying to study for what was acknowledged to be a very difficult test while continually falling asleep was an interesting challenge.

It took the German driver about two years of mandatory *Fahrschulen* (driving schools) to qualify for the driving examinations, at an out-of-pocket expense of hundreds of Deutschmarks. Whereas Americans could be licensed with a passing grade of 75 percent, Germans either had to have a score of 100 percent or return the next year for a re-test. The German drivers tended to be aggressive, but they were skilled. Luckily, there was abundant information available about driving in Germany and how to cope with the unlimited speeds on the Autobahns. All the driving I did in Germany was defensive, and I tried to remain passive behind the wheel. If a German driver came up behind me at speeds well over a hundred miles an hour with lights flashing, I got out of the way—fast. The only drivers who scared me were the Americans who tried to drive like the Germans but lacked their skill.

Somehow, even in my jet lag fog, I managed to pass the driving test. I had to because our little MGB, which I had shipped from Los Angeles eight weeks earlier, had arrived in Bremerhaven and was ready to be picked up.

The journey to Bremerhaven was another eye opening experience—our first on German railroads. I set the trip up using a travel agency that we were to use many more times in the next three years. I noted that in Bremen we had to switch trains for the final hour to Bremerhaven, but that there were only four minutes allotted between our arrival and the departure of the second train. I questioned the agent about this but was reassured that four minutes was an ample amount of time. He was correct. We had two minutes and forty seconds to spare. German trains are clean, comfortable, precise, smooth, and serve excellent food. The tracks are seamless, hence we didn't hear the clickety-clack so familiar in the United States. German trains put our once great railroad system to shame. We traveled to many places during our time in Europe and were never disappointed by the train system. We returned from Bremerhaven in about half a day, a bit shaken after driving speeds undreamed of in the States. Driving at 90mph, I never passed anyone, but I was passed by an assortment of Audis, Mercedes, and BMWs driving so fast that I could not believe what I was seeing.

The work at the hospital was busy from the first day, and it steadily increased. My first meeting with our commander, Col. Gino Signorino, was a revelation. He was the first hospital commander I met who set forth his priorities very clearly at the outset. He was one of only three hospital commanders I had during my career that I respected.

In the European theater in 1982, there were three priorities for the medical corps: productivity, quality control, and war readiness. Each hospital commander set his own emphasis. For Gino, it was productivity. "Bean counting" was the basis for increased or decreased budgets and for adequate staffing. Quality control was a given, and war readiness was something that had to be accepted—boring, but necessary. However, trying to function in a chemical warfare costume (cumbersome coveralls, nerve gas resistant gloves, gas masks, etc.) was ludicrous. There were those who did not necessarily agree with Gino's priorities but at least he was clear.

My staff of clinicians, nurses, aides, and corpsmen was an interesting mix of personalities. At full strength, the staff was adequate to carry out the mission, but it was rarely at full strength. Our catchment area was all of Europe and parts of Africa, but not the United Kingdom. We were authorized five physicians, two nurse midwives, one nurse practitioner, several nurse's aides, and corps women. Bill Birdsong, who was well-trained and a hard worker, was the one physician who was with me full-time for the full three years. Rita Bieson-Bradly was a dynamo, a skilled clinician and surgeon, and very popular with our patients. Unfortunately, we lost her for months when, unable to control her diet and weight, she developed a severe toxemia of pregnancy. Vern Wagner was likeable and diligent but was not well-trained or skilled at surgery and had to be closely monitored. His first love was flight medicine and would have much preferred staying in that career field rather than being forced into the role of full-time obstetrician. Bill Ayers was a well-trained and rather contemplative physician whose full three years at Wiesbaden was cut short when he developed a severe, symptomatic herniated spinal disc problem and had to be sent to Wilford Hall Medical Center for corrective surgery. And then he developed a life-threatening post-operative complication. One of our dedicated nurse midwives was diagnosed with breast cancer and had to be transferred to the States for treatment and was never replaced. The other nurse midwife, Bobby Jo Roe, was a godsend. She delivered more of our uncomplicated obstetrical patients than any of the rest of us and we could not have functioned without her.

Thus, though the authorized staff was present only part of the time, productivity steadily increased to levels that had not been seen for a dozen years. To further complicate matters, there were serious personality conflicts, especially between our nurse practitioner and the clinic charge nurse as well as between the two German nurse's aides. The latter two didn't like each other and never had. For three years it was an unending battle trying to maintain harmony and adequate staffing. Eighty-hour work weeks were routine and one-hundred-hour weeks not rare. Furthermore, with such a large workload, there were many unhappy patients who, having waited weeks for an appointment, were seen for fifteen minutes. It was not an ideal situation but we had to play with the cards we were dealt. The saving factor that made it all worthwhile for me and Eileen was the experience of living in Europe.

Our house was a revolving door for houseguests, who included not only many of our friends but also friends of the children from Colorado and California. It was always fun to introduce people to Wiesbaden and its many charms. John and Liz were the first to arrive a few days before Christmas 1982. They had escaped the great Colorado blizzard of '82 just minutes before the airport was closed. After visiting her siblings in Denver, Boulder, and Florida during the summer and fall of 1982, Liz was, at first, a little overwhelmed and suffered culture shock the first few weeks in Germany. In restaurants, she would only order spaghetti, applesauce, and cokes because they were the only menu items she recognized. John got a job at the large shopping center at Mainz-Kastel and soon was comparing skiing in the Alps with the Rockies. In the spring of 1983, he applied for a job as assistant manager of the pro shop at the Rheinblick Golf Club, where he met Grant Porter, who was the teaching professional at Rheinblick. Grant's family, originally from Kansas, had moved to Germany in 1967. Grant's father had spent his career as an administrator in the Department of Defense school system and his mother was a special education teacher. When John introduced Grant to Liz, the summer of 1983, her culture shock magically disappeared and she enjoyed the rest of her years in Europe as only a twenty-year-old in love can.

In the spring of 1983, Kathy and her new husband, Matt Wicklund, arrived. Kathy was able to fulfill her student teaching requirement for her Bachelor's degree at Arnold High School, the Department of Defense high school in Wiesbaden. On the appropriate day, her students gave her a college graduation replete with the University of Colorado colors, gown, and mortar board. The five of us, Matt, Kathy, Liz, Eileen, and myself, then celebrated with our first trip to Paris. At that time, Kathy had declared herself to be a vegetarian and we discovered that one way to make waiters in Parisian restaurants unhappy, especially elderly ones, was to have to adapt to the tastes of a strict vegetarian.

In the summer, Ellen, David, and their toddler, Ryan, arrived, rented a Volkswagen camper, and took off on a trip through Germany and Switzerland. I shall never forget two-year-old Ryan bidding German people *guten tag* on our walks in the Kurpark. The middle-aged German women especially melted at our beautiful, blond-headed little grandson trying his hand at their language.

In October 1983, Norm and Deb arrived to celebrate their thirtieth wedding anniversary. We had a marvelous time showing them all the sights in our part of Germany, had a fabulous dinner at *L'Auberge de l'Ill*, and took a trip down the Romantic Road to Rothenberg where Norm, with his lifelong fascination with crime and criminals, both fictional and non-fictional, was especially interested in the Medieval Crime Museum. On the way home, we stopped for a few hours in Heidelberg, toured the castle, and enjoyed an excellent lunch in the student quarter. None of the romanticism celebrated by German writers is exaggerated when one sees the gardens of that beautiful place. The only mix-up in our itinerary was missing the barge at Biebrich for a Rhine River cruise. That cruise, which we enjoyed many times, traveled north through the narrows at Lorelei to Koblenz. We would then return home by train. It was a beautiful day trip. In good weather, the vistas of the wine country and the villages of the Rheingau were especially lovely.

Many of our warmest memories of Wiesbaden are of times spent with our friends in the German-American Friendship Club. It was another reason to be grateful to Tom and Aria, who first introduced us to them. There were a dozen or more couples our age and we kept in touch with many of them for a decade after we came home, especially Wolf and Christa Mitscher, Ernst and Anita Fisher-Bothof, Katie and George Billings, Frau Lilo Mach, and Frau Waltraud Lewinski. There were others we knew less well, but all were hospitable and kind. Wolf Mitscher had been a Luftwaffe pilot during the war and was the grand nephew of the great American World War II hero, Admiral Mark Mitscher—Wolf's grandfather and Admiral Mitscher's father were brothers. Wolf was in his seventies, a most knowledgeable wine expert, and had more joy in life than most men of thirty. Christa was aristocratic, very beautiful, warm hearted, and a delightful person to talk to. We seldom talked about the war during our evenings together, but Ernst Fisher-Bothof told me one evening what life had been like in Berlin before and during the airlift. He was not given to hyperbole or emotion, but said that life would have been impossible without the Americans. The club met monthly, and whoever hosted the cocktail party before dinner picked the restaurant for the evening meal. In the years we were there, I think we dined at every fine restaurant in the area and returned often to many of them.

Dining out in Germany is "grown-up time." As much as Germans love children, they almost never take them out to dinner, and if one saw children with their parents, they were invariably Americans. But this was not so for pets. Unlike in the United States at the time, well-mannered dogs were common in restaurants. Germans did not understand why they were prohibited in the United States. We were at dinner one night at Luigi's, our favorite Italian restaurant, when I glanced up directly into the eyes of an extremely large Harlequin Great Dane. He stood at least thirty inches at the shoulders. After exchanging greetings, he spent the rest of the evening at the feet of his owner, causing no disturbance at all.

After Liz and John returned to the States during the summer of 1984, Liz to be with Grant and John to begin his career in the ski industry, we continued to have guests and visitors. In January of 1985, I was promoted and pinned on colonel's "eagles" and immediately noticed a difference in my co-workers. They tended to listen when I spoke. Of course, nothing else changed. I've discussed this phenomenon with others and the consensus is that since no one can be quite sure which of the five percent of the colonels will someday become generals, it's best to play it safe and be attentive.

All too soon, it became necessary to start thinking about our departure and our next duty station. In May, Grant and Liz, after a civil ceremony in Kansas, returned to Wiesbaden for a traditional wedding in the garden of Grant's home in Medenbach. After the wedding, we had a reception at a hotel on the Rhine near Hallgarten for the Porter's friends, our German friends, and our colleagues at the hospital. It was a lovely ceremony, with beautiful weather, which is unpredictable in the spring, and everyone seemed to enjoy themselves. In the late afternoon, Liz and Grant left for their honeymoon in Evian.

After a last series of farewell parties, we were ready for the packers and, sadly, our time in Wiesbaden drew to a close. We were assigned to

Scott Air Force Base in O'Fallon, Illinois, and decided to go home on the Cunard Line's *Queen Elizabeth 2 (QE2)* as a fortieth wedding anniversary present to ourselves. I sold the Volvo that I had bought three years earlier, bought an Audi, but had to have a catalytic converter installed before I could bring it home, which involved one more trip, to Emden on the North Sea.

Lead-free gasoline was available in Germany but not in France, so driving to Cherbourg to meet the *QE2* took careful planning. From Wiesbaden we drove to Saarbrucken, bought two five-liter containers and filled the car to the brim before entering France. After spending the night in a once grand but now decaying resort hotel, we drove through Reims and beyond to the village of Fère-en-Tardenois to a magnificently restored thirteenth-century chateau where we enjoyed a memorable seven course meal and spent the night. Walking the grounds of the chateau after dinner, with the ruins dramatically lit with indirect lighting, was a theatrical and beautiful sight. In the morning we were off to Cherbourg and made it with a few liters of gas to spare. We spent the day touring that interesting city, with its memorabilia of Operation Overlord, the Allied invasion of Europe on June 6, 1944. In the late afternoon, the magnificent *QE2* arrived from Southampton.

Once aboard, we were shown to our cabin. Norm and Deb, ever thoughtful, had ordered flowers for our room and a magnum of Dom Perignon to be opened on our anniversary. After unpacking, we went to the dining room and found we were to be seated at the Captain's table. Our mess mates were an older couple from Naples, Florida, an attractive English lady who was celebrating a recent divorce, a young English couple, Nancy and Andrew Gilchrist, and Captain Lawrence Portet, master of the *QE2*. Captain Portet was the perfect embodiment of what the master of the flagship of the Cunard Line should look like. At six feet four inches tall, he was perfectly cast. I could not imagine anyone on the *QE2* daring not to do what he ordered. He was also perfectly charming and most interesting when answering questions about his great ship—questions he had probably heard a hundred times. The couple from Florida was retired, spent most of their time traveling, and they were excellent company. The English lady was very cheerful and if at all depressed about her marital problems, never showed it. But the young English couple became our favorites. Nancy was absolutely stunning, with auburn hair and flawless coloring; and Andrew, recently discharged from the British Army, was attractive and amusing. Nancy was not only lovely to look at but beautifully educated and very bright and was an expert on all facets of wine production and the wine industry. Andrew was on his way to Harvard to begin work on his degree in business administration.

Having cleared the English Channel during the night, we awoke to what I considered to be mountainous seas in the Atlantic. Captain Portet later referred to it as a "moderate" sea, but moderate or not, green water washed over our porthole, which was nearly a hundred feet above the water line. Dressing was impossible as we pitched and rolled. Getting to the dining room was too difficult to contemplate. Neither of us became ill, but I remember being very dizzy. As I lay on the bed, I timed the waves and they seemed to come in sets of three, with the first always the most severe. As the ship pitched up, we were pressed into the bunk, and as it went down, we were momentarily airborne. This kept up all day, and our meals were limited to fresh fruit, crackers, and water. There was no steward service. By nightfall, things eased a bit and the next day, though still rough, it was possible to get to and from the dining room. The next day after that, and for the rest of the trip, the seas were calm and one could enjoy the countless amenities the QE2 offered. Though we were never in any danger, experiencing what the sea can do to one of the mightiest machines built by man, tossing it about like a cork in a bathtub, was impressive.

On our arrival in New York, I offered Nancy and Andrew transportation to their destination in the city, as soon as our car was off-loaded. Nancy, charming and affectionate as always, declined saying that she was sure her "Daddy" would be meeting them. A little later, after our good-byes, we saw them getting into the first of two Rolls Royces, both bearing United Nations flags on their fenders. It was then that I learned the "Daddy" was the British Ambassador to the United Nations.

When our car was rolled onto the dock, we left the ship, and with our luggage stored, we headed out of New York for Rhode Island and a wonderful three-day visit with the Armentrouts, which included a fascinating walking tour of Newport, to look at the summer "cottages" of the obscenely wealthy robber barons of the nineteenth century. Even the very wealthy of today do not live in that kind of splendor. When we had recovered our land legs, we were off to our final destination, Scott Air Force Base, in O'Fallon, Illinois.

The first priority in Illinois was, as usual, housing. But this time, getting settled was complicated by the fact that all our effects were arriving from two different places, Germany and California, at about the same time. We found a roomy three bedroom condominium about a ten minute drive from the hospital at Scott. Once again, thirty-five cartons of books had to be stored, unopened, in the garage. By August we were comfortably settled and the familiar routines of clinic, delivery room, operating room began again.

The hospital at Scott was a teaching hospital staffed by military physicians and residents in training from two teaching hospitals in St. Louis. This was a new experience for me and had advantages and disadvantages. It was pleasant not to have to do a complete history and physical examination on every patient when they were admitted, or long narrative summaries when they were discharged. It was even more pleasant not to have to be in the hospital at all times when on call. However, I always had the feeling that I was giving up a certain amount of control over the care of patients. I was also worried about risk management and quality assurance. I did not like the idea of being called in only to deal with some actual or potential problem, which, in some cases, should never have occurred in the first place. I was not chief of service when I arrived and did not become head of the department until Dr. Bill Gerber retired the summer of 1986. I was, therefore, not in a position to change protocols and routines that had prevailed for many years and, for better or worse, went along with established practice. In the final two years, I elected not to institute basic changes for two reasons: I had no mandate to do so and, with the way the department was set up, it seemed to be working reasonably well most of the time.

The obstetrical service was structured to include a so-called family practice residency program. It was popular for many patients because they saw the same physician throughout their pregnancies. However, an equal number of patients elected to be seen by OB/GYN specialists, with no guarantee that a particular doctor would be in attendance at delivery. As might be expected, the competence of the general practice residents varied, and if complications arose, they were expected to call their chief of service. However, if he was not available, the obstetrical specialist was to be called. This was a situation with which I was never comfortable. There were too many instances where the safety of the mother or the baby was compromised by the inexperience of the attending physician. Most crises in obstetrics develop very rapidly, and not having a specialist in the room, scrubbed, gowned, and ready to intervene, created risk factors that I found very unsatisfactory.

The civilian residents from hospitals in St. Louis were an interesting group of young people, and it was from them that I learned how drastically the new techniques and basic concepts of the specialty were changing compared to my training and years of practice. They were third-year residents and yet they knew very little about operative obstetrics. Some of them had never delivered an infant in the breech position (or even seen a delivery of a baby presenting in the breech position), had no expertise in the use of forceps, and would opt for cesarean delivery over straightforward mid-forceps delivery. They were still using mediolateral episiotomies instead of midlines and were ignorant of the technique of pudendal block anesthesia. On the other hand, they were more knowledgeable of the significance of variations in electronic fetal heart monitoring than I, and they were far more skilled at epidural anesthesia. They had a pathological fear of the slightest evidence of meconium-stained amniotic fluid and seemed to be convinced that it was always associated with fetal distress. None of them quite grasped the fact that some meconium staining is so common as to be considered normal. I recall having to restrain one young trainee from blindly intubating a neonate as soon as the head stemmed the perineum because of the presence of flecks of meconium. When I told her that blind intubation with a rigid plastic tube could cause laryngospasm, she simply didn't believe me.

All babies delivered vaginally are born with some degree of cerebral edema—obviously the longer and more difficult the labor the greater the degree of edema. Someone once said that being born is about the equivalent of boxing three rounds with Mohammed Ali. At birth, after a clear airway is established, a newborn should be kept warm and snug in a quiet environment with subdued light and carefully observed for any genetic or developmental anomalies that might not have been immediately apparent at birth. The practice of promptly putting the baby to the mother's breast and challenging it to start nursing is, I think, unfair. It has never been shown that a newborn is hungry. Suckling is instinctive but the process of eating is learned behavior. "Bonding" is important as are the benefits of colostrum, but both can wait an hour or two. Bonding is not an all-or-none phenomenon in the first minutes of life and colostrum isn't going anywhere. When I was last practicing medicine, the contemporary vogue, promulgated by natural childbirth enthusiasts, of taking a newborn infant who one minute is in a very secure environment and in the next is thrust more or less violently into a hostile one, and offering it to the mother to begin nursing, may appeal to the parents but I'm not so sure it's good for the baby. For months, the infant has been warm, wet, and secure; but then it suddenly finds itself in a cold, dry, noisy, and brightly lit place.

Furthermore, the infant is about to undergo the most profound phys-iologic changes of its existence—changes that natural childbirth enthu-siasts in my time were either unaware of or chose to ignore. With the first breath and the clamping of the umbilical cord, the entire circulatory system of the baby essentially reverses itself. The foramen ovale undergoes physiologic closure, the ductus arteriosus, which is vital in intrauterine life, becomes irrelevant and begins the process of closure, and the lungs, for-merly dependant on maternal oxygen via the umbilical artery, immediately begin processing atmospheric oxygen for the first time. All of these chang-es occur naturally in a healthy infant, but in the first thirty minutes or so of life, careful observation is essential to be sure that the baby is healthy. Meanwhile, the obstetrician—after assuring that the baby's airway is un-obstructed—should busy himself with the third stage of labor, the delivery of the afterbirth. Mismanagement of the third stage can lead to the final greatest hazard in childbirth (i.e., after toxemia and infection), maternal hemorrhage. Again, in the vast majority of cases, problems are rare and there are reliable drugs available to aid the process, but should the after-birth become retained or "trapped," there is an immediate threat to the mother's safety.

As much as I supported the concept of natural childbirth for decades, I've never been convinced that prenatal classes have sufficiently stressed all these inconvenient facts. Enthusiasm by the laity for impermanent fads that come and go have been the curse of medical practice, in all probability, since the time of Hippocrates.

A final assault on what I knew to be good obstetric practice was the prevailing attitude of the members of the Pediatric Department who, for lack of a better word, were activists. Though none of the pediatricians had delivered a baby since medical school, they were convinced that they knew more about resuscitation of the newborn than did the obstetricians. They did not fully understand the Apgar scoring system and this, unfortunate-ly, led to some unpleasant confrontations and, occasionally, unnecessary complications which were entirely due to inappropriate intervention and over-treatment. When the pediatrician was actually in the delivery room, I deferred to him, but when he arrived ten or fifteen minutes after delivery and started doing meddlesome things, it drove me to distraction.

Our hospital commander, Colonel Mike Torma, was the third hospital commander I thoroughly respected. He was highly intelligent, a knowledgeable surgeon, and a natural leader. It was no surprise that he later became a brigadier general and the Strategic Air Command surgeon. He understood quality control and risk management better than any commander with whom I had ever worked and had a well-grounded interest in the mission and doctrine of the Air Force. Unfortunately, when the SAC ceased to exist in 1992, so did Mike's job, which forced his retirement. It was the Air Force's loss. He had all the prerequisites and qualifications to have been an excellent air surgeon general.

Life in America's heartland was pleasant, and there was much of interest in the St. Louis area. In southern Illinois, one could tour the smaller towns and enjoy many "mom and pop" antique stores, and we were able to add many pieces of Tea Leaf Ironstone china to our growing collection. We became instant fans of the St. Louis Cardinals and could get to Busch Stadium in thirty minutes. When the "interstate world series" of 1985 was played with Kansas City, our interest peaked. There are still those who do not believe that St. Louis lost.

The Lewis and Clark Museum of Western Expansion at the base of the Gateway Arch in St. Louis is probably the most complete exhibit in the country of the great expedition; it is remarkably rich in memorabilia of the epic journey. Whether or not my great grandfather, William Lewis, who came across the plains and settled in Petaluma, was the great grandson of John Lewis, Meriwether Lewis's uncle, is difficult to prove. Aunt Edith, who kept track of such things, insisted it was so. But my cousin, Robin De

Graf, a professional genealogist, who has spent decades researching the Hall-Lewis families, has never been able to prove the relationship.

Our condominium in O'Fallon was large enough to accommodate frequent guests and visitors. Kathy arrived on my birthday in 1985 with a kitten, Jaguar, who, after a rocky start health-wise, remained our pet and companion for thirteen years. "Jag" was always a little cranky, but was handsome and vain. I don't think he ever forgave us for de-clawing him, but we had no choice after he nearly destroyed the living room curtains chasing a moth. One trip to Columbia, Missouri, to visit Liz and Grant, was a near disaster when he went berserk in the car, probably because we were driving in very heavy, noisy freeway traffic.

Norm and Deb came for their traditional visit in 1986, this time by Amtrak from Seattle. Norm made it sound funny, but their trip was actually a nightmare. They were both overweight and his description of getting in and out of bed and getting caught in the webbing was hilarious. It wasn't until fifteen years later when we experienced the horrors of train travel in the U.S., on a trip from Denver to Portland, that I fully understood what they went through.

Life in O'Fallon was pleasant and we soon met compatible neighbors with whom we shared many enjoyable activities, dinners, and events at the base. Sunday brunch at the Officer's Club with Liz and Grant was a particular favorite and the golf course was challenging. Work at the hospital was neither difficult nor especially interesting. To my surprise, I began to experience diminishing interest in the work that had sustained me for thirty-five years. I found myself almost resenting those rare occasions when I was called to the hospital for an all-nighter. It was this realization that forced me into thinking about retirement not only from the military, which would soon be mandatory, but also from the practice of medicine. Whether it was my age, the changing nature of the specialty, the new technology with which I was increasingly unfamiliar, or a combination of all three, I couldn't be sure. But I was aware that my dynamic interest in obstetrics and

gynecology was waning. I never seriously considered reopening a practice
after military retirement. The idea of working hard just to pay tens of thousands of dollars for malpractice insurance seemed ridiculous. Moreover,
with a guaranteed retirement income, there were too many other things
I wanted to do and too many interests in academia that I had not had a
chance to pursue during the days when I was preparing for medical school.

The passage of time during our last year at Scott seemed to acceler-
ate as it never had before, and soon we were planning our future, which
would begin after the first of May, 1988. There was never any doubt that we
would return to Colorado, but we never considered returning to Colorado
Springs. With Clayt and Sherry in Greeley, and Ellen, David, and Kathy
in Denver, and John in Boulder, we decided Denver or one of its suburbs
would be best. In October 1987, we spent a week with David and Ellen,
met a realtor, and began house hunting. We looked at several properties
in the city and then heard of a new development south of Denver called
Castle Pines. Homes in Castle Pines Village were too expensive, but those
in the adjacent Castle Pines North were not. After reviewing available lots
and many architectural styles, we were attracted to an enclave called The
Retreat. The imaginative way the builders, McStain Enterprises, had plot-
ted the lots and situated the houses on them, avoiding the cookie-cutter
look of so many developments, appealed to us. The home prices were in our
range, and we soon decided on a floor plan on a well-situated lot with an
unobstructed view to the west. We were advised that the house could be
available by April 1988. For the next few months, we were kept up to date
on every detail of construction with snapshots taken by David and Ellen.
The view from the back of the house of the rolling scrub-oak covered hills
and the distant foothills of the front range of the Rockies, would remain
unobstructed permanently.

Castle Pines North had all the advantages we had hoped for. It was
near enough to Denver so that we could enjoy all the cultural advantages,
music, museums, and restaurants, but far enough away so that we could
enjoy the clean air, the wildlife, the quiet, and the pristine beauty of the

country. At this writing, we have never had cause to regret the decisions we made in 1987.

The last few weeks at Scott flew by and my retirement date was set for May 1, 1988. I took my accrued terminal leave the month of April so that we could make final decisions on the décor of the house—paint colors, tile colors, floor coloring, and the like. Our house closing was accomplished the first week of April and the house was to be ready for occupancy any time thereafter. I had completed out-processing in March and was amazed to learn of a stroke of great good luck when I talked to the clerk in charge of retirement pay and allowances. In 1945, when we were discharged from wartime active duty, we were routinely asked if we wished to stay in the Reserves. Since no one thought, at that time, there would be another war in our lifetime and because the inactive reserve did not require any commitment to train so many days or week-ends per year, there did not seem to be any reason not to stay in the reserve component. Therefore, all the years between 1945 and 1954, in conjunction with my twenty-plus of active duty, counted for pay purposes. So instead of receiving fifty percent basic pay as a colonel, my retirement pay was to be seventy-five percent, which made a difference of tens of thousands of dollars over the years. Thus, the most astute financial move I ever made was done without planning or thought.

My retirement ceremony at Scott was formal, somewhat unexpected, and not without emotion. I was awarded the Meritorious Service Medal and discovered I was the last of the thousands of young men who went through pilot training in World War II (from 7 December 1941 to 14 August 1945) to retire from the Air Force. I was not the last combat crew member, however. That honor went to my old friend Tom Cock, when he retired in 1990. As we left Scott a few days later, the message at the main gate was, "Thank you and good luck, Colonel Dinmore, on your retirement." And so ended the last chapter of my military career, which, altogether, spanned forty-five years.

In retrospect, I enjoyed it all tremendously. I met countless bright, dedicated, outstanding people; I had traveled, experienced different cultures, and never regretted for a second the decision to leave private practice in 1979. Practicing medicine in the military offers unique professional freedom. I was able to function to the best of my ability, without the worry of malpractice litigation or the maddening interference in medical decisions by insurance companies. In general, I found the military was about ten years ahead of private practice in the critical areas of quality control and risk management. Additionally, the disparity in income is largely off-set by retirement benefits as well as the freedom from worry about the business aspects of private practice. Though I knew I would miss many of the customs and traditions of military service, both Eileen and I faced the future with optimism and hope.

Eileen, Norm, and Deb
England 1978

Heli and Gordon Gray, Eileen and Me
Air Force Academy, 1960

Me, Walt and Ann Hurd, Eileen
Vandenberg Air Force Base, 1980

Eileen, Ted and Phyllis Marvis, Tom and Aria Cock
Alsace, 1982

Russ "Guppy" and Cecily Armentrout

Eileen with Bill and Betty Lilly
Charlottesville, 1993

At the Captain's Table on the QE2

Eileen and Me
Captain's Dinner aboard the QE2
August 4, 1985

VII
1988 AND BEYOND

Moving into our new home in Castle Pines North was easy. After four moves in nine years, we were getting good at it and this time we had Ellen, David, Kathy, and John helping. Landscaping went well, and I decided to build a large deck extending from the lower level of the house out into the garden because the larger the deck, I cleverly reasoned, the less grass there would be to mow. Building the deck, all seven hundred and fifty square feet of it, kept me busy through the summer and into the fall. In the years to come, we would use all of it for parties and barbecues. Though the original plan for the house included three bedrooms, we eliminated one of them, choosing, rather, to make a large family room with enough space for a pool table, couches and chairs for the TV, and enough room for bookshelves. At last, after nine years, all our books were unpacked and put away.

Our first house guests were Walt and Ann Hurd and they were enthusiastic about the house and its location overlooking the scrub oak and rolling hills of Castle Pines. We were to see them a year later when the 349th Troop Carrier Group had its thirty-fourth reunion in Colorado Springs. Although I have mixed feelings about reunions, whether they be school, military, or medical, it is interesting and even fun to reminisce with old friends about times past and to see who is still alive and who has led an interesting life. But it is sometimes shocking to see what time, stress, and disability can do to people one remembers in the prime of their lives. Of the many reunions we have attended over the years, a few stand out as being especially enjoyable. One of the best was the fiftieth reunion of the Punahou class of '41. All of Honolulu seemed to be involved in the gala that was presented honoring the school and alumni.

After the first year in our new home, with the deck built and we comfortably settled in, I had time to study current events, philosophy, and the contemporary political scene. I began to think about pursuing the study of law. Before making a commitment or applying to law school, I thought it would be a good idea to take some undergraduate pre-law courses at Arapahoe Community College. I also wanted to take some classes in subjects that I had not had time for in the 1940s. So, for the next three years, I registered for courses in political science, anthropology, economics, philosophy, and four law courses—an introductory survey, torts, property law, and contracts.

The quality of the teaching at Arapahoe Community College was excellent and as good as any I remembered as an undergraduate at Hawaii and the University of Virginia. The survey law course was so interesting that it motivated me to go on with three more. Torts and contracts were fascinating but property law was a little dull. My many talks about civil litigation with David, who by 1989 had become a successful plaintiff's attorney, were especially motivating. After three years, I did learn two things of fundamental importance: first, I lacked the passion and commitment necessary for law school, and second, I did not have the turn of mind to think like a lawyer. It seemed to me that prosecutors and plaintiff's attorneys pursued truth and justice as it is generally perceived by the layman, but that defense lawyers are more interested in the process of the law. I once heard a famous defense lawyer on television say that he did not care whether his client was guilty or not and did not want to know. His sole concern was mounting the best possible defense. This is commendable and consistent with our constitutional principles. But after a lifetime in a profession that demanded one be unsatisfied with anything less than scientifically arrived at facts as "truth," I doubted that I could ever be content with anything as esoteric as "the process" being an end unto itself, nor could I feel content about someone I knew to be guilty going unpunished.

I thoroughly enjoyed all my other courses. Political science was great fun. The text was written by a moderate conservative, John Q. Wilson, but taught by a moderate liberal, like myself, so it was a well-balanced course.

Our teacher in economics was an amusing ex-stockbroker from New York and he made the "dismal science" entertaining. But the highlight of the course was the text, *The Worldly Philosophers*. It is a classic that has been enjoyed by students for decades. I enjoyed anthropology as much as any liberal arts course I ever studied. A few years later, after reading two books by Jared Diamond, I realized that I could have been very content had I made anthropology a career. Philosophy, too, was interesting, as was the teacher—up to a point. Contemplating the age old questions of good vs. evil, man's relationship with God, etc., was good clean fun. But when I learned that our teacher, by his own description, had been a troubled teenager who "found God" and became a "born-again" Christian (whatever that is), I began to lose interest. But, exposing one's self to the thinking of St. Augustine, Descartes, Pascal, and some of the moderns, especially John Hick, was challenging and worthwhile.

Many years before, in the 1960s, I was interested in the works of Baruch Spinoza, especially his *Ethics*; so, in studying philosophy, my interest in the work of this kindly ascetic was rekindled. Reading and understanding Spinoza, even the best translations, is not easy, and in trying to comprehend his methodology, I relied heavily on Joseph Ratner, Kenneth Brown's translation of Chïam Perelman, Will Durant, the Encyclopedia of Philosophy, and others.

Spinoza was born into the Jewish community of Amsterdam in 1632. Like so many teachers who challenge orthodoxy, he came to be reviled, feared, and was ultimately excommunicated. One only needs to recall the fates of Jesus Christ, Mahatma Gandhi, and Martin Luther King for parallels. The Jews in the Netherlands of the seventeenth century were accepted without violent persecution, but they were expected to be quite circumspect in their behavior. Anyone, Jew or Gentile, who questioned the status quo by espousing doctrines thought to be heretical, was not tolerated. To paraphrase Ratner, Spinoza's philosophic intent was to establish ethics on a thoroughly tested, scientific foundation; and geometry, the exemplar of all mathematical thought, embodied the highest scientific ideal. Even though the method of geometry with its propositions, theorems, and axioms may not be the perfect one to define God, nature, and man, it is certainly more rational than accepting, on faith, the unprovable dogmas of Catholicism or Judaism.

Having studied Catholic dogma, I am aware of its beauty—and of its cruelty. It has always been disconcerting to me that the Church promulgates clericalism, anti-intellectualism, and parochialism (for the laity), and the bizarre notion that poverty is somehow ennobling to the human spirit. Nonetheless, if one accepts certain preposterous tenets—the virgin birth, miracles, the mystery of transubstantiation, the ascension, and papal infallibility among them—there is perfect logic to the dogma. I have never understood, as a Christian is supposed to, the necessity of believing that Jesus Christ is divine. His teachings of love, forbearance, humility, and tolerance are valid no matter how or by whom he was conceived but, as Bernard Shaw once said, He taught a message that the world has never quite learned, nor quite forgotten. Many Christians apparently think of God as an anthropomorphic entity, probably a middle-aged, bearded, powerful, white male residing in Heaven someplace, directing the affairs of man and the universe. This notion is an obvious affront to common sense. Rationalism is far more challenging and, since man has only one advantage over other animals—his mind—he has only one obligation—to use it. Whether the mind of man will ever be capable of understanding all the mysteries of the universe is moot, but there is no reason for him not to keep trying.

To Spinoza, man is part of nature, and nature is governed by exact, eternal, and immutable laws. Thus it must be possible to determine with exactitude man's relevance in the cosmos. Since God and nature are one, divine revelation becomes unnecessary and the concept of the supernatural—something greater than nature itself—blasphemous. Some have said that rationalism leads inevitably to a belief in predestination when, in fact, it does nothing of the sort. Man, as a part of nature, is perfectly free to make mistakes, violate the laws of nature, and do evil. The most appealing aspect of rationalism is that it permits one to believe that the mind of man, potentially, has the capability of discovering the mysteries of the universe. I much prefer that challenge than to simply surrender to the notion of a perfect, all powerful, omniscient father figure. Man has learned much already. We know when the universe started, give or take a few million years, and possibly how. Learning why it was created will take a little longer.

Moses and the many other biblical scribes of a few thousand years ago were learned, spiritual men whose collected work, the Bible, is interesting as history, perhaps valuable as a guide to morals, and beautiful as literature—though the archaic language of the King James version makes it difficult for me to read. But because it was written by fallible men, no more intelligent than we, to believe every word is the literal truth is ridiculous. To believe it is "the word of God" takes faith, and "having faith," to me, is not necessarily a virtue. Accepting any doctrine solely on faith requires neither initiative, nor intelligence, nor curiosity. The biblical scribes of the Old Testament, over the centuries, who may or may not have been men of great intellect, were doing their best to record history as they had heard it from their forebears and, coincidentally, were seeking to direct men and women into leading virtuous lives. I've heard it said, but I do not know by whom, "what a book they might have written had they had even a rudimentary knowledge of modern science." Finally, the biblical injunction that "man is made in the image of God," is a conceit that I do not necessarily believe. Why should he be?

As for my own beliefs, I revere nature, the power of the sea, the majesty of the mountains, the diversity of plant and animal life, cosmology, particle physics, and the ability for man to think. All of these things fill me with awe and inspire me. I have spent a professional lifetime studying one small aspect of nature—human reproductive physiology—and am aware of how much more there is to learn. I also believe in the ethics of the recorded teachings of Jesus but have very little patience with man-made institutions that often interpret His teachings to further their own ends. Spending millions of dollars on magnificent churches so that parishioners can spend an hour on Sunday contemplating good and evil is, to me, obscene when one considers how much poverty and misery there exists in the world. Jesus preached an imperishable philosophy in open fields without costumes, trappings, or rituals. If someone were to ask me if I believed in God, I would first ask them to define what they meant. Usually such a question means, *Do you believe in my conception of God?* If, as Spinoza taught, God and nature are one, then I most certainly do believe in God; and if asked if I were a Christian, I would say that I was because I know of no more ethical premise than Jesus' teachings.

However, a belief in an afterlife eludes me. I think to promote Jesus' philosophic message—that believers would be with him in Heaven—as *literal* truth is a promulgation by ordinary men aimed to assuage the wretchedness of life on earth for most people for most of recorded history. It has only been in the past hundred years that man has seen a measure of success in the triumph over pain, hunger, disease, and, in parts of the world, grinding, soul-destroying poverty. Humanity would be much better served by disseminating scientific progress than by perpetuating fairy tales of saints and devils or Heaven and hell. Even if there was such a place as Heaven, I'm not at all sure that I would want to spend eternity happy, satisfied, and unchallenged. An eternity of bland pleasantness would, I think, be insufferably dull. Each person's uniqueness, or soul, is locked in their DNA, the product of their forebears, and is passed on to their progeny. Their DNA is their immortality and the end of life for an individual is just that and no more. However, contrary to Shakespeare, I believe that the evil men do is (oft) interred with their bones but the good men do lives after them. Surely the legacies of nature's noblemen—the great teachers and ethicists—are more significant and enduring than are the legacies of evil men.

Early in 1993, I responded to a questionnaire from the Air Force seeking physicians to help in the gynecology outpatient clinic after normal duty hours at the Air Force Academy Hospital. Schoolwork was not so demanding that I could not afford three or four hours three evenings a week doing the sort of work that I had been doing for decades. There was, however, one requirement that I lacked, which was skill at colposcopy and colposcopic-directed cervical biopsies. To become proficient, I enrolled in a course offered by the Planned Parenthood Clinic in Denver. After a three week learning period, I felt I was ready to attend eight or ten Air Force dependents each evening.

After a year's experience in the clinic, I was able to compare the new procedures with the old. For years, the precise method of collecting Pap smears as taught by Dr. Traut, the use of Schiller stains, step biopsies with adequate instruments, radial electro-cauterizations, and cone biopsies had worked well for me. There are perhaps advantages to colposcopy of which I am not aware, but they did not become obvious. In many years of practice, I never saw a cervical cancer develop in a patient that I attended at regular intervals. Though one person's experience is not conclusive, neither should it be ignored.

After one year at the Academy Clinic, I was becoming concerned and dissatisfied with the quality control aspect of my duties. Ostensibly, we were to see only healthy individuals for routine check-ups, but not a week went by that there were not two or three individuals who presented with worrisome signs and symptoms. I had no admitting authority, and if I thought someone presented with symptoms that demanded emergency care, I had to summon the on-call Air Force physician. This did not happen often, but there were too many close calls, and I was concerned. There was no available diagnostic X-ray, and laboratory back-up was limited to routine blood counts and urinalyses. Accordingly, I decided not to apply for a second year. Coincidentally, I was advised I was not going to be invited to return for a second year by the doctor who ran the program because they wanted the services of a younger physician. I was satisfied, even relieved, at this turn of events and decided to terminate all my medical duties permanently and irrevocably.

During the 1990s, I became increasingly aware that I was developing the classic signs and symptoms of prostatic hypertrophy. I knew what the trouble was and carefully monitored the symptoms with biannual physical exams and PSA tests. The PSA was gradually rising but not at an alarming rate. Finally, in 1994, feeling ill and very much out of sorts, I consulted with my physician, who ordered me into the hospital immediately.

I had developed an acute obstructive uropathy, felt very weak, and was profoundly anemic. After catheterization and two days of rest, I was sent home with medication to prepare for surgery in about six weeks. Almost immediately, with the in-dwelling catheter, I began to feel better. In six weeks, my serum creatinine was nearly normal and the anemia much improved, so I felt fit for surgery. The morning after admission, I was taken to the operating room for the removal of a large, benign adenoma. It was to be done under epidural anesthesia. Sitting on the operating table, I could feel the anesthesiologist pressing on and preparing my lower back when I heard the dreaded words, "Oh no!" I knew immediately what had happened—a wet tap with a large caliber needle. I was placed in the supine position, given a general anesthesia, and the operation proceeded. I awoke in some discomfort but less than I had anticipated and my surgeon, Dr. Noel Stanky, advised me that a very large benign adenoma had been removed, that the operation had gone well, and that only one unit of blood replacement was required.

My post-operative course was uneventful and I was sent home four days after surgery. It was then that the real discomfort began—a post-spinal tap headache. I had had patients in the past who had complained of this misery but was never aware of how incapacitating it could be. The post-operative pain was nothing by comparison. The constant, pulsating headache was unrelieved by various positions, from supine to Trendelenberg, and several conventional pain killers. The anesthesiologist was sympathetic and supportive, but the fact that he had not had a misadventure like that in years didn't help much. Finally, after two weeks, the pain subsided and I began to feel better than I had in months.

Contemplating the future, I gave up the idea of law school as well as any more college courses. I had taken all that interested me and was quite content to catch up on several new books and to begin a little writing—a memoir of my mother. I collected all her mini-essays, poems, and the many writings of others that she had admired well enough to jot down. I collected fifty or sixty pages, had them bound in a loose-leaf jacket, and sent the book to the family and those close friends who remembered her.

Following that project, I began pursuing an interest in model building that had always been a hobby. I found a source for highly-detailed models of historic ships, and for the next several years built models of James Cook's HMS *Endeavour*, the USS *Constitution*, Charles Darwin's HMS *Beagle*, the famous HMS *Bounty*, and finally, the most ambitious project of all, Nelson's flagship at Trafalgar, the HMS *Victory*. All of these took months to finish. The *Victory* took almost a year. But altogether, building the model ships and reading the books associated with the models were thoroughly engrossing projects.

In the spring of 1996, we began making plans to attend our fifty-fifth Punahou class reunion, see Norm and Deb, and this time, take all the Porters for a week at the Hale Koa Hotel in Waikiki. There is no better armed-forces facility, or one with more amenities than the Hale Koa. Matt and Brad loved the four interconnected swimming pools, the proximity to the beach, the snack bars, and the two excellent dining rooms. The highlight of the trip for the boys was snorkeling at Haunama Bay. It was a marvelous vacation in all respects, and Liz's foresight in bringing many tubes of sun screen lotion saved our pale little Coloradans from serious sunburn.

The alumni activities at Punahou were, as usual, fun and brought back many memories of years past. The luau was as it always had been and I found I still enjoyed poi, lau lau, and lomi lomi salmon. Eileen's dinner was also as it always had been—iced tea, fresh pineapple, and a small piece of cake. The luau tent covered most of Alexander Field on campus and it was packed. The reunion lacked the excitement of 1991, but it was still fun to greet old classmates who, for the most part, seemed to be in good shape.

Norm and Deb's hospitality was as warm and thoughtful as ever and we were relieved to see that Deb had come through the radiation and chemotherapy for lung cancer in good spirits; however, though it remained unspoken, we all knew that the prognosis was not good. Sadly, there was a recurrence of the tumor and Deb died four months later in October. I went back to the Islands for her memorial service primarily to give Norm a little moral support. My last memory of Deb was seeing her enjoy a big dinner at one of their favorite restaurants, the Swiss Inn, in Aina Haina. Norm's health began to deteriorate in early 1997, and I returned that summer for a final visit. He was frail, suffering from heart and kidney failure, and except for bits and pieces, his memory was gone. In a man who had performed *King Lear* not so many years before, this was hard to accept. He was well attended by two practical nurses but more importantly, by John's son Peter. Peter and Norm had a virtual father-son relationship that was very touching. I returned home, and in October, on the day that would have been Norm and Deb's forty-fourth anniversary, he died in his sleep. As Peter said, "He and Deb had a final date."

Though Norm was not himself during my visit, I'm glad I made that final visit because he still recognized me and even shared a few memories. As my mother once said, Norm had a rare gift for friendship not given to many people. In fact, we never had a more loyal friend. Within a year, his considerable estate was settled and he left the majority of it to John and Nini's five and our six children, a final gift of uncommon generosity to our family, a family that he always considered his. For over fifty years, there was no one with whom we shared more good times, laughter, and interesting experiences. For twenty-five years, he and Deb had sent us beautiful little gold and silver snowflake and star ornaments from the New York Metropolitan Museum of Art, the last one arrived during the Christmas holidays. He had somehow remembered that last parting gift.

Nineteen ninety-eight was a year characterized by some new health problems, travel, visits with old friends, and, finally, excitement. In the spring, I noted that Eileen was developing a tremor in both hands, which was especially obvious when she was holding a newspaper but which tended to disappear when she was sewing. There was also a change in her posture when walking. A consultation with a neurologist confirmed the fact that she was showing the early signs of Parkinson's disease. She was started on a dopamine agonist, which improved the symptoms for the next five years. However, I noted a short-term memory-loss problem at about the same time which was not affected one way or the other by medication, which grew worse, almost imperceptibly, over the years.

In April, we visited Margaret and Karen in their new home in Sonora. I had never seen the "mother lode" country of California and it was most interesting to see the area and the several small communities where the great gold rush of the mid-nineteenth century began. While there, we spent one day in Yosemite, enjoyed lunch in the famous Ahwahnee Lodge, and drove through a blizzard getting in and out of the park. The many little towns in the vicinity of Sonora were rich in antique shops offering a lot of early California memorabilia.

In May 1998, we returned to Charlottesville for our forty-fifth medical school class reunion. About half our class of seventy members was on hand, and it was enjoyable catching up on all their activities since our last reunion. Seeing Barby and Oscar for the first time since Honolulu in 1991 was great fun. We had lunch at their club, toured the developing wine country in Albemarle County, and drove by the many familiar neighborhoods of so many years before. The Thorups seemed in excellent health and as interested in current events, hobbies, books, art, and travel as ever. We drove out to Chinquapin and were pleased to see how well the grounds and house had been maintained over the years. A few days later, we drove to White Stone for a three-day visit with the Armentrouts, which included a trip to Norfolk and to the Maritime Museum, where we saw the greatest collection of model ships in the country. We ended the trip with a return to Washington and pleasant visits with Kent and Shirley Thorup and Bill and Robin DeGraf.

In October, on the spur of the moment, we decided to go with David and Ellen to see Ryan's college environment for the next few years at Middlebury, Vermont. Never having seen that part of New England, we were tremendously impressed with the beauty of the fall colors, the tidy little towns, the friendly people, and the charm of the Woodstock Inn. Early fall is without doubt the best time to visit Vermont. The locals say that by then, the damage of the preceding winter has been repaired and the harsh winter to come is still several weeks in the future.

In November, a few weeks after we returned, we were saddened to hear of Yale Lewis's death. Another old friend of over sixty years was gone. Yale's last few years had been very difficult and plagued with chronic ill health, incapacitating back problems, and finally, macular degeneration. Little by little all the things he loved doing—travel, golf, and even gin rummy—were taken from him. Although we hadn't seen Bobby and Yale as often as we had in the past, Yale's generosity and kind heart were imperishable memories. His wartime exploits, typical of the "greatest generation," included the award of the Silver Star for heroism. He was involved in every campaign in the Pacific that the Air Force was called upon to support, from Guadalcanal to the bombing raids over Japan, and like every member of the armed forces I ever knew, those who saw the most of war talked the least about it. Whenever he did, it was always some amusing anecdote. We were once talking about dyslexia and he surprised me by saying, in a very off-hand way, that he had that problem. I don't know to this day if he was precisely accurate, but if he was, it certainly never compromised his success in college, the military, or in business. In 1941, when he and Bobby became officially engaged and I first met him, he soon became my role model. Later, when my children came to know his war record, his daring exploits at the gaming tables, his enthusiasm for golf, and his considerable success in the oil business, he became their hero as well.

The final event of a busy year came on Christmas Eve. As we arrived at Ellen's for dinner, we found her standing at the front door, telephone in hand, almost screaming, "I don't believe it! You've got to be joking!" It was Clayt calling from Greeley with the news that he had just won the Colorado State Lottery. I don't think, until that moment, I ever believed that real people ever won lotteries. Nineteen ninety-eight had not been the best year for Clayt, Sherry, and the children, so this turn of events could not have happened to a nicer person or at a more opportune time.

During the 1990s, particularly the last five years of the decade, the country was mesmerized by the difficulties of President William Jefferson Clinton—the most gifted politician of the age, and one of the most intelligent men ever to hold the office of the Presidency as well as one who inspired as much hate among his enemies as admiration from his admirers. His enemies loathed him with a deep, visceral, almost pathological intensity not seen since the days of Franklin Roosevelt. They presented manufactured "evidence" (never facts) that he was a rapist, a drug dealer, and even that he was complicit in the "murder" of one of his best friends, Vincent Foster. If there was not, in Hillary Clinton's words, a "vast right-wing conspiracy" against him, there was certainly a cabal of conservatives who sought to destroy his presidency from the day of his inauguration. The so-called Arkansas Project, largely financed by the infamous Richard Mellon Sciafe and supported by right-wing, homophobic, segregationists in Arkansas, was organized with the goal of impeaching Clinton long before Paula Jones and Monica Lewinski were ever heard of.

Unfortunately, the president's self-indulgence proved to be his undoing. His enemies cleverly politicized a private indiscretion and constructed a perjury trap that led to a vote of impeachment. Though found not guilty by the Senate, his legacy was poisoned. He was put in the position of either being a liar if he evaded personal questions or a cad if he answered them. None of his activities ever threatened the republic, as had Richard Nixon's, but were enough to give his enemies all the ammunition they needed to defame him. "Greatness" is a word that can be applied to only two presidents in the twentieth century—the two Roosevelts; but no one can deny that President Clinton was the leader of the most successful administration since Franklin Roosevelt.

President Clinton's enemies invariably dwell on "character" and his apparent lack of it, as demonstrated by his relationships with women. But if he lost "the moral authority to lead" by his dalliances, then so too did Thomas Jefferson with Sally Hemings, Franklin Roosevelt with Lucy Mercer, Dwight Eisenhower with Kay Summersby, Douglas MacArthur with his Eurasian mistress, and John Kennedy with his many affairs. The qualities of leadership and character have little to do with sex. The most disgusting aspect of President Clinton's critics was their hypocrisy since many were guilty of the same offenses—Dan Burton, Newt Gingrich, Bob Barr, Henry Hyde, *et al.*, had all had similar indiscretions—and worse.

Character has to do with courage and steadfastness to core beliefs, no matter what the outcome. In my opinion, just about all the men who have occupied the Oval Office who have simply shown up for work every day—whether a ridiculous figure like Calvin Coolidge or a psychologically disturbed creature like Richard Nixon—have demonstrated some degree of courage and steadfastness. The fate of the nation and even the world is a responsibility that few men want and even fewer can handle successfully. A man's relationship with women may reflect on his maturity, wisdom, and judgment but not necessarily on his character. Some of the self-appointed (conservative) moralists of the contemporary scene—Bill Bennett, Cal Thomas, and even the loathsome Jerry Falwell—never miss an opportunity to politicize their conception of character deficiencies.

The turmoil of the Clinton years, including the farcical Ken Starr investigation, culminated in the remarkable presidential election of 2000. It was the most confused event in modern political history. The popular winner was denied the office by a conservative majority in the United States Supreme Court in one of the most disgraceful episodes in the history of the court. All that can be said of this episode is that politicians have long memories and that conservatives will one day rue their temporary triumph.

I have tried to be a liberal Democrat all my adult life, and there have been some very lonely times. As a member of the medical community and of the military, I found few like-minded liberals. Republican Party professionals have a penchant for finding and running for office citizens who, allegedly, disavow, distrust, dislike, and even hate government, which, it seems to me, borders on lunacy. Mainstream Republicans have a talent for promoting mediocrities for public office and are neither impressed by, nor trusting of, great intellect. There have been a few exceptions: Theodore Roosevelt was brilliant; Herbert Hoover and Richard Nixon were highly intelligent but the former did not understand the economic forces of the time and the latter was psychologically disturbed; President Eisenhower was a gifted soldier, an effective president, but a political anomaly.

It is the reactionary, far-right conservative, primarily, but not exclusively, of the Republican Party, that menace the country. Countless fair-minded, mainstream Republicans have helped Democrats improve and pass social legislation that has benefited most of the people. But it is a fact that since 1900, right-wing, militant conservatives have not conceived, promulgated, or caused to be passed into law a single piece of legislation that has benefited the majority of Americans. (Tax cuts are not social legislation.) Conservatives fought the Sherman anti-trust laws, the graduated income tax, the Internal Revenue Service, the League of Nations, the New Deal, Social Security, the Marshall Plan, the United Nations, integration of the Armed Services, and the Civil Rights movement. Conservatives do not dispute the point, they proudly proclaim it. Conservatives are unable to grasp the fact that there is a causal relationship between the social legislation passed in the twentieth century, which they invariably refer to as "creeping socialism," and the fact that the United States emerged from the two most destructive wars in world history, and the most devastating depression in its own history, as the world's only superpower.

One contemporary conservative spokesman, Rush Limbaugh, who allegedly has a following of several million people, though a despicable, cruel, ignorant, and uneducated buffoon, did precisely enunciate the fundamental difference between right-wing conservatives and the rest of the body politic (middle-of-the-roaders and liberals) by stating: "It's not the job of government to help people." This remarkable statement sums up the conservative philosophy and rejects that part of the preamble to the United States Constitution that states, among other things, that the business of government is to "promote the general welfare." Committed conservatives ridicule liberals as "muddle-headed, bleeding-heart do-gooders." Conservatives apparently prefer hard-headed, cold-hearted do-badders. Conservative stand-patters have always been with us. Even at the birth of our country, more than half the population preferred the *status quo* with England and considered our national heroes troublesome radicals. The only worthwhile function conservatives serve is to modulate ill-considered progressive legislation since not everything new is automatically workable.

There are, however, among the far-right conservatives, some who are more than a menace, they are dangerous. They are the ones that invariably have simple-minded solutions to complex problems—the ones of whom Voltaire said, "Beware the simplifier." If the twentieth century has taught us anything, it is that complex problems are not easily solved. The chaos in Germany following World War I—political instability, hyperinflation, unemployment, and despair—was fertile ground for the rantings of an Adolf Hitler. His solution was "simple." The mythical "pure Aryans" had been betrayed by the Communists and the Jews, so his solution was to liquidate them. The world then watched as an erudite, civilized culture degenerated into the madness of Nazism. It is this "us" versus "them," the "good" versus the "bad" mentality that is antithetical to democracy. It is seen today in "good" conservatives versus the "bad" liberals. The essence of fascism is not economic or political, it is philosophic. The crypto-fascists of today do not believe in intelligent discourse, concession, or compromise, and they pose the greatest threat to our American traditions. I believe H. L. Mencken's dictum, "To every complex problem there is a simple solution—which is invariably wrong."

In December 1999, at a regular follow-up physical examination, my doctor noted a small irregularity in the prostate gland and a slight but significant rise in the PSA level. A biopsy revealed a well-differentiated cancer. The treatment options were expectancy, surgery, or radiation (brachytherapy). In view of my age and good general health, I chose the latter. As a pre-radiation step, I was given a testosterone-suppression hormone and definitive treatment scheduled for May 2000. The choice I made was influenced by the medical histories of two old friends—Walt Hurd and Tom Cock.

Walt's history was similar to mine. His obstructive uropathy, due to a benign growth, was treated surgically just as mine had been. But because of his work, he let careful follow-up visits slide by. Walt was chief of quality assurance at Lockheed, which was a big job requiring a great deal of travel, lecturing, and decision making for both the civilian and military aerospace industries. He remained well for five years and then when dressing one morning, he noted unilateral ankle swelling, which proved to be due to metastatic prostate cancer involving the lymph nodes of the groin. In spite of radiation and surgery, he was dead in a year.

Tom's history was remarkably the same, first a benign growth then a malignant one, though his choice of therapy, chemotherapy followed by external radiation, was complicated by unpleasant side effects. The lesson to be learned in all our cases is that proper treatment for a benign growth does not preclude the development of a malignant one later. Careful follow-up is essential. As to the choice of definitive treatment, it seemed to me that brachytherapy was the least likely to offer major complications. Both my surgeon and radiotherapist were of the opinion that it would replace radical surgery altogether in time. The insertion of seventy or eighty palladium pellets, under general anesthesia, is well-tolerated, requires no blood replacement, and avoids the hazards of major surgery. After four years, I have had no side effects and the PSA remains about 0.1. The only reaction to the entire treatment program that was annoying (to some people almost funny) were the intense hot flashes in response to the hormone shot I received pre-operatively. For years I had tried to help women who complained of peri-menopausal hot flashes (sympathetically, I hope), but I never realized how annoying they can be. Drenching night sweats were common for weeks. Just as a surgical procedure would make all surgeons wiser, so would a hormone shot or two make gynecologist more empathetic.

Before radiation treatment, Eileen and I traveled to Palm Springs to visit Penn and Nancy and the Marvises. I had not been to Palm Springs for sixty-five years—when Jack Cooper and I had spent our cowboy weekend. The place had undergone remarkable change with now more than a hundred golf courses in the valley. The Marvis's home in Rancho Mirage was lovely and seeing them was a treat, and, in spite of Phyllis's heart problems and Ted's back ailments, they were in good spirits and as much fun as ever. After three days in Rancho Mirage, we drove to La Quinta for three more days with Penn and Nancy and a round of golf at PGA West. The city of Palm Springs showed its age and was not as chic at it had been in the 1930s when it was a favorite retreat for the Hollywood stars, but it appeared to be trying hard for a renaissance. The area is ideal for the winter months, with near perfect weather, but playing golf is a virtual necessity for one to enjoy the complete ambiance of the community.

In the summer, Nancy and Penn visited us, and we had a good time showing them the Broadmoor, the Air Force Academy, and playing a round of golf at our course, The Ridge at Castle Pines. Penn had spent winters at Aspen and Vail but never had seen much of the Front Range.

After their visit, we, like the rest of the country, were plunged into the spectacle of the November 2000 elections. The results were the exact opposite of my predictions. Vice President Al Gore lost to George W. Bush—the Texas preppy-buckaroo (New Haven, Connecticut, out of Midland, Texas); Hillary Clinton won the Senate seat in New York; the

House of Representatives stayed Republican; and the Electoral College failed to reflect the will of the majority or the voters. So much for my political acumen.

To ease the disappointment of the election results, we rented a condominium at Vail for Thanksgiving and, in all, fourteen children and grandchildren were on hand for a memorable dinner. It was a huge success—so much so that we planned to do it again in two years.

After Christmas, we returned to Palm Springs for an encore visit with the Marvises and the Arnetts. It was even more fun the second time around. This time, Penn had passes for all of us to the Bob Hope Invitational golf tournament. It was, as usual, fascinating to watch the masters of the great game.

Planning for the summer became our next priority. We were undecided whether to choose the Punahou reunion or a bike tour through Tuscany with Margaret, Karen, Julie and a group of their friends. Finally, after studying the pros and cons of both, we did neither. A three thousand mile trip to Honolulu, absent Norm and Deb, for a luau neither of us was enthusiastic about, seemed impractical and a six thousand mile trip to Italy even less so. At our age, not having ridden bicycles for years, trying to peddle fifty kilometers a day for the better part of two weeks seemed too arduous to contemplate. We briefly considered renting a two-man Moped but decided against that as well. Renting a car and just tagging along behind the cyclist was another option, but matching wits with rural Italian drivers had very little appeal.

The Marvises had invited us to visit them at their summer home on the Oregon coast at Oceanside. Having just read Stephen Ambrose's, *Nothing Like It In The World*, which retraces the Union Pacific route over the mountains to California, it seemed like a worthwhile adventure. So, in a moment of madness, we decided to go by Amtrak from Denver to Portland via Sacramento.

It was a trip from hell and I found out why Amtrak is perpetually on the verge of bankruptcy. The problem is the lack of maintenance on the roadbed. At twenty miles an hour over the Rockies and the Sierras, the scenery was spectacular, but on the flat at seventy or more miles per hour, the ride was not only uncomfortable but downright dangerous. Schedules were meaningless. We were two hours late leaving Denver, two hours late leaving Sacramento, and two hours late arriving in Portland. At high-speed, reading is impossible, walking hazardous, and eating (very mediocre food) is like a scene out of a Three Stooges movie. Our compartment, advertised as "the ultimate in train travel luxury," was obviously designed by a deranged midget. There was no place to store a medium-sized suitcase. The wardrobe was six inches wide and twenty-four inches high and had no hangers. The shower and the commode were in a nineteen-inch square closet. To shower, one stood on the commode and rinsed with a removable shower head then risked breaking both elbows toweling off. With both berths made up for sleeping, there was so little room that if one wanted to pass another, one would have to exit into the companionway. The only positives were the spectacular scenery and the helpful people on the train crew doing their best to make an intolerable situation bearable.

The hospitality of the Marvises was as pleasant and thoughtful as ever and their part of the coast of Oregon was beautiful. We flew home on a clean, smooth, quiet airplane that departed and arrived precisely on time and vowed never again to complain about air travel. The food is better and airports are far more user-friendly than gloomy, old, dirty, cold train stations.

A few days after our return home, watching the *Today* show on television, I witnessed the events of September 11, 2001, as they happened. I could not believe what I saw. It was like watching a violent Hollywood movie with incredible special effects. To see those magnificent buildings collapse was beyond belief, as was the story as it unfolded over the next several hours. It was an act of such malignant fanaticism that it was beyond comprehension for a time. Nothing like it had ever occurred in the history of our country. In some ways it was comparable to the attack on

Pearl Harbor, but there were even more casualties and it was directed at helpless civilians, not military targets. I have never been convinced that the Al Qaeda perpetrators knew in advance the devastation that two airplanes could cause. I suspect they were thinking in terms of severe damage and a few hundred casualties but not the collapse of both towers of the World Trade Center and thousands dead. I've always wondered if the designers and builders of the towers, given the hypothetical, could have foreseen such devastation.

The United States, even when provoked, has been traditionally slow to anger, but the events of September 11, 2001, like Pearl Harbor, galvanized the nation instantly. But the problem was that the enemy, international terrorism, is amorphous. There is no one enemy, one country, one army, navy, or air force. The leaders are scattered throughout the world including, in all probability, our own country. We face an enemy like no other in our history. By comparison, Hitler's Germany and Hirohito's Japan were out-law states whose armed forces could be dealt with in conventional ways. The United States has always been able to rise to the occasion and it is our nature to deal with enemies quickly and decisively, but we have never had to deal with an entire culture disseminated throughout the world that despises our way of life, our material wealth, our ignorance of the teachings of Mohamed, and our perceived indifference to the misery of have-not nations. Militant Muslims are great haters; they've hated infidels, Jews, and Western Civilization for centuries. In the decades ahead, it is not yet certain that we will have the staying power to match their enmity and prevail over people who hate with such passion and who have hated for so long. Whether conventional victory over such people is even possible is not clear. A rapprochement, perhaps in decades, if we are imaginative, compassionate, and patient enough, and maintain overwhelming military superiority, will be the best that we can hope for.

One year after the tragedy in New York, the Bush administration be-gan saber rattling and talking of war in the near future against Iraq, justifying such talk by alleging that Iraq had a cache of weapons of mass destruction and that they would use them against U.S. citizens. By comparison, in 1962, when the world was on the verge of nuclear war with Russia, the Kennedy administration showed pictures at the United Nations that proved, without doubt, that nuclear missiles in Cuba were becoming operational—unequivocal evidence of a clear and present danger. That was sufficient. That should have been the kind of evidence to justify preventive war with Iraq. But the Bush "go-it-alone" foreign policy, without clear evidence of imminent danger, was short-sighted; starting the war without the unified support of our traditional allies proved to be disastrous. Pre-emptive war based on "coulds" or "mights" or "possibilities" led us into a quagmire from which there was no easy exit.

By late October 2001, even though the enormity of the 9/11 catastrophe had barely been absorbed by the national psyche, though it will never be forgotten, Eileen and I were invited to join Kathy and Annette for a week at their time-share condominium in Orlando and a visit to Disneyworld. Liz and her boys and Katherine Struthers made up a party of eight. We rented two cars at the airport in Orlando and headed for the park. We had not seen the place for twenty years and the enlargement and improvements were so many and so varied it was like seeing it for the first time. The place is really a work of genius. It is not only well maintained with imaginative crowd control but also remarkably free of flying insects. With billions of gallons of water, plenty of heat, and innumerable places to eat, I do not remember seeing a single fly or mosquito. I have no idea how this is accomplished. The children were enthralled by the array of amusements, thrill rides, countless presentations, parades, and diversions. We all felt the trip, which had actually been planned before 9/11, was therapeutic in light of recent events. We even felt a bit patriotic heeding the president's advice to carry on with our lives and the normal pleasures that Americans enjoy and not succumb to the kind of inertia that is sometimes seen in the aftermath of great tragedies.

Soon after our return from Florida, we were caught up in the spirit of the holidays. We were also considering a third trip to Palm Springs after the New Year. We had originally planned to fly to Phoenix, visit the family, and rent a car to drive to Palm Springs, but I developed an unpleasant bronchitis and we had to abort the trip after just three days in Phoenix. Soon the pleasant activities of summer—golf for me and gardening for Eileen—began again and we participated, though with perhaps a little less vigor than in the past.

Over dinner one night in May, I decided that it was an appropriate time for a week stay at the Hotel del Coronado in San Diego to celebrate our fifty-seventh wedding anniversary. It was a trip I had hoped to make one day ever since Eileen and I had spent our thirty-fifth anniversary at La Valencia Hotel in La Jolla in 1980. I thought it would be even more fun to invite as many of the children and grandchildren as could come to join us. In all, there were eighteen people in six rooms at the "Del" for five days. It was wildly extravagant but well worth it. The hotel is one of the last of the great resorts. Places like it—the Greenbrier, the Broadmoor, and Mackinac are not being replaced. Theme parks, golf courses, and tennis resorts are currently in vogue. The vacation was a great success and our mountain-raised young people were fascinated by the small surf and tidal marine life. The hotel was "Five Star" in every particular with great service, superb food, and an ambiance that lived up to its reputation as a playground for everyone from celebrities to heads of state for over one hundred-twenty years.

In the year that followed the trip to the Del, we lost three more old and dear friends. Oscar Thorup died of a recurring lymphoma in the fall of 2002, Guppy Armentrout died in the spring of 2003 with a very rare gastrointestinal stromal tumor, and Jim Gustafson died in the summer of 2003 with amyloidosis.

No one had a greater effect on my career choice than Oscar. He, more than anyone else, influenced my decision to attend the University of Virginia, and he and Barby, by putting us in touch with Jeff and Monica Baker, were the ones that enabled us to live at Chinquapin Hill for six years, the last two years of college and the four years of medical school. Oscar was one of those rare people whose interest in so many things—the arts, the sciences, sports, people, current events—was infectious. His brilliant mind more or less swept one along in an effort to keep pace.

Guppy and I could not have disagreed more on the questions of race relations and politics—he was as much a product of his up-bringing as I was of mine, so we just didn't discuss matters that might have ruptured our friendship. He was highly intelligent and well read, and a thoughtful, warm host, and we both loved each other's wives. I don't think he enjoyed anything more than conversation (with a good drink in hand), his hobbies, tennis, and sailing his beautiful boat.

Jim Gustafson, too, was a loyal friend and, though we didn't see each other again after he and Margaret divorced, we kept in touch. My fondest memories of Jim were countless games of golf and pleasant evenings with Margaret, Julie, and their many friends in Florida.

Final Thoughts

As I close this autobiography, I realize that I have often diverted from just a chronicle of what I, and we, have done during the last eight decades. From time to time I have written my thoughts on politics and religion, but nothing about the third leg of that triad, which, traditionally, one should avoid lest one alienate friends—sex. The reason for this omission is simply because I don't know very much about it. But of the two sexes, in general, I have always admired women more than men. Perhaps that is why I was so comfortable for so many years in the specialty of obstetrics and gynecology. I am certainly not an expert on the feminine mystique, but I do understand the male psyche. I think women are more admirable than men and more interesting. They are more stable, more well-balanced emotionally, tolerate physical pain more stoically, and react to stress with more maturity. As a gynecologist, I have heard hundreds of stories of marital discord and the fault in the vast majority of cases is male immaturity. Women are the care givers, the givers of life, and the nurturers; men are the hunter-gatherers and the warriors. The former is much more difficult than the latter.

Having seen my eightieth birthday, I face the fact, with equanimity, that there is a strong possibility that I have seen more birthdays than I will see. I have never feared death—which would be an awful way to have to live—but I do not particularly look forward to the process of dying. No one, of course, knows how and when that will happen; but no sane person looks forward to pain, disability, humiliation, embarrassment, or indignity. It was an ancient Greek who, when asked what manner of death he preferred replied, "A sudden one." I think there is much wisdom in that. I hope that when I "cross the river," to use Stonewall Jackson's quaint phrase, people I know and love will celebrate the occasion with a party or an old-fashioned wake with plenty to drink and plenty of traditional Irish music.

The greatest happiness in life is a steadfast, loyal wife and children who do you no dishonor or precede you in death; the greatest blessing in life is good health and a strong constitution; the greatest joy in life is derived from work that one loves and to which one devotes all of one's spiritual, physical, and intellectual gifts in the pursuit of excellence.

EPILOGUE
(2009)

Eileen's ten-year struggle with Parkinson's disease and related dementia ended early in the morning of June 1, 2007, five days after her eighty-third birthday. Although I was the primary caregiver for many years, I had lots of support as the two afflictions progressed. In the last five years of her life especially, I learned a good deal about Parkinson's disease, about dementia, and about myself.

Eileen's gifts were many and varied, and she gave meaning to the term domestic arts. She could mend or make anything with needle and thread or on her little portable Singer sewing machine that her mother had given us as a wedding present. When we were students in Virginia, she supplemented our modest income by making everything from clothes to draperies for our friends and neighbors, to alter cloths for the local church. Later she made most of the children's clothes and repaired a thousand rips and tears. In her later years she became interested in quilting and created many beautiful pieces.

If the expression "you are what you eat" is valid, then our children's good health is attributable to Eileen's innate knowledge of nutrition. She was a gifted nutritionist long before it became a vogue. She could assemble or create unforgettable meals out of almost anything and rarely had to consult a cookbook. Her "casserole cookery" was particularly memorable and many of her meals are still popular today with the girls and their families. Her special talent was seasoning food to perfection and, as a corollary, the same is true of her talent with table settings. She and her friend, Helen Smith, won the popular "Tournament of Tables" event twice in Colorado Springs in the 60s and 70s.

Eileen had artistic talent, which the responsibilities of parenting prevented her from fully developing. She had an excellent eye for color and painted many little still-lifes for friends that she often gave as Christmas presents. She was also a knowledgeable horticulturalist. With her close friends in the Hobby Garden Club of Colorado Springs, Eileen spent years tending and beautifying the grounds of the Colorado School for the Deaf and Blind.

In our many travels from Honolulu to Europe and back again, Eileen carefully researched the places we were to visit, which was a task I lacked the time to do. Without her studies ahead of time, we would not have seen the Fan Museum in Greenwich or the Medieval Crime Museum in Rothenberg or a hundred other places of special interest.

As a hostess, Eileen was unparalleled. We lived in many places and adapted to many cultures from Hawaii to Europe and had countless friends both in and out of the military and the medical communities. Her ability to put all sorts of people at ease in a welcoming environment was unique.

To witness all these attributes gradually stripped away by not one but two cruel diseases was difficult. I could not have dealt with this tragic progression without the support of old friends and, especially, our children, whose maturity and judgment, where mine might have failed, were invaluable. Of our sixty-two years together, only the last five and especially the last year-and-a-half were truly difficult and it is far better to dwell on the first sixty years which were full of joy, interest, and happiness.

In 1997, the first symptoms of Parkinson's disease—a tremor when she was reading the paper—became apparent; this was accompanied by a mild instability and loss of balance. In 1998, she tripped and fell in the garden and suffered a Colles fracture of the right wrist. Soon after, she was prescribed the principle medicine for Parkinson's, dopamine and a dopamine agonist, Mirapex. Coincidentally, I noticed what I later learned were the first signs of dementia—the early repetition of certain observations like the particular color of a house in the neighborhood or the size of a tree in the backyard and how much lumber I thought it would yield if it were milled. The repetitive nature of these observations was, at first, not alarming, and occurred once or twice a week. But when they began occurring two or three times a day it was obvious that something serious was happening. At this point, a well known drug, Aricept, was offered, but after six weeks of persistent nausea, it had to be stopped. About three years into her illness, it was obvious that she could no longer safely drive a car. Without discussing the matter, we (Elizabeth, Kathy, Ellen, and I) simply removed her car keys from her key ring. We did not want to hurt her feelings by making an issue of it and, happily, there really was none—though even in the last months of her life, she maintained that she "was a good driver." I had long since sold our second car, so there was no reason for her to drive.

As Eileen drifted into a more profound dementia, there were a few moments of despair and self-pity, but they were infrequent and fleeting. Only rarely would she say things like, "What's happening to me?" or "Why can't I remember...?"

As her condition deteriorated, I began reading what I could find about dementia, Alzheimer's disease, and related matters. Early on I learned that Alzheimer's is quite different than Parkinson's dementia (PD), although, from the point of view of the caregiver, there are similarities.

Eileen, until the last weeks of her life, rarely exhibited mood changes or depression. Psychologically she was "flat"—not necessarily cheerful nor necessarily depressed. She enjoyed family dinners, people, conversation, an occasional movie, and the activities associated with Christmas, Thanksgiving, and Halloween. She rarely complained of pain other than stiffness getting in and out of bed in the morning or out of a chair to walk. Once she became mobile, however, with or without a walker, there was little complaint of discomfort. Until the last few weeks of her life, she enjoyed food and sitting at the table with friends and family. In vain, I tried to find a monograph about the natural history of Parkinson's and especially what the end stages were apt to be. I never could find one.

The fact that "people with Parkinson's die with the disease not of it" is true. Many people with advanced Parkinson's fall and die of complications of their injuries; the father of one of Eileen's nurses simply choked to death on a bolus of food. There is apparently no specific end-stage. In only the last ten days of her life did Eileen have swallowing difficulties. I noticed that she would chew her food then discreetly put what was in her mouth into her napkin. Drinking fluids became possible only through a straw. If there is a typical end-stage of the disease, it is apparently a breakdown of primitive motor skills. To the extent that one disease, Parkinson's, aggravates the other, dementia, is unclear, but expert clarification would certainly be helpful to the layman.

The principal role of the caregiver is to maintain a non-threatening, safe environment. Though wandering away from home is a worrisome behavior in Alzheimer patients, it did not appear to be so in Eileen's PD. Only twice did she walk out of the house unexpectedly and unaccompanied and both times she was found within the hour. In the last year of her life, Parkinson's had made walking any considerable distance impossible. Offering too many choices to people with dementia is a mistake. Asking, "What would you like for dinner?" should be the simpler, "Do you want chicken or salad tonight?" And, "What would you like to wear?" should be "Do you want tan or blue slacks today?" And, "Is there anything you want to do today?" should be, "Shall we go for a walk or take a drive in the car?" It is also a mistake to plan any activity too far in advance. It is far better to take advantage of the moment for any activity outside the normal routine.

If there was a particularly difficult time of day in the last two years of Eileen's life, it was the late afternoon—the so-called "sundown effect." Most afternoons she would begin setting the dining room table for six or eight people, convinced we were having guests for dinner. The place settings, unthinkable in the past, would be a hodge-podge of kitchen silver, sterling, and stainless steel. Discouraging this activity, I finally discovered, was a poor idea. Simply stating that no one was coming for dinner—most often they were people who lived in different states or were long dead—was met with disbelief or resentment. So the table was set then ignored, and we had our TV dinners as usual two hours later.

In the last months of her life, Eileen would awake between one and three in the morning complaining of pain "all over." Sometimes the pain was in the lower abdomen, sometimes the lower back, sometimes in the legs, but it was always hard to locate specifically. Once back to sleep, there was no residual the next day and I was never able to be sure whether or not the discomfort was real, exaggerated, or imagined. A heating pad or an aspirin was helpful but there never seemed to be any continuing discomfort.

In retrospect, one of the first signs that her health was seriously deteriorating was a small thing—her indifference and even an aversion to a cup of black coffee first thing in the morning. For decades, her morning coffee had been a ritual. Two weeks before her final hospitalization she began refusing her coffee and this simple thing had ominous implications.

In the past ten years, I learned many other important lessons as a caregiver. Perhaps the most important was to never, ever, become critical or judgmental towards the afflicted one. This obvious fact is not always so obvious. There is a tendency to say to someone who has always been totally competent and capable to "snap out of it" or "you know perfectly well that...." One must never forget that he or she does not want to descend into a second childhood. Self-pity on the part of the caregiver is another trap that must be avoided. It is perhaps understandable but it is also unforgivable and can only make matters worse.

To watch a loved one slip into dementia, to know that conversation becomes impossible and reduced to single words like "cold," "hungry," or "tired," is sad but all too often is part of life. Dealing with it gives meaning to the vows one took with one's spouse—solemn pledges to look after one another until death. This is why, I believe, mature people weep at weddings. To see two young people untouched by sadness or tragedy pledging eternal devotion and fidelity to one another without the slightest inkling of the vicissitudes they may face in their lives is both beautiful and sad.

II

Concurrent with Eileen's declining years, I was sustained by a life-long interest in the history of our country—especially the contemporary political scene and the misadventures of the 43rd President of the United States, George W. Bush.

In my lifetime, I have come to believe that conservatives are habitually more comfortable trying to reduce complicated issues to simple ones. They tend to be confused and even irritated when "elitist intellectuals" or (worse) "elitist liberals" muddy the waters by pointing out that many complex matters like health care, tax policies, the problem of illegal immigration, entitlement programs, and international relations defy simplistic solutions. Conservatives have even managed to give the word "elite" a pejorative connotation. For the conservative, issues are either true or untrue, good or evil, black or white, or yes or no. Thus, for the dyed-in-the-wool Republican conservative, people either admire President Bush or they hate him—nothing in between—and critics of the president are automatically "Bush haters." This is, of course, simplistic nonsense.

President G. W. Bush had many faults: he was ignorant of history, incompetent, arrogant, and stubborn; but he was not without virtues. He had the strength of character to give up alcohol abuse before it created permanent brain damage, the grace to never criticize publicly his successor, and he had the good sense to marry a thoroughly admirable woman. But there is nothing about the man to hate. During his eight-years in office, he did inestimable damage to the country and to our nation's rightful place in the world. From being the most admired country in the world, the United States became the most feared and despised. Contrary to the respected and traditional Republican principals of governance, Bush created an unparalleled federal debt and an intrusive bureaucracy that would have fulfilled the Founding Fathers' worst fears. But it was not because President Bush was an evil man or a man to be hated. One can hate an unctuous hypocrite like Jerry Fallwell or a classic "presstitute" like Ann Coulter, who say and/

or write anything no matter how outrageous just to make money, or an uneducated bully and coward like Rush Limbaugh, but one cannot hate an incompetent blunderer who was trying his best to do a job for which he had inadequate training and that was simply too big for him. In private, George Bush may be a pleasant individual and one who might be good company discussing inconsequential matters, but as President of the United States, his term in office was an unmitigated disaster. There was nothing there to hate; one can only be dismayed.

In less dangerous times, as in the early decades of the twentieth century, little permanent damage could be done by a ridiculous figure like Calvin Coolidge or a dishonest political hack like Warren Harding. Even after World War II, the country survived a mentally disturbed (but brilliant) Richard Nixon. But at a time when the alienation of one-sixth of the world's population is a fact, the United States could not afford an incompetent blunderer. President Bush's "core belief" was that it was the mission of the United States to impose our form of representative democracy on unstable parts of the world, where such a governmental form is neither understood nor wanted. This belief is simply breathtaking in its arrogance. He was apparently unaware that it took one hundred and fifty years for the American colonists to try to make a republic and two hundred and thirty years for its citizens to try to improve it—and it is still a work in progress. Even if the invasion of Iraq was high-minded and had nothing to do with oil, or the enrichment of Halliburton, the notion that an ancient culture (which most Americans know very little about) would eagerly adopt America's form of democracy just because we removed a contemporary tyrant is almost unbelievable in its ignorance and arrogance. If Talleyrand-Périgord was right, and he probably was, that great nations may commit crimes but cannot commit blunders, the United States is paying a heavy price for the Bush administration's blunders. The greatest tragedy of the Bush presidency was the Iraq conflict, but from its earliest days, there were miss-steps after miss-steps that mesmerized the public. The first event, which was not entirely the president's responsibility, was the disgraceful and unprecedented partisan intervention of the Supreme Court awarding the presidency to the candidate (George W. Bush) who polled half a million fewer votes than his opponent (Al Gore). Subsequently, there were many more events and incidents—some funny, some tragic, and some infuriating.

First was the famous seven minutes of 9/11 when, without Vice President Cheney's neo-con brain trust to tell him what to do, George W. Bush sat befuddled and uncertain in the presence of kindergarten children when advised that the country was under attack. *Seven minutes*, or half the time it would have taken a missile launched from Pakistan to reach the United States—the president was frozen with indecision.

Early in his campaign for the office, President Bush announced that he would be a "uniter" when elected as well as a "compassionate conservative." Neither descriptor proved to be true. The congress became more polarized than at any time since the Civil War, and compassion became a joke. Soon the basic and honorable tenets of conservatism were forgotten. By the second year of his presidency, the long-term goals of the vice president and the president's handlers became apparent. A relatively weak attorney general, John Ashcroft, allowed the beginning of politicalization of the federal judiciary which, by 2007, had become so scandalous that it forced the resignation of the president's lackey and second attorney general, Roberto Gonzales.

By 2003, the president and his vice-president, Dick Cheney, promoting spurious "facts," committed the country to war in Iraq. The truth was that Iraq posed no threat to the United States, had no weapons of mass destruction, harbored no terrorists, and played no part in the destruction of the Twin Towers of the World Trade Center—even though for years, the president, the vice president, and their sycophants perpetuated the notion that Saddam Hussein was involved in the 9/11 attack to fester in the public mind. Using illegal "war powers" (we were not at war since only the congress has the authority to declare war) the infamous "Patriot Act" became law. Suddenly, basic civil liberties began to erode and any criticism of the administration became synonymous with treason. From Genghis Kahn to Adolf Hitler, this ploy—equating criticism with treason at a time of alleged national peril—has been a fact of history. The "national peril" of "Islamofascism" was eerily similar to Hitler's tactic of blaming the communists and the Jews for all of Germany's problems after World War I. Some of the provisions of the Domestic Security Enhancement Act of 2003 were absolutely unprecedented: stripping citizenship from Americans supporting organizations labeled "terrorist," providing immunity to federal agents who conduct illegal surveillance, expanding home search and wire taps without warrant, and creating a DNA national data base on "suspected terrorists." It was not until 2006 that Americans awoke and realized that once lost, civil liberties are hard to regain.

One of the most egregious abuses of power that President G.W. Bush carried out repeatedly—and with a surprising lack of interest on the part of the public—has been the "signing statement" scandal. In his first six years, the president did not veto a single measure passed up to him from the congress. He signed everything into law and then issued a "signing statement" which, in effect, stated that he would enforce only those provisions of the new law with which he agreed. The president cannot do this. It is illegal. The president has only three options when considering new legislation: he can veto it, he can sign it into law, or he can do nothing—the so-called pocket veto. However, once the president signs legislation, it becomes the law of the land and he is bound by his oath of office and the constitution to enforce it—*all* of it. He cannot enforce only those parts of the law he approves, which would clearly be an impeachable offense. Sooner or later this matter will get the attention it deserves.

By the fall of 2007, the Bush administration had begun saber rattling again and this time the target was Iran. Almost unbelievably, in statements similar to those before the Iraq invasion, the American people were advised that "we" would not permit Iran to proceed with their plans to achieve nuclear weapons capability and "to do whatever it takes" to prevent such an eventuality. According to the then current group of neo-cons, since Iran is pledged to the destruction of Israel, Israel would be the target of such weapons. Apparently President Bush did not know what every informed person in the world knew—if Iran had been mad enough to use nuclear weapons against Israel, a country decades ahead of Iran in weapons development, Tehran, and probably other large cities in Iran, would have ceased to exist. Assuming President Bush was in full possession of his faculties, it is inconceivable that he would have been thinking of military options against Iran rather than exploiting, diplomatically, President Ahmadinejad's relative weakness. It was a further manifestation of how dangerous it is for an ignorant and stubborn man, absolutely convinced of the rightness of his beliefs and intolerant of anyone who would offer contrary opinions, to be the most powerful of all the world's leaders.

Finally, during the years of the Bush administration, we saw a political party welcome a worrisome and un-American intrusion of religious fundamentalism into politics. United by their hatred of legalized abortion, Catholics, political conservatives, and evangelicals formed a kind of alliance and large voting bloc that threatens the principles of the First Amendment of the Constitution, the "wall of separation" between church and state. The alliance does not understand that freedom *from* a theocracy is the best guarantee of freedom *of* religious choice. In a wonderfully lucid article in the autumn 2007 edition of *The American Scholar*, Ethan Fishman reminded us that from Roger Williams to Thomas Jefferson, the Founders stressed that the role of government was to establish order—not enforce morality. Fishman reminded us that the only acceptable standard for statutory law in our republic is reason—not the Bible, or the Koran, or the Torah, or *Grimm's Fairy Tales*—but *reason*.

The years 2000-2007 were unprecedented in American history. We witnessed the ascendancy and eventual decline of one of the most inept presidents in American history, how fragile a democracy can be, and how easily tyranny can insinuate itself in the guise of patriotism.

III

In the mid-1930s, James Hilton, a friend of my parents, typed out, autographed, and gave to them his paean, *Let Us Give Thanks*. I found it going through my mother's correspondence after her death and enjoyed reading it so much that I had it framed and it has hung in my library for nearly forty years. James Hilton, an Englishman, lived nearly the last half of his life in this country. He was one of the most popular and widely read novelists of the day and several of his books were made into successful motion pictures; among them were *Lost Horizon, Goodbye Mr. Chips*, and *Random Harvest*.

Because it is wise and true and because I think it is unpublished, I'm including it in this book lest it be lost. I have read and re-read it many times over the years and found it to be comforting and reassuring, especially in times of depression or sadness.

LET US GIVE THANKS

LET US GIVE THANKS—
For Love that offers us escape from the unquiet world into
    the universe of private happiness....
For the freemasonry of reasonable men amidst extremists—
    and yet—
For the unreasonable courage of man which would
    destroy the earth for a new thrill on a fragment of new
    knowledge, and which may end by destroying him unless
    controlled by wisdom....
For Youth that makes us desire things, and for Age that
    gives us contentment without them....
For the freedom that growing older gives us from the
    puzzles and problems of youth, so that we have more

big things to care about and fewer little things to worry
about....

For Health, if we have it; and if not, for the chance of
Health; and if not that, for the hope of Health; and if
not that, then for the power of medicine and surgery to
relieve ultimate suffering....

For the gift of Sleep that comes unawaited; and for the
first faint ebb of the tide of physical pain....

For Pleasures of all kinds—waking to sunshine, the smell
of farmland, string quartets, the whack of a dog's tail on
the carpet....

For the ease with which a healthy memory remembers
good and forgets evil....

For the Second Law of Thermodynamics and the
Quantum Theory of Relatively and all the new
mathematics which has banished the doom of
predestination by suggesting that though some things
are very probable indeed, nothing is absolutely inevitable
tomorrow....

For the Law of Diminishing Returns which operates to
make more and more propaganda less and less effective....

For the past greatness of England and for the future
greatness of America, and for the Declaration of
Independence which freed them both for their present
mission of peace....

For the man who is honest even when he knows it is not
the best policy. For the man who does not do good in
hope of reward or avoid evil in fear of punishment; and
for the increasing millions of people all over the world—
teachers, preachers, doctors, etc.—who prove by their
lives that greed for gain is not the only human incentive
to good work....

For the unflagging mirth of the poor. For good intentions,
   which are not enough, but are better than bad intentions.
For great art, which is a fingerpoint of meaning in the vast
   randomness of events....
For the curiosity of children, and for the faithfulness of
   animals....
For the glory of knowing oneself necessary to someone or
   something near to one's heart....
For the twilight of the wise, which is brighter than the
   noonday of the blind....
For the powerlessness of action to control thought—which
   is the ultimate victory of wise men over fools.

                                        By James Hilton

Final Thoughts

The original manuscript for this book was completed in 2004 and the Epilogue in 2009. During the ensuing years leading up to the printed version of my book, I have enjoyed good health and the enduring support of my children, most especially Lizzy, Ellen, and Kathy.

Among the highlights of the past six years have been several trips: to California to see Margaret and my beautiful great-granddaughters; to Honolulu with all four daughters for the seventieth reunion of my class at Punahou; many visits with old and dear friends and family; and to Charlottesville, in 2013, for my sixtieth medical school class reunion, which was coincidental with my granddaughter's graduation from my beloved University of Virginia.

I've been lucky enough to remain an active learner and observer of the current political scene, witnessing the steady, competent leadership of President Barack Obama as he brought the country back from the edge of an economic disaster and who will, I am sure, ultimately enter the pantheon of great presidents of the United States. I have also had the good fortune to take many of the courses offered by the University of Denver's Enrichment Program—courses in philosophy, history, religion, science, and the art of writing memoirs and biographies.

Golf has been a continuing diversion ever since I first took it up over seventy-five years ago. My favorite companions at the game have been my sons, my grandsons, my son-in-law, Kathy, and her life partner Annette. With Annette and Kathy, I often managed to play at least once in every month of the year—no mean feat during the winter months in Colorado. Whether or not this passion for the great game fulfills Einstein's definition of insanity, doing the same thing over and over again expecting a different result, which never happens, I will leave to the opinion of the gentle reader.

Finally, over the past nine decades, although there have been moments of despair and sadness, there have been few tragedies involving people I love. For the most part, I have had the inestimable joy of seeing my children and grandchildren grow, mature, and lead honorable, useful, praiseworthy lives. So, I have done and seen many things but, as the title of this book suggests, the trip so far has been so good.

Philosophia Biou Kybernētēs

Knowledge is the Essence of Life

Index